BARRON'S
BILINGUAL BUSINESS GUIDES

TALKING BUSINESS IN
GERMAN

Dictionary and Reference
for International Business

Phrases and Words You Need to Know

by Henry Strutz, M.A.
Former Associate Professor of Languages
SUNY Agricultural and Technical College
at Alfred, New York

BARRON'S

BARRON'S EDUCATIONAL SERIES, INC.
New York • London • Toronto • Sydney

All inquires should be addressed to:
Barron's Educational Series, Inc.
250 Wireless Boulevard
Hauppauge, New York 11788

Library of Congress Catalog Card No. 86-22360
International Standard Book No. 0-8120-3747-2

Library of Congress Cataloging-in-Publication Data
Strutz, Henry.
    Talking Business in German.

    1. Commerce—Dictionaries. 2. Commerce—
Dictionaries—German. 3. Business—Dictionaries.
4. Business— Dictionaries—German. 5. English
language—Dictionaries—German. 6. German
language—Dictionaries—English. I. Title.
HF1002.S79   1987   650'.03'31   86-22360
ISBN 0-8120-3747-2 (pbk.)

PRINTED IN THE UNITED STATES OF AMERICA

7 8 9   9 6 9   9 8 7 6 5 4 3 2 1

CONTENTS

PREFACE

It is the nature of business to seek out new markets for its products, to find more efficient ways to bring its goods to more people. In the global marketplace, this often means travel to foreign countries, where language and customs are different. Even when a businessperson knows the language of the host country, the specific and often idiosyncratic terminology of the business world can be an obstacle to successful negotiations in a second language. Pocket phrase books barely scratch the surface of these problems, while standard business dictionaries prove too cumbersome.

Now there is a solution—Barron's *Talking Business in German*. Here is the essential pocket reference for all international business travelers. Whether your business be manufacturing or finance, communications or sales, this three-part guide will put the right words in your mouth and the best expressions in your correspondence. It is a book you'll carry with you on every trip and take to every meeting. But it is also the reference you'll keep on your desk in the office. This is the business dictionary for people who do business in German.

This book is one of a new series of business dictionaries. We welcome your comments on additional phrases that could be included in future editions.

Acknowledgments

We would like to thank the following individuals and organization for their assistance on this project:

Hubert Astegher, Deputy Trade Commissioner, Austrian Trade Commission in the United States; John Downes, Business Development Consultant, Office for Economic Development, New York, New York; Peter Felix, Consul, Swiss Consulate General in New york; Peter-Christian Haucke, Vice-Consul, Consulate General of the Federal Republic of Germany; Gunter Nitsch of the German-American Chamber of Commerce; and Warren T. Schimmel, Senior Vice-President, Academic Affairs, The Berkeley Schools.

Portions of this book are reprinted with permission from *German at a Glance* by Henry Strutz and from *Travel Diary—German*, both published by Barron's Educational Series, Inc.

PRONUNCIATION GUIDE

This book assumes you are already somewhat familiar with the basic pronunciation rules of German, but for those whose knowledge is a little rusty, here are some tips.

German pronunciation is not difficult because in German spelling, letters consistently represent the same sounds. The phonetic transcriptions in this book are English approximations of the German sounds and should be read as you would normally read them in English. Capitalized syllables indicate stress and should be pronounced with more emphasis than lower-case syllables in the same word.

Vowels

Vowels may be long or short. A vowel is long when:

1. doubled (B*ee*thoven, B*oo*t, W*aa*ge);
2. followed by an *h* Br*a*hms, *O*hm, F*e*hler);
3. followed by a single consonant (Sch*u*bert, M*o*zart, T*o*n).

When followed by two or more consonants, a vowel is usually short, as in B*a*ch.

VOWEL	SOUND IN ENGLISH	EXAMPLE
a	aa (long; f*a*r)	h*a*ben (H*AA*-ben)
	ah (short; h*o*t)	h*a*tte (H*AH*-teh)
ä	ay (long; w*ay*)	B*ä*der (B*AY*-duh)
	eh (short; m*e*t)	Gep*ä*ck (geh-P*EH*K)
e	ay (long; h*ay*)	l*e*ben (L*AY*-ben)
	eh (short; *e*nd)	h*e*lfen (H*EH*L-fen)
	e (unstressed syllables ending in -*n*, -*l*, and -*t* (like -*en* in hidd*en*)	li*e*ben (LEE-b*e*n)
	uh (unstressed syllables ending in -*er*, moth*er*)	Ritt*er* (RIT-*uh*)
i	ee (long; fl*ee*t)	*I*hnen (*EE*-nen)
	i (short; w*i*t)	w*i*ssen (V*I*ss-en)
ie	ee (always long; mart*ini*)	L*ie*be (L*EE*-beh)
o	oh (long; r*o*se)	R*o*se (R*OH*-zeh)
	o (short; l*o*ve)	k*o*mm (k*o*m)

VOWEL	SOUND IN ENGLISH	EXAMPLE
ö	er (like h*er*, but sounded with the lips forward and rounded)	hören (H*ER*-en)
u	oo (long; bl*oo*m)	Sch*uh* (sh*oo*)
	u (short; b*u*ll)	B*u*lle (B*U*L-eh)
ü	ew (like dr*ea*m, but with lips forward and rounded)	Br*ü*der (BR*EW*-duh)
y	ew (like the German *ü*)	l*y*risch (L*EW*-rish)

Diphthongs

DIPHTHONGS	SOUND IN ENGLISH	EXAMPLE
ai, ay ei, ey	eye (*eye*)	schr*ei*ben (SHR*EYE*-ben)
au	ow (br*ow*n)	br*au*n (br*ow*n)
ä, eu	oy (j*oy*)	tr*eu* (tr*oy*)

NOTE: German is pronounced more vigorously and with sharper vowels than English.

Consonants

CONSONANTS	SOUND IN ENGLISH	EXAMPLE
f, h, k, l, m, n, p, t, x	usually pronounced as in English	
b	p (between vowel and consonant or at end of word: ma*p*)	Lei*b* (leye*p*)
	b (elsewhere as in English)	*b*in (*b*in)
c	ts (before *e, i, ö,* and *ä*: wi*ts*)	*C*äsar (*TS*AY-zahr)
	k (elsewhere; *c*old)	*C*oburg (*K*OH-boork)
ch	kh strongly aspirated (breathy) sound; ("*Ha*-waiian" or "*Hugh*")	dur*ch* (door*kh*)
chs	k (sometimes: *k*ind)	La*chs* (lah*ks*)
d	t (between vowel and consonant and at end of word; ca*t*)	Hun*d* (hun*t*)
	d (otherwise *d*ollar)	*D*ank (*d*ank)

CONSO-NANTS	SOUND IN ENGLISH	EXAMPLE
g	g (hard; *g*ods)	*G*eist (*g*eyest)
	k (at end of word; ba*ck*pack)	Ta*g* (taa*k*)
	kh (words ending in *ig*, see *ch* above)	windi*g* (VIN-di*kh*)
j	y (*y*ear)	*J*ahr (*y*aar)
qu	kv (*k*, followed by *v* as in *v*eal)	*Qu*ell (*kv*ehl)
r	r preferably rolled in the throat, as in French, or trilled with the tip of the tongue, as in Spanish or Irish or Scottish brogues)	*R*eise (*R*EYE-zeh)
s	z (preceding vowels or between them; *z*ap)	*S*ee (*z*ay)
	sh (at beginning of syllable, before *p* and *t*: *sh*ell)	*s*pielen (*SH*PEE-len)
	s, ss (elsewhere: *s*ing)	Wa*s* ist da*s*? (vah*s* ist dah*s*)
ß, ss	s, ss (always: *s*ell)	(weiß veye*s*) wi*ss*en (VI-*ss*en)
sch	sh (*sh*ow)	*sch*lau (*sh*low)
tsch	ch (*ch*eer)	Ki*tsch* (ki*ch*)
tz	ts (wi*ts*)	Ka*tz*e (KAH-*ts*eh)
v	f (*f*ather)	*V*ater (*F*AA-tuh)
	v (words of non-Germanic origin: *v*iolin)	*V*ioline (*v*ee-o-LEE-neh)
w	v (*v*est)	*W*asser (*V*AH-suh)
z	ts (gri*ts*)	*Z*eit (*ts*eyet)

INTRODUCTION

DOING BUSINESS IN GERMAN-SPEAKING COUNTRIES

Doing business with another culture and in another language can be a difficult and mystifying experience. Customs and procedures may be quite different from what is perceived as the "normal" way of conducting oneself in a business circumstance.

In this introduction, some of the customs and economic aspects of German-speaking countries are outlined, in order to assist you in effectively conducting business in these areas. Basic knowledge of these factors will help in becoming more accustomed to the business situation of the German-speaking world.

Usual Hours of Operation

Hours of operation can vary considerably in each country, and the following are only general guidelines. It will be wise to telephone in advance to determine the precise hours of the business or government office you plan to visit.

West Germany: Monday to Friday 8:00 AM – 4:00 PM, with 1 – 2 hours lunch.
East Germany: Monday to Friday 8:00 AM – 4:00 PM, with a lunch break.
Switzerland: Monday to Friday 7:30 AM – 5:30 PM, with 1 – 2 hours lunch.
Austria: Monday to Friday 8:00 AM – 5:00 PM, with 1 hour for lunch.

Business Customs

West Germany: Business people in West Germany tend to be formal and reserved, but many will be more open when they become familiar with you. An increasing number have had contact with Americans and will try to behave like an American business person. It's best to let your German business partner set the tone to avoid unnecessary friction. German business people are usually very efficient, and they will expect you to be well-informed, particularly because they are very interested in American techniques. It's very important to be punctual.

East Germany: This is a single-party, centrally controlled people's republic, and one must follow highly structured procedures in doing business. Don't expect instant deals — in fact, expect drawn-out negotiations as matters are considered at various levels of the bureaucracy. Your relations with officials concerned with industry will rarely stray from the very formal though polite level.

Switzerland: Swiss business people are usually very formal and serious. Their businesses are generally very efficiently managed, and you will be expected to be well-informed and well-organized. As in West Germany, it is best to let your business partner set the tone of your contacts.

Austria: Business people in Austria tend to be polite and formal, though they may become more open in an on-going relationship.

General Government Policy and Economic Situation

West Germany: The West German economy is based on free enterprise but the German federal and state governments as well as the European Community have considerable influence over economic affairs. West Germany has one of the world's largest economies and foreign trade is an extremely important component. The West German economy grew spectacularly in the 1950s and '60s, but economic growth has slowed in the 1980s and unemployment has increased. Major manufacturing products include motor vehicles, iron and steel, chemicals, machinery, processed food, clothing, and electrical and electronic equipment.

Main imports: crude and refined petroleum, food, machinery, chemicals, clothing.

Main exports: machinery, motor vehicles, chemicals, textiles and clothing.

Principal trade partners: France, the Netherlands, Belgium and Luxembourg, Italy, the United States.

Population: 62 million.

Language: German.

Religion: Protestant (47%), Roman Catholic (45%).

Gross Domestic Product: $600 billion.

East Germany: The East German economy is dominated by the state, and all large enterprises have been nationalized. There is relatively little local control of important economic matters, though somewhat more than 20 or 30 years ago. Economic reconstruction and growth after World War II started slowly in East Germany, but by the 1960s there was considerable economic development. In the 1980s the country was a major industrial power, albeit oriented to East European nations and the Soviet Union. Major manufacturing products include iron and steel, chemicals, electrical and electronic equipment, textiles, and precision instruments.

Main imports: crude petroleum, food, industrial raw materials, transportation equipment.

Main exports: machinery, chemicals, textiles, transportation equipment.

Principal trade partners: Soviet Union, Czechoslovakia, Hungary, West Germany.

Population: 17 million.

Language: German.

Religion: Protestant (50%), Roman Catholic (6%)

Switzerland: The Swiss economy is based on free enterprise, with relatively little government regulation. The Swiss have long been noted as efficient business people, and today the country's economy is highly developed. Manufactures are important, and so are financial services and tourism. Agriculture plays a small role in the economy. Principal products of Switzerland include precision machinery, timepieces, textiles and clothing, chemicals and pharmaceuticals, foodstuffs, and refined metal.

Main imports: machinery, transportation equipment, crude and refined petroleum, textiles and clothing, metals.

Main exports: machinery, chemicals and pharmaceuticals, timepieces, electronic equipment, precision instruments, chocolate.

Principal trade partners: West Germany, France, Italy, Great Britain, United States.

Population: 6.5 million.

Language: German (65%), French (18%), Italian (12%), Romansh (1%).

Religion: oman Catholic (50%), Protestant (43%).

Gross Domestic Product: $95 billion.

Austria: The state plays an important role in the Austrian economy, with most major industries controlled by the government. Manufacturing is key to the economy, though agriculture and tourism also are important. Major manufacturing products include iron and steel, transporation equipment, chemicals, textiles and clothing, forest products, processed food, and handicrafts.

Main imports: machinery, transportation equipment, chemicals, petroleum, foodstuffs.

Main exports: forest products, textiles, machinery, chemicals, handicrafts.

Principal trade partners: West Germany, Italy, Switzerland, Great Britain.

Population: 7.6 million.

Language: German.
Religion: Roman Catholic (90%), Protestant (6%).
Gross Domestic Product: $67 billion.

BEFORE YOU GO . . .

Passports

All permanent U.S. residents must carry a valid passport in order to travel to, from, and within Europe. Application should be made by mail or in person at least eight and preferably twelve weeks in advance to either (1) a U.S. Passport Agency office located in thirteen major cities in the U.S.; (2) designated U.S. post offices throughout the country; or (3) State and Federal courthouses. You may also consult your travel agent or international airline office. All of these offices will let you know what documents you need and the proper procedures to follow. Requirements for citizens and non-citizens differ somewhat. No international travel tickets will be issued by an airline or travel agent to persons without valid passports.

Visas

No visas are required by western European countries for travelers with U.S. passports whose stay does not exceed three months. If planning to stay longer, contact the consulate or national tourist organization of the country in the nearest major city or in New York City, or ask your travel agent or international airline office about visa applications. Visas may also be acquired while abroad before the 3-month limit expires.

Immunizations

There are no immunization requirements (for smallpox or other diseases) for entry into western European countries or upon return to the United States. If you plan to include travel outside Europe to Asia, Africa or the Middle East, consult your doctor or the nearest U.S. Public Health Service office.

Customs and Currency Regulations

In general, travelers to and within western Europe with U.S. passports are allowed to bring in fairly generous amounts of duty-free items for their own personal use. These items include tobacco, alcohol, and perfumes and are typically allowed in the following quantities (despite local variation):

    400 cigarettes or 100 cigars or 500 grams of
            tobacco (about 1 lb.)
    2 liters of wine
    1 liter of liquor
    2 ounces of perfume

If you are not well in excess of these amounts, a simple statement of "nothing to declare" will be respected by most customs officials.

For gifts whose final destination is the country you are entering, the rules are a bit stricter and vary greatly among the different countries. If you are planning to bring in a large number of such gifts, it would be wise to check on the duty-free limits beforehand and to declare whatever is in excess.

For personal valuables like jewelry or furs and foreign-made items like watches, cameras, typewriters or tape recorders (acquired before your trip) you should have proof of prior possession or register with U.S. Customs before departure. This will ensure that they are not subject to duty either by the United States upon return or by the country you visit.

Upon return to the United States, each person (including children) has a duty-free allowance of $400, including 100 cigars and 1 carton of cigarettes. Each adult may bring in only 1 liter of wine or other liquor duty-free. Gifts worth $50 or less may be sent home subject to certain restrictions. For further up-to-date details ask your travel agent or airline to provide a copy of U.S. Customs regulations or write: U.S. Customs, P.O. Box 7407, Washington, DC 20044 (202-566-8195).

There are usually no restrictions on the amounts of foreign currency (or checks) which foreign nationals may bring into western Europe. Some countries, however, do restrict the amount of local currency that may be brought in or out. Consult a travel agent or national tourist organization office either in the United States or abroad on these restrictions.

Traveler's Checks, Credit Cards, Foreign Exchange

Although all major international traveler's checks and credit cards are accepted by large travel agencies and most of the better (more expensive) hotels, restaurants and shops in Europe, it is always best to check at each establishment beforehand. The checks most recognized are: American Express, Barclays, Visa, CitiBank, Bank of America and Thomas Cook & Sons. The cards most acceptable are: American Express, Bank Americard, MasterCard, Visa, Diners Club, and Carte Blanche.

However, be advised that the exchange rate on dollar traveler's checks is almost always disadvantageous. If you want, you can buy foreign currency checks and/or actual currency in the United States before leaving at rates equivalent to or better than the bank rate you will get over there. Currency or checks may be purchased from retail foreign currency dealers. The largest of these, Deak-Perera, will send information if you write them at: 29 Broadway, New York, NY 10006.

A warning to credit card users: When charging, make sure that the following information appears on the original and all copies of your bill: the correct date; the type of currency being charged (francs, marks, kroner, etc.); the official exchange rate for that currency on that date (if possible); and, the total amount of the bill. Without this information, you may end up paying at an exchange rate less favorable to you and more favorable to your European host, and for a larger bill than you thought!

Drivers' Licenses

A valid American (state) license is usually respected throughout Europe, if you are 18 years old or over. However, if you have time, and want to avoid language problems on the road, it is a good idea to get an international drivers' document through the AAA or a local automobile club. Also, despite local rules, car rental agencies may restrict rentals to people 21 years old or over. **And remember**, drive on the *left* in Great Britain and Ireland!

BASIC WORDS AND PHRASES

Fundamental Expressions

Yes.	Ja. (yaa)
No.	Nein. (neyen)
Maybe.	Vielleicht. (fee-LAYEKHT)
Please.	Bitte. (BIT-eh)
Thank you very much.	Vielen Dank. (FEEL-en dahnk)
Excuse me.	Verzeihung! (fehr-TSEYE-ung)
I'm sorry.	Es tut mir leid. (ehs toot meer leyet)
Just a second.	Augenblick mal! (OW-gen-blik maal)
It doesn't matter.	Das macht nichts. (dahs mahkht nikhts)
That'll be fine.	Schon gut. (shon goot)
Good morning.	Guten Morgen. (GOOT-en MORG-en)

Good afternoon.	Guten Tag. (GOOT-en taak)
Good evening.	Guten Abend. (GOOT-en AAB-ent)
Good night.	Gute Nacht. (GOOT-en nahkht)
Good-bye!	Auf Wiedersehen! (owf VEED-uh-zayen) auf Wiederschauen! (owf VEED-uh-show-en) Uf Wiederluege! (Swiss) (uf VEED-uh-lueh-geh)
How are you? (How do you do?)	Wie geht es Ihnen? (vee gayt ehs EEN-en)
How are things?	Wie geht's? (vee gayts)
Fine, thank you. And you?	Gut, danke. Und Ihnen? (goot DAHNK-eh) (unt EEn-en)
See you later.	Bis später. (bis SHPAYT-uh)
See you soon.	Bis bald. (bis bahlt)
Do you speak English?	Sprechen Sie Englisch? (SHPREHKH-en zee EHNG-lish)
I don't speak German.	Ich kann kein Deutsch sprechen. (ikh kahn keyen doytsh SHPREHKN-en)
Do you understand?	Verstehen Sie? (fehr-SHTAY-en zee)
I (don't) understand.	Ich verstehe (nicht). (ikh fehr-SHTAY-eh [nikht])
What was that you said?	Wie bitte? (vee BIT-eh)
I speak little German.	Ich spreche wenig Deutsch. (ikh SHPREHKH-eh VAYN-ikh doytch)
Does anyone here speak English?	Spricht hier jemand Englisch? (shprikht heer YAY-mahnt EHNG-lish)
Please write it down.	Bitte schreiben Sie es auf. (BIT-eh SHREYEB-en zee ehs owf)
Please speak more slowly.	Bitte sprechen Sie langsamer! (BIT-eh SHPREKH-en zee LAHNG-zaam-uh)
Please repeat.	Wiederholen Sie bitte! (VEED-uh-hoh-len zee BIT-eh)
What does that mean?	Was bedeutet das? (vahss be-DOYT-et dahs)
How do you say that in German?	Wie heißt das auf deutsch? (Vee heyest dahs owf doytch)
What's your name?	Wie heißen Sie? (vee HEYESS-en zee)
(The) gentlemen, Mr.	(Der) Herr. ([dehr] hehrr)

(The) lady, Mrs.	(Die) Frau. ([dee] frow)
(The) girl, Miss.	(Das) Fräulein. ([dahs] FROY-leyen)
Here's my address and telephone number.	Hier ist meine Adresse und Telefon Nummer. (heer ist meyen-eh aa-DRESS-eh unt TAY-leh-fohn NUM-uh)
Where are you staying?	Wo sind Sie einquartiert? (voh zint zee EYEN-kwaa-teert)
Where can I reach you?	Wo kann ich Sie erreichen? (voh kahn ikh zee ehr-REYEKH-en)
I'll pick you up at your house (hotel).	Ich hole Sie in Ihrem Haus (Hotel) ab. (ikh HOHL-eh zee in EER-em hows [ho-TEL] ahp)
Nice to have met you.	Nett, daß ich Sie kennengelernt habe. (neht dahss ikh zee KEHN-en-geh-lehrnt HAAB-eh)

Common Questions and Phrases

Where is ___?	Wo ist ___? (voh ist)
When?	Wann? (vahn)
How?	Wie? (vee)
How much does that cost?	Wieviel kostet das? (VEE-feel KOST-et dahs)
Who?	Wer? (vayr)
Why?	Warum? (vah-RUM)
Which?	Welcher? (VEHLKH-uh)
Here is ___.	Hier ist ___. (heer ist)
There is ___.	Dort ist ___. Da ist ___. (dort ist) (daa ist)
That is ___.	Das ist ___. (dahs ist)
It is ___.	Es ist ___. (ehs ist)
Arrival/Hotel	Hotelankunft. (hoh-TEL-ahn-kunft)
My name is ___	Ich heiße ___ (ikh HEYESS-eh)
I am an American.	Ich bin Amerikaner. (ikh bin aa-meh-ri-KAAN-uh)
I'm staying at ___.	Ich bin im ___. (ikh bin im)
Here is my passport.	Hier ist mein Paß. (heer ist meyen pahss)
I'm on a business trip.	Ich bin auf Geschäfts reise hier. (ikh bin owf geh-SHEHFTS-reye-zeh heer)
I'm just passing through.	Ich bin nur auf der Durchreise. (ikh bin noor owf dehr DOORKH-reye-zeh)
I'll be staying ___.	Ich bleibe ___. (ikh BLEYEB-eh)

• a few days	• einige Tage (EYEN-ig-eh TAAG-eh)
• a few weeks	• einige Wochen (EYEN-ig-eh VOKH-ehn)
• a month	• einen Monat (EYEN-en MOHN-aat)
I have nothing to declare.	Ich habe nichts zu verzollen. (ikh HAAB-eh nikhts tsoo fehr-TSOL-en)

Useful Nouns

address	die Adresse (dee ah-DRESS-seh)
amount	der Betrag (dehr beh-TRAHK)
appointment	die Verabredung (dee fehr-AHP-ray-dung)
bill	die Rechnung (dee REKH-nung)
business	das Geschäft (dahs geh-SHEHFT)
car	der Wagen, das Auto (dehr VAA-gen) (dahs OW-toh)
cashier	die Kassee (dee KAHSS-eh)
check	der Scheck (dehr shehk)
city	die Stadt (dee shtaht)
customs	der Zoll (dehr tsol)
date	das Datum (dahs DAA-tum)
document	das Dokument (dahs doh-koo-mehnt)
elevator	der Aufzug (dehr OWF-tsook)
flight	der Flug (dehr flook)
friend	der Freund, die Freundin (dehr froynt) (dee FROYN-din)
hanger	der Kleiderbügel (dehr KLEYE-duh-bew-gel)
key	der Schlüssel (dehr SHLEWSS-el)
list	die Liste (dee LISS-teh)
maid	das Dienstmädchen (dahs DEENST-mayt-khen)
mail	die Post (dee post)
magazine	die Zeitschrift (dee TSEYET-shrift)
manager	der Geschäftsführer (dehr geh-SHEHFTS-few-ruh)
map	die Karte (dee KAAR-teh)
mistake	der Fehler (dehr FAY-luh)
money	das Geld (dahs gelt)
name	der Name (dehr NAA-meh)
newspaper	die Zeitung (dee TSEYE-tung)
office	das Amt, das Büro (dahs ahmt) (dahs bew-ROH)

package	das Paket (dahs pah-KAYT)
paper	das Papier (dahs pah-PEER)
passport	der Pass (dehr pahss)
pen	der Kugelschreiber (deh-KOO-gel-shreye-buh)
pencil	der Bleistift (dehr BLEYE-shtift)
porter	der Gepäckträger, der Hausdiener (dehr geh-PEHK-tray-guh) (dehr HOWSS-dee-nuh)
post office	das Postamt (dahs POST-ahmt)
postage	die Postgebühr (dee POST-GEH-bewr)
price	der Preis (der preyess)
raincoat	der Regenmantel (dehr RAY-gen-mahn-tel)
reservation	die Reservvierung (dee reh-zehr-VEE-rung)
rest room	die Toilette (dee foy-LET-te)
restaurant	das Restaurant (dahs res-toh-RANG)
road	die Strasse (dee SHTRAHS-seh)
room	das Zimmer (dahs TSIM-muh)
shirt	das Hemd (dahs hehmt)
shoe	der Schuh (dehr shoo)
shower	die Dusche (dee DOOSH-eh)
store	der Laden (dehr LAA-den)
street	die Strasse (dee SHTRAHS-seh)
suit	der Anzug (dehr AHN-tsook)
suitcase	der Koffer (dehr KOF-fuh)
taxi	die Taxe (dee TAHK-seh)
telegram	das Telegramm (dahs tay-leh-GRAHM)
telephone	das Telefon (dahs TAY-leh-fon)
terminal	die Endstation (dee END-stah-tzee-ohn)
ticket	die Karte, die Fahrkarte (dee KAAR-teh) (dee FAAR-kaar-teh)
time	die Zeit (dee tseyet)
tip	das Trinkgeld (dahs TRINK-gelt)
train	der Zug (dehr tsook)
trip	die Reise (dee REYE-zeh)
umbrella	der Schirm (dehr shirm)
waiter	der Kellner (dehr KEL-nuh)
watch	die Uhr (dee oor)
water	das Wasser (dahs VAHS-suh)

Useful Verbs (infinitive forms)

accept	annehmen (AHN-nay-men)
answer	antworten (AHNT-vor-ten)

arrive	ankommen (AHN-kom-men)
ask	fragen (RAA-gen)
assist	beistehen, helfen (BEY-shtay-en) (HEL-fen)
be	sein, werden (zeyen) (VEHR-den)
begin	beginnen (beh-GIN-nen)
bring	bringen (BRING-en)
buy	kaufen (KOW-fen)
call	rufen (ROO-fen)
carry	tragen (TRAA-gen)
change	wechseln (VEHK-seln)
close	schliessen (SHLEES-sen)
come	kommen, ankommen (KOM-men) (AHN-kom-en)
confirm	bestätigen (beh-SHTAY-tee-gen)
continue	fortsetzen (FORT-zet-sen)
cost	kosten (KOS-ten)
deliver	bringen (BRING-en)
direct	anweisen, leiten (AHN-vey-sen) (LEY-ten)
do	tun (toon)
eat	essen (EHS-sen)
end	beenden (beh-EN-den)
enter	betreten, herein kommen (beh-TRAY-ten) (hehr-EYEN-kom-en)
examine	erwägen, untersuchen (ehr-VAY-gen) (un-tuh-ZOO-khen)
exchange	wechseln (VEHK-seln)
feel	füklen (FEW-len)
finish	beenden (beh-EHN-den)
fix	reparieren (reh-paa-REE-ren)
follow	folgen (FOL-gen)
forget	vergessen (fehr-GEHS-sen)
forward	schicken (SHI-ken)
get	bekommen (beh-KOM-men)
give	geben (GAY-ben)
go	gehen (GAY-hen)
hear	hören (HER-en)
help	helfen (HEL-fen)
keep	behalten (be-HAHL-ten)
know	kennen (KEN-en)
learn	lernen (LEHR-nen)
leave	lassen (LAHS-sen)
like	mögen (MERG-en)
listen	hören (ER-en)
look at	ansehen (AHN-zay-en)
lose	verlieren (fehr-LEE-ren)

make	machen (MAHKH-en)
mean	bedeuten (beh-DOY-ten)
meet	treffen (TREF-en)
miss	versäumen (fehr-ZOY-men)
need	brauchen (BROWKH-en)
open	aufmachen (OWF-mahkh-en)
order	bestellen (beh-SHTEL-en)
park	parken (PAHRK-en)
pay	zahlen (TSAA-len)
prefer	vorziehen (FOR-tsee-hen)
prepare	vorbereiten (FOR-beh-reye-ten)
present	vorlegen (FOR-lay-gen)
prove	beweisen (beh-veye-sen)
pull	ziehen (TSEE-hen)
purchase	kaufen (KOW-fen)
put	stellen (SHTEHL-en)
read	lesen (LAY-zen)
receive	bekommen (beh-KOM-men)
recommend	empfehlen (ehmp-FAY-len)
remain	bleiben (BLEYE-ben)
repair	reparieren (reh-pah-REE-ren)
repeat	wiederholen (VEE-duh-hoh-len)
return	zurückbringen (tsoo-REWK-bring-en)
run	laufen (LOW-fen)
say	sagen (ZAA-gen)
see	sehen (ZAY-hen)
send	senden (ZEN-den)
show	zeigen (TSEYE-gen)
sit	sitzen (ZIT-sen)
speak	sprechen (SHPREHKH-en)
stand	stehen (SHTAY-en)
start	anfangen (AHN-fahng-en)
stop	anhalten (AHN-hahl-ten)
take	nehmen (NAY-men)
talk	sprechen (SHPREHKH-en)
tell	sagen, erzählen (ZAA-gen) (ehr-TSAY-len)
think	denken, glauben (DEHNK-en) (GLOW-ben)
try	versuchen (fehr-ZOOKH-en)
turn	drehen, wenden (DRAY-en, VEHN-den)
use	benutzen (beh-NUTS-en)
visit	besuchen (beh-ZOOKH-en)
wait	warten (VAAR-ten)
walk	gehen (GAY-en)
want	mögen (MERG-en)
wear	tragen (TRAAG-en)
work	arbeiten (AHR-beye-ten)
write	schreiben (SHREYE-ben)

Useful Adjectives and Adverbs

above/below	über/unter (EW-buh/un-tuh)
ahead/behind	vorwärts/hinter (FOR-vayrts/ HIN-tuh)
best/worst	beste/am schlechtesten (BEH- ste/am SHLEHKH-te-sten)
big/small	gross/klein (grohss/kleyen)
early/late	früh/spät (frew/shpayt)
easy/difficult	einfach/schwierig (EYEN- fahkh/SHVEE-rikh) leicht/ schrer (leyekht/shreyr)
few/many	einige/viele (eye-nee-ge/VEE-le)
first/last	erstens/letztens (EHRS-tens/ LEHTS-tens)
full/empty	voll/leer (foll/layr)
good/bad	gut/schlecht (goot/shlehkht)
hot/cold	heiss/kalt (heyess/kahlt)
high/low	hoch/neidrig (hohk/NEE-rikh)
large/small	gross/klein (grohss/kleyen)
more/less	mehr/weniger (mayr/VAYN- ikh-uh)
old/new	alt/neu (ahlt/noy)
open/shut	offen/geschlossen (OFF-en/geh- SHLOSS-en)
right/wrong	richtig/falsch (RIHKH-ikh/ fahlsh)
slow/fast	langsam/schnell (LAHNG- zaam/shnell)
thin/thick	dünn/dick (dewn/dik)

Other Useful Words

a, an	ein, eine, einer (eyen) (EYE- neh) (EYE-nuh)
across	über (EW-buh)
after	nach (nahkh)
again	wieder (VEE-uh)
all	alle, ganz (AHL-leh) (gahns)
almost	fast (fahst)
also	auch (owkh)
always	immer (IM-uh)
among	unter (UN-tuh)
and	und (unt)
another	andere (AHN-de-reh)
around	um (um)
away	weg (vek)
back	zurück (tsoo-REWK)
because	weil (veyel)
before	vor (for)
behind	hinter (HIN-tuh)
between	zwischen (TSVI-shun)
both	beide (BEYE-deh)

but	aber (AAB-uh)
down	unter (UN-tuh)
each	jede, jeder, jedes (YAY-deh) (YAY-duh) (YAY-des)
enough	genug (geh-NOOK)
every	jede (YAY-deh)
except	sonst, ausser (zonst) (OWSS-uh)
few	wenig (vaye-nikh)
for	für (fewr)
from	von (fon)
however	jedoch (yay-dohkh)
if	wenn (vehn)
in	in (in)
instead	anstatt (ahn-SHTAHT)
into	in (in)
maybe	vielleicht (fee-LAYEKHT)
more	mehr (mayr)
much	viel (feel)
next to	neben (NAYE-ben)
not	nicht (nikht)
now	jetzt (yetst)
of	von (fon)
often	oft (oft)
only	nur (noor)
or	oder (OHD-uh)
other	andere, anderer, anderes (AHND-eh-reh) (AHND-eh-ruh) (AHND-eh-res)
perhaps	vielleicht (feel-LEYEKHT)
same	dasselbe (dahs-ZEHL-beh)
since	seit (zeyet)
some	einige (EYEN-ig-eh)
still	noch (nokh)
that	dass, das (dahs) (dahs)
these	diese (DEE-seh)
this	dies (dees)
to	zu, nach (tsoo) (nahkh)

Directions

Which way do I go?	In welche Richtung soll ich gehen? (in VELKH-en RIKHT-ung zol ikh GAY-en)
• straight ahead	• geradeaus (ge-RAAD-eh-OWS)
• north	• der Norden (NOR-den)
• south	• der Süden (dehr ZEW-den)
• east	• der Osten (dehr OS-ten)
• west	• der Western (dehr VEHS-ten)
• left	• links (links)
• right	• rechts (rehkhts)

Is this the road to ___?	Ist dies die Straße nach ___? (ist dees dee SHTRAASS-eh nahkh)
Am I on the right road now?	Bin ich jetzt auf der richtigen Straße? (bin ikh yetst owf dehr RIKHT-ig-en SHTRAASS-en)
Can you show it to me on the map?	Können Sie ihn mir auf der Karte zeigen? (KERN-en zee een meer owf dehr KAART-eh TSEYEG-en)

Days of the Week

Today is ___.	Heute ist ___. (HOYT-eh ist)
• Monday	• Montag (MOHN-taak)
• Tuesday	• Dienstag (DEENS-taak)
• Wednesday	• Mittwoch (MIT-vokh)
• Thursday	• Donnerstag (DON-ehrs-taak)
• Friday	• Freitag (FREYE-taak)
• Saturday	• Samstag/Sonnabend (ZAHMS-taak / ZON-aab-ent)
• Sunday	• Sonntag (ZON-taak)
yesterday	gestern (GEST-ehrn)
the day before yesterday	vorgestern (FOHR-gest-ehrn)
tomorrow	morgen (MORG-en)
the day after tomorrow	übermorgen (EWB-ehr-morg-en)
in the morning	am Morgen (ahm MORG-en)
• afternoon	• Nachmittag (NAHKH-mit-taak)
• evening	• Abend (AAB-ent)
tonight	heute abend (HOYT-eh AAB-ent)
this afternoon	heute nachmittag (HOYT-eh NAHKH-mit-taak)
every day	jeden Tag (YAYD-en taak)

Months of the Year

January	Januar/Jänner (Austria) (YAA-noo-aar/YEH-nehr)
February	Februar (FAY-broo-aar)
March	März (mehrts)
April	April (ah-PRIL)
May	Mai (meye)
June	Juni (YOON-ee)
July	Juli (YOOL-ee)
August	August (ow-GUST)
September	September (zep-TEHM-buh)
October	Oktober (ok-TOH-buh)
November	November (no-VEHM-buh)

December	Dezember (deh-TSEHM-buh)
What is today's date?	Der wievielte ist heute? (dehr VEE-feelt-eh ist HOYT-eh)
Today is May 3.	Heute ist der 3. Ma. (HOYT-eh ist dehr DRIT-eh meye)
monthly	monatlich (MOHN-aat-likh)
this month	in diesem Monat (in DEEZ-em MOHN-aat)
next month	im nächsten Monat (im NAYKHST-en MOHN-aat)
last month	im letzten Monat (im LETST-en MOHN-aat)

The Four Seasons

spring	der Frühling (dehr FREW-ling)
summer	der Sommer (dehr ZOM-uh)
autumn	der Herbst (dehr hehrpst)
winter	der Winter (dehr VINT-uh)
during the spring	während des Frühlings (VEHR-ent dehs FREW-lings)
every summer	jeden Sommer (YAYD-en ZOM-uh)
in the winter	im Winter (im VINT-uh)

Time

What time is it?	Wieviel Uhr ist es? (VEE-fee oor ist ehs)
• hour	• Stunde (SHTUND-eh)
• minute	• Minute (mi-NOOT-eh)
• second	• Sekunde (zeh-KUN-deh)
• half an hour	• eine halbe Stunde (EYEN-eh HAHLB-eh SHTUND-eh)
• an hour and a half	• anderthalb Stunden (AHN-dehrt-haalp SHTUND-en)
twenty after twelve OR	zwanzig nach zwölf (TSVAHNTS-ikh nahkh tsverlf)
twelve-twenty	zwölf Uhr zwanzig (tsverlf oor TSVAHNTS-ikh)
one-thirty OR	ein Uhr dreißig (eyen oor DREYSS-ikh)
half an hour (30 minutes)	halb zwei (hahlp tsveye)
9:37	neun Uhr siebenunddreißig (noyn oor ZEEB-en-unt-dreyess-ikh)
eight to three (2:52)	acht vor drei (ahkht for drey)
five to seven (6:55)	fünf vor sieben (fewnf for ZEEB-en)
nine after four (4:09)	neun nach vier (noyn nahkh feer)

a quarter after three (3:15)	viertel nach drei (FEERT-el nahkh dreye) drei
At what time shall we meet?	Um wieviel Uhr treffen wir uns? (um VEE-feel oor TREHF-en veer uns)
We'll eat at eight (o'clock).	Wir essen um acht (Uhr). (veer ESS-en um ahkht [oor])

Arrival/Hotel

My name is . . .	Ich heiße . . . (ikh HEYESS-eh)
Here is my passport.	Hier ist mein Paß. (heer ist meyen pahss)
I'm on a business trip.	Ich bin auf Geschäfts reise hier. (ikh bin owf geh-SHEHFTS-reye-zeh heer)
I'm just passing through.	Ich bin nur auf der Durchreise. (ikh bin noor owf dehr DOORKH-reye-zeh)
I'll be staying ___.	Ich bleibe___. (ikh BLEYEB-eh)
• a few days	• einige Tag (EYEN-ig-eh TAAG-eh)
• a few weeks	• einige Wochen (EYEN-ig-eh VOKH-ehn)
• a month	• einen Monat (EYEN-en MOHN-aat)
I have nothing to declare.	Ich habe nichts zu verzollen. (ikh HAAB-eh nikhts tsoo fehr-TSOL-en)
I'm looking for the ___ hotel.	Ich suche das Hotel ___. (ikh ZOOKH-eh dahs hoh-TEL)
Where is the taxi stand?	Wo ist der Taxistand? (voh ist dehr TAHK-see-shtahnt)
Please call a taxi for me.	Rufen Sie bitte eine Taxe fürmich. (ROOF-en zee BIT- eh EYEN-eh TAHKS-eh fewr mikh)
I (don't) have a reservation.	Ich habe (nicht) reservieren lassen. (ikh HAAB-eh [nikht] reh-zehr-VEER-en LASS-en)
I'd like a single (double) room for tonight.	Ich möchte ein Einzelzimmer (Doppelzimmer) für heute nacht. (ikh MERKHT-eh eyen EYEN-tsel-tsim-uh (DOP-el-tsim-uh) fewr HOYT-eh nahkht)
Is breakfast included in the price of the room?	Ist der Zimmerpreis mit Frühstück? (ist dehr TSIM-uh-preyes mit FREW-shtewk)
Where is the elevator?	Wo ist der Aufzug? (voh ist dehr OWF-tsook)

Please wake me tomorrow at ___ o'clock.	Bitte wecken sie mich morgen um ___ Uhr. (BIT-eh VEHK-en zee mikh MORG-en um oor)
Are there any letters (messages) for me?	Gibt es Briefe (Nachrichten) für mich? (gipt ehs BREEF-en [NAHKH-rikht-en] fewr mikh)
May I leave this in your safe?	Darf ich dies in Ihrem Tresor lassen? (dahrf ikh dees in EE-rem treh-ZOHR LASS- en)
Please send someone up for the bags.	Bitte schicken Sie jemanden fuer das Gepaeck hoch. (BIT-eh SHIK-en zee YAY-mahnd-en fewr dahs geh-PEHK hohkh)
Please prepare my bill.	Bitte bereiten Sie meine Rechnung vor. (BIT-eh beh-REYET-en zee MEYEN-en REKH-nung for)

Transportation

Street cars	Strassenbahn (SHTRAASS-en-baan)
Buses	Busse (BUSS-eh)
Suburban commuter trains of German Rail	S-Bahn (EHS-baan)
Subway	U-Bahn (OO-baan)
• the men's room	• die Herrentoilette (de HEHR-en-toy-let-eh)
• the ladies' room	• die Damentoilette (dee DAAM-en-toy-let-eh)
• the bus stop	• die Bushaltestelle (dee BUS-hahl-teh-shteh-leh)
• the nearest subway station	• die nächste U-Bahn Station (Untergrund-bahn) (dee NAYKH-steh oo-baan shtah-TSYOHN [UNT-uh-grunt-baan])
Where can I buy a ticket?	Wo kann ich eine Fahrkarte kaufen? (voh kahn ikh EYEN-eh FAAR-kahr-teh KOWF-en)
Do I have to change trains?	Muß ich umsteigen? (muss ikh UM-shteyeg-en)
Drive me to the hotel.	Fahren Sie mich zum Hotel. (FAAR-en zee mikh tsoom ho-TEL)
• railroad station	• Bahnhof (BAAN-hoht)

• airport	• Flughafen(FLOOK-haa-fen)
Let me off at the next corner.	Lassen Sie mich an der nächsten Ecke aussteigen! (LASS-en zee mikh ahn dehr NAYKST-en EK-oh OWS-shteye-gen)
Please wait for me.	Warten Sie auf mich bitte. (VAART-en zee owf mikh BIT-eh)
Please tell me arrival and departure time again.	Bitte sagen Sie mir noch einmal Ankunft-und Abflugzeiten. (BIT-eh ZAAG-en zee meer parture timesnoch EYEN-maal AHN-kunft unt AHP-flook-tseye-ten)
I want a seat next to the window in the (non) smoking section.	Ich möchte einen Fensterplatz (Nicht) Raucher haben. (ikh MERKH-teh EYEN-en FEHNST-uh-plahts [nikht] ROWKH-uh HAAB-en)
When do I have to check in?	Wann muß ich mich melden? (vahn muss ikh mikh MEHLD-en)
May I take this with me as carry-on luggage?	Darf ich dies als Handgepäck mit-nehmen? (daarf ikh dees ahls HAHNT-ge-pehk MIT-nay-men)
Is there a car rental office nearby?	Gibt es eine Autovermietung in der Nähe? (gipt ehs EYEN-eh OW-toh-fehr-meet-ung in dehr NAY-eh)
What sort of cars do you have available?	Was für Wagen haben Sie ze vermieten? (vahs fewr VAAG-en HAAB-en zee tsoo fehr-MEET-en)
How much does it cost per ____ ?	Wieviel kostet es pro ____? (VEE-feel KOST-et ehs proh)
• day	• Tag (taak)
• week	• Woche (VOKH-eh)
• month	• Monat (MOH-naat)
• kilometer	• Kilometer(kee-loh-MAYT-uh)
How much is the insurance?	Was kostet die Versicherung? (vahs KOST-et dee fehr-ZIKH-ehr-ung)
Do I have to pay for gas?	Muß ich das Benzin bezahlen? (muss ikh dahs behn-TSEEN beh-TSAAL-en)
Do I have to leave a deposit?	Muß ich etwas hinterlegen? (muss ikh EHT-vahs hin-tehr-LAYG-en)

I want to rent the car here and leave it in Munich.	Ich will das Auto hier mieten und es in München wieder abgeben. (ikh vil dahs OW-toh heer MEET-en unt ehs in MEWN-khen VEED-uh AHP-gayb-en)
Is there an additional charge for that?	Entstehen mir dadurch zusätzliche Kosten? (ehnt-SHTAY-en meer daa-DURKH TSOO-zehts-likh-eh KOST-en)
Here is my driver's license.	Hier haben Sie meinen Führer-schein. (heer HAAB-en zee MEYEN-en FEWR-ehr-sheyen)
Where is the nearest gas station (with service)?	Wo ist die nächste Tankstelle (mit Bedienung)? (voh ist dee NAYKST-eh TAHNK-shtehl-eh [mit beh-DEEN-ung])
Fill it up, please.	Voll, bitte. (fol, BIT-eh)

Drivers should recognize these international road signs.

Guarded railroad crossing

Yield

Stop

Right of way

Dangerous intersection ahead

Gasoline (petrol) ahead

Parking

No vehicles allowed

Dangerous curve

Pedestrian crossing

Oncoming traffic
has right of way

No bicycles allowed

No parking allowed

No entry

No left turn

No U-turn

No passing

Border crossing

Traffic signal ahead

Speed limit

Traffic circle (roundabout)
ahead

Minimum speed limit

All traffic turns left

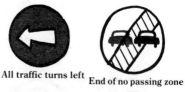

End of no passing zone

One-way street

Detour

Danger ahead

Entrance to expressway

Expressway ends

Leisure Time

I'd like to go to an interesting nightclub tonight.	Ich möchte gerne in ein interessantes Nachtlokal heute abend gehen. (ikh MERKHT-eh GEHRN-eh in eyen in-teh-ress-AHNT-es NAKHT-lo-kaal HOYT-eh AAB-ent GAT-en)
Is a reservation necessary?	Muß man reservieren lassen? (muss mahn reh-zehr-VEER-en LASS-en)
I'd like a good table.	Ich möchte einen guten Tisch. (ikh MERKHT-eh EYEN-en GOOT-en tish)
Where is the check-room?	Wo ist die Garderobe? (voh ist dee gahr-deh-ROHB-eh)
May I smoke?	Darf ich rauchen? (dahrf ikh ROWKH-en?)
Where can I buy English newspapers?	Wo kann ich englische Zeitungen kaufen? (voh kahn ikh EHNG-lish-eh TSEYET-ung-en KOWF-en?)
I'm looking for ____.	Ich suche ____. (ikh ZOOKH-eh)
• a tennis court	• einen Tennisplatz (EYEN-en TEN-is-plahts)
• a golf course	• einen Golfplatz (EYEN-en GOLF-plahts)
Where can I find a swimming pool?	Wo kann ich ein Schwimmbad finden? (voh kahn ikh eyen SHVIM-baat FIND-en)

Restaurants

Breakfast	Frühstück (FREW-shtewk)
Lunch	Mittagessen (MIT-aak-ehs-en)
Dinner	Abendessen (AAB-ehnt-ehs-en)

spoon	einen Löffel (EYEN-en LERF-el)
fork	eine Gabel (EYEN-eh GAAB-el)
knife	ein Messer (eyen MESS-uh)
glass	ein Glas (eyen glaas)
plate	einen Teller (EYEN-en TEL-uh)
chair	einen Stuhl (EYEN-en shtool)
ashtray	einen Aschenbecher (EYEN-en AHSH-en-bekh-uh)
napkin	eine Serviette (EYEN-eh zehr-VYEHT-eh)
Is there a good, not too expensive, German restaurant around here?	Gibt es ein gutes, nicht zu teures deutsches Restaurant in der Nähe? (gipt ehs eyen GOOT-es mikht tsoo TOYR-es DOY-ches restow-RAHNG in dehr NAY-eh)
Waiter!	Kellner! (KELN-uh)
Waitress!	Fräulein! (FROY-leyen)
Do you have a table for me?	Haben Sie einen Tisch für mich? (HAAB-en zee EYEN-en tish fewr mikh)
May we see the menu, please?	Können wir die Speisekarte haben? (KERN-en veer dee SHPEYEZ-en-kaart-eh HAAB-en)
What do you recommend?	Was empfehlen Sie? (vahs ehmp-FAYL-en zee)
May I take a look at the wine list please?	Darf ich mir bitte die Wein-karte ansehen? (daarf ikh meer BIT-eh dee VEYEN-kaart-eh AHN-zay-en)
Beer, please.	Ein Bier, bitte. (eyen beer BIT-eh)
Where can I wash my hands?	Wo kann ich mir die Hände waschen? (voh kahn ikh meer dee HEHND-eh VAHSH-en)
The check, please.	Die Rechnung, bitte! (dee REKH-nung BIT-eh)

Shopping

I must do some shopping today.	Ich muß heute einige Einkäufe machen. (ikh muss HOT-teh EYE-ni-geh EYEN-koy-feh NAH-khen)
I'm looking for ____.	Ich suche ____. (ikh ZOOKH-eh)
• a department store	• ein Warenhous (eyen VAAR-en-hows)
• a camera shop	• ein Photogeschäft (eyen FOH-toh-geh-shehft)

• a book store	• eine Buchhandlung (EYEN-eh BOOKH-hahnt-lung)
• a china shop	• einen Porzellanladen (EYEN-en por-tseh-LAAN-laad-en)
How much does that cost?	Wieviel kostet das? (VEE-feel KOST-et dahs)
Will you accept this credit card?	Nehmen Sie diese freditkarte an? (NAYM-en zee DEEZ-eh kray-DIT-kaar-teh ahn)

Medical Care

I don't feel well.	Ich fühle mich nicht wohl. (ikh FEWL-eh mikh nikht vohl)
I think I'm sick.	Ich glaube, ich bin krank. (ikh GLOWB-eh ikh bin krahnk)
I need a doctor.	Ich brauche einen Arzt. (ikh BROWKH-eh EYEN-en ahrtst)
Is there a doctor here who speaks English?	Gibt's hier einen Arzt, der Englisch spricht? (gipts heer EYEN-en ahrtst dehr EHNG-lish shprikht)
I've had this pain since yesterday.	Seit gestern habe ich diese Schmerzen. (zeyet GEHST-ehrn HAAB-en ikh DEEZ-eh SHMEHRTS-en)
I am a diabetic and take insulin.	Ich bin Diabetiker und nehme Insulin. (ikh bin dee-ah-BEH-tik-uh unt NAYM-eh in-zoo-LEEN)
I have heart trouble.	Ich bin herzkrank. (ikh bin HEHRTS-krahnk)
Unfortunately I must go to the dentist.	Leider muß ich zum Zahnarzt. (LEYED-uh muss ikh tsoom TSAAN-ahrtst)
Do you know a good one?	Kennen Sie einen guten? (KEN-en zee EYEN-en GOOT-en)
Where can I find the nearest (all-night pharmacy?	Wo finde ich die nächste Apotheke (mit Nachtdienst)? (voh FIND-eh ikh dee NAYKST-eh ah-poh-TAYK-eh [mit NAHKHT-deenst])
I'm looking for something for ____.	Ich suche etwas gegen ____. ikh ZOOKH-eh EHT-vahs GAYG-en ____.
• a cold	• eine Erkältung (EYEN-eh ehr-KEHLT-ung)
• constipation	• Verstopfung (fehr-SHTOPF-ung)

- a cough
- a fever
- diarrhea
- a hangover
- indigestion

- headache

- insomnia

- Husten (HOOST-en)
- Fieber (FEEB-un)
- Durchfall (DOORKH-fahl)
- Kater (KAAT-uh)
- Magenverstimmung (MAAG-en-fehr-shtim-ung)
- Kopfschmerzen (KOPF-shmehrts-en)
- Schlaflosigkeit (SHLAAF-loh-zikh-keyet)

Telephones

I'm looking for ____.

- a telephone booth
- a telephone directory

May I use your phone?

Here is the number.

Can you help me?

It's a local call.

- a long-distance call

- a person-to-person call

- a collect call

Can you dial direct?

May I speak to Mr. (Mrs., Miss) ____?

Speak louder (more slowly).

Don't hang up.

I'll call again later.

Ich suche ____. (ikh ZOOKH-eh)

- eine Telefonzelle (EYEN-eh tay-leh-FOHN-tsel-eh)
- ein Telefonbuch (eyen tay-leh-FOHN-bookh)

Darf ich Ihr Telefon benutzen? (dahrf ikh eer tay-leh-FOHN beh-NUTS-en)

Hier ist die Nummer. (heer ist dee NUM-uh)

Können Sie mir helfen? (KERN-en zee meer HELF-en)

Es ist ein Ortsgespräch. (ehs ist eyen ORTS-geh-shpraykh)

- ein Ferngespräch (eyen FEHRN-geh-shpraykh)
- ein Gespräch mit Voranmeldung (eyen geh-SHPRAYKH mit FOHR-ahn-mehld-ung)
- ein R-Gespräch (eyen ehr-geh-SHPRAYKH)

Kann man durchwählen? (kahn mahn DOORKH-vayl-en)

Darf ich bitte Herrn (Frau, Fräulein) ____ sprechen? (dahrf ikh BIT-eh hehrn [frow, FROY-leyen] SHPREHKH-en)

Sprechen Sie lauter (langsamer). (SHPREHKH-en zee LOWT-uh [LAHNG-zaam-uh])

Bleiben Sie am Apparat. (BLEYEB-en zee ahm ah-pah-RAAT)

Später rufe ich noch einmal an. (SHPAYT-uh roof ikh nokh EYEN-maal ahn)

I'd like to leave a message.	Ich möchte etwas ausrichten lassen. (ikh merkht EHT-vahs OWSS-rikht-en LAHSS-en)
Where is the post office?	Wo ist das Postamt? (voh ist dahs POST-ahmt)
Where can I find a mailbox?	Wo finde ich einen Briefkasten? (voh FIND-en ikh EYEN-en BREEF-kahst-en)
Where is the stamp window?	Wo ist der Schalter für Briefmarken? (voh ist dehr SHAHLT-uh fewr BREEF-mahrk-en)
Where can I send a telegram?	Wo kann ich ein Telegramm aufgeben? (vo kahn ikh eyen tay-leh-GRAHM OWF-gayb-en)
I want to send it collect.	Ich möchte, daß der Empfänger es bezahlt. (ikh MERKHT-eh dahs dehr ehmp-FEHNG-uh ehs beh-TSAALT)
At what time will it arrive?	Um wieviel Uhr wird's ankommen? (um VEE-feel oor veerts AHN-kom-en)

Signs

Abfahrten	Departures
Aufzug	Elevator
Ausgang	Exit
Auskunft	Information
Belegt	Filled Up
Besetzt	Occupied
Betreten des Rasens verboten	Keep off the grass
Damentoilette	Ladies' room
Drücken	Push
Eingang	Entrance
Gefahr	Danger
Geschlossen	Closed
Herrentoilette	Men's room
Nicht berühren	Do not touch
Nichtraucher	Nonsmoking section
Notausgang	Emergency exit
Rauchen verboten	No smoking
Ziehen	Pull

Numbers

Cardinal Numbers

0	null (nul)
1	eins (eyenss)
2	zwei, zwo (tsveye), (tsvoh)
3	drei (dreye)

4	vier (feer)	
5	fünf (fewnf)	
6	sechs (zehks)	
7	sieben (ZEEB-en)	
8	acht (ahkht)	
9	neun (noyn)	
10	zehn (tsayn)	
11	elf (elf)	
12	zwölf (tsverlf)	
13	dreizehn (DREYE-tsayn)	
14	vierzehn (FEER-tsayn)	
15	fünfzehn (FEWNF-tsayn)	
16	sechzehn (ZEHKH-tsayn)	
17	siebzehn (ZEEP-tsayn)	
18	achtzehn (AHKHT-tsayn)	
19	neunzehn (NOYN-tsayn)	
20	zwanzig (TSVAHN-tsikh)	
21	einundzwanzig (EYEN-unt-tsvahn-tsikh)	
22	zweiundzwanzig (TSVEYE-unt-tsvahn-tsikh)	
23	dreiundzwanzig (DREYE-unt-tsvahn-tsikh)	
24	vierundzwanzig (FEER-unt-tsvahn-tsikh)	
25	fünfundzwanzig (FEWNF-unt-tsvahn-tsikh)	
26	sechsundzwanzig (ZEHKS-unt-tsvahn-tsikh)	
27	siebenundzwanzig (ZEEB-en-unt-tsvahn-tsikh)	
28	achtundzwanzig (AHKHT-unt-tsvahn-tsikh)	
29	neunundzwanzig (NOYN-unt-tsvahn-tsikh)	
30	dreißig (DREYESS-ikh)	
31	einundreißig (EYEN-unt-dreyess-ikh)	
40	vierzig (FEER-tsikh)	
41	einundvierzig (EYEN-unt-feer-tsikh)	
50	fünfzig (FEWNF-tsikh)	
60	sechzig (ZEHKH-tsikh)	
70	siebzig (ZEEP-tsikh)	
80	achtzig (AHKH-tsikh)	
90	neunzig (NOYN-tsikh)	
100	(ein)hundert ([eyen]HUN-dehrt)	
101	hunderteins (HUN-dehrt-eyenss)	
102	hundertzwei (HUN-dehrt-tsveye)	

200	zweihundert (TSVEYE-hun-dehrt)
300	dreihundert (DREYE-hun-dehrt)
400	vierhundert (FEER-hun-dehrt)
500	fünfhundert (FEWNF-hun-dehrt)
600	sechshundert (ZEHKS-hun-dehrt)
700	siebenhundert (ZEEB-en-hun-dehrt)
800	achthundert (AHKHT-hun-dehrt)
900	neunhundert (NOYN-hun-dehrt)
1,000	(ein)tausend ([eyen] TOW-zehnt)
2,000	zweitausend (TSVEYE-tow-zehnt)
3,000	dreitausend (DREYE-tow-zehnt)
4,000	viertausend (FEER-tow-zehnt)
5,000	fünftausend (FEWNF-tow-zehnt)
6,000	sechstausend (ZEHKS-tow-zehnt)
7,000	siebentausend (ZEEB-en-tow-zehnt)
8,000	achttausend (AHKHT-tow-zehnt)
9,000	neuntausend (NOYN-tow-zehnt)
10,000	zehntausend (TSAYN-tow-zehnt)
20,000	zwanzigtausend (TSVAHN-tsikh-tow-zehnt)
30,000	dreißigtausend (DREYESS-ikh-tow-zehnt)
40,000	vierzigtausend (FEER-tsikh-tow-zehnt)
50,000	fünfzigtausend (FEWNF-tsikh-tow-zehnt)
60,000	sechzigtausend (ZEHKH-tsikh-tow-zehnt)
70,000	siebzigtausend (ZEEP-tsikh-tow-zehnt)
80,000	achtzigtausend (AHKH-tsikh-tow-zehnt)
90,000	neunzigtausend (NOYN-tsikh-tow-zehnt)
100,000	(ein)hunderttausend (eyen)HUN-dehrt-tow-zehnt)

200,000	zweihunderttausend (TSVEYE-hun-dehrt-two-zehnt)
300,000	dreihunderttausend (DREYE-hun-dehrt-tow-zehnt)
400,000	vierhunderttausend (FEER-hun-dehrt-tow-zehnt)
500,000	fünfhunderttausend (FEWNF-hun-dehrt-tow-zehnt)
600,000	sechshunderttausend (ZEHKS-hun-dehrt-tow-zehnt)
700,000	siebenhunderttausend (ZEEB-en-hun-dehrt-tow-zehnt)
800,000	achthundertausend (AHKHT-hun-dehrt-tow-zehnt)
900,000	neunhunderttausend (NOYN-hun-dehrt-tow-zehnt)
1,000,000	eine Million (EYEN-eh mil-YOHN)
2,000,000	zwei Millionen (TSVEYE mil-YOHN-en)
10,000,000	zehn Millionen (TSAYN mil-YOHN-en)
100,000,000	(ein)hundert Millionen (eyen)HUN-dehrt-mil-YOHN-en
1,000,000,000	eine Milliarde (EYEN-eh mil YAHRD-eh)

Examples

540	fünfhundertvierzig (FEWNF-hun-dehrt-feer-tsikh)
1,540	eintausendfünfhundertvierzig (EYEN-tow-zehnt-fewnf-hun-dehrt-feer-tsikh)
11,540	elftausendfünfhundertvierzig (ELF-tow-zehnt-fewnf-hun-dehrt-feer-tsikh)
611,540	sechshundertelftausendfünfhundertvierzig (ZEHKS-hun-dehrt-elf-tow-zehnt-fewnf-hun-dehrt-feer-tsikh)
1,611,540	eine Million sechshundertelftausendfünfhundertvierzig (EYEN-eh mil-yohn zehks-hun-dehrt-elf-tow-zehnt-fewnf-hun-dehrt-feer-tsikh)

Years

1900	neunzehnhundert (NOYN-tsayn-hun-dehrt)

1987	neunzehnhundertsiebenun- dachtzig (NOYN-tsayn-hun- dehrt-seeb-en-unt-ahkh-tsikh)
1988	neunzehnhundertachtundacht- zig (NOYN-tsayn-hun-dehrt- ahkht-unt-ahkh-tsikh)
1989	neunzehnhundertneunundacht- zig (NOYN-tsayn-hun-dehrt- noyn-unt-ahkh-tsikh)
1990	neunzehnhundertneunzig (NOYN-tsayn-hun-dehrt- noyn-tsikh)

Ordinal Numbers

first	erst- (ayrst)
second	zweit- (tsveyet)
third	dritt- (drit)
fourth	viert- (feert)
fifth	fünft- (fewnft)
sixth	sechst- (zehkst)
seventh	siebt- (zeept)
eighth	acht- (ahkht)
ninth	neunt- (noynt)
tenth	zehnt- (tsaynt)

In writing, ordinals are abbreviated by placing a period after the number.

the first day	der erste Tag (der 1. Tag) (dehr AYRST-eh taak)
for the second time	zum zweiten Mal (zum 2. Mal) (tsoom TSVEYET-en maal)
once	einmal (EYEN-maal)
twice	zweimal (TSVEYE-maal)

German Abbreviations

Abt.	Abteilung	compartment
ACS	Automobil-Club der Schweiz	Automobile Association of Switzerland
ADAC	Allgemeiner Deutscher Auto-mobil Club	General Automo-bile Association of Germany
Bhf	Bahnhof	railway station
BRD	Bundesrepublik Deutschland	Federal Republic of Germany (West Germany)
BMW	Bayerische Motorenwerke	Bavarian Motor Works
CDU	Christlich-Demokratische Union	Christian Demo-cratic Union

DB	Deutsche Bundes-bahn	West German Railways
DBP	Deutsche Bundes-post	West German Postal Service
DDR	Deutsche De-mokratische Republik	German Demo-cratic Republic (East Germany)
DZT	Deutsche Zentrale für Tourismus	German National Tourist Board
d.h.	das heißt	that is (i.e.)
e.V.	eingetragener Verein	registered associa-tion corporation
FKK	Freikörperkultur	Free Physical Culture (nudism)
Frl.	Fräulein	Miss
GmbH	Gesellschaft mit beschränkter Haftung	limited-liability corporation
Hr.	Herr	Mr.
JH	Jugendherberge	youth hostel
km	Kilometer	kilometer
KG	Kommandit-gesellschaft	limited partnership
LKW	Lastkraftwagen	truck
Mill.	Million	million
ÖAMTC	Österreichischer Automobil-Motorradund Touring-Club	Austrian Automo-bile, Motorcy-cle, and Touring Assocation
ÖBB	Österreichische Bundesbahnen	Austrian Federal Railroad
PKW	Personenkraft-wagen	passenger car
PTT	Post, Telefon, Telegraph	Postal, Telephone, and Telegraph Office
SSB	Schweizerische Bundesbahnen	Swiss Federal Railways
SPD	Sozialdemokra-tische Partei Deutschlands	Social Democratic Party of Germany
Str.	Straße	street
TCS	Touring-Club der Schweiz	Swiss Touring Association
usf./usw.	und so fort/und so weiter	et cetera (etc.)
Ztg.	Zeitung	newspaper
z.Z.	zur Zeit	at the present time

BUSINESS DICTIONARY

All nouns in German are capitalized. They come in three genders: masculine, feminine, and neuter. **Der, die** and **das** all mean *the* and indicate the noun's gender—masculine, feminine and neuter, respectively. *The,* for all nouns in the plural, is **die**. The feminine forms for nouns of agent usually end in **in** and sometimes they take an umlaut.

der Anwalt lawyer (m)   **die Anwältin** lawyer (f)

A few nouns, like **das Firmenmitglied**, do double duty for males and females. But few such nouns exist. For the sake of simplicity and space, we've limited the definitions to masculine forms when necessary. When referring to a female in this position, use the feminine form, as illustrated above.

Many of the definitions in this dictionary contain a noun modified by an adjective or an adverb. Fortunately, adverbs always stay the same. But German adjectives are variable, depending on the gender and grammatical usage of the noun. The English-German dictionary defines *competitive price* as **der konkurrenzfähige Preis.** The ending on the adjective is *e* because the word for *the* is given. In the German-English dictionary, however, *competitive price* is listed without the word *the* and is therefore **konkurrenzfähiger Preis** (note the final **r** on the adjective). The English-German dictionary gives you the word *the,* thus indicating gender. If there is an adjective, it has the correct ending necessary when *the* is used.

Verbs change endings, too, depending, as in English, on the subject and the time (tense). But that need not concern you here since verb forms are given in the infinitive, which in German usually ends in **en.**

kaufen to buy   **verkaufen** to sell

German has an abundance of commercial terms. Many are of Latin origin by way of Italian or French. There are usually Germanic synonyms. Note:

die Gleichheit	die Herstellung
parity	production
die Parität	die Produktion

If you don't know the German term, use an English one and it's probable that you'll be understood. Whether you use the Germanic or Germanized term in German, try to pronounce the word distinctly and sharply, since German is a more strongly accented language than English (see Pronunciation Guide).

ENGLISH TO GERMAN

A

abandon (v)   aufgeben, abandonnieren, ausbuchen

abandonment   die Preisgabe, die Ausbuchung

abatement (reduction)   der Abschlag, die Herabsetzung

abatement (suspension)   die Einstellung

ability-to-pay concept   die Zahlungsfähigkeit

above mentioned   obenerwähnt, obengenannt

above par   über pari

above-the-line   über der Linie, über dem Strich

above-the-line (short term)   kurzfristig

absentee owner   der Eigentümer ohne Leitungsfunktion

absenteeism   die Abwesenheit

absorb (v)   absorbieren

absorb the loss (v)   den Verlust auffangen

absorption costing   das Kostenaufteilungsverfahren

accelerated depreciation   die erhöhte Abschreibung

accelerating premium   die produktivitätsabhängige Leistungsprämie

acceleration clause   die Fälligkeitsklausel

accept (v)   annehmen, akzeptieren

acceptable quality level   das annehmbare Qualitätsniveau

acceptance agreement   der Annahmevertrag

acceptance bill   das Akzept, der Wechsel

acceptance (bill of agreement)   das Akzept

acceptance credit   der Wechselkredit

acceptance house   die Wechselbank, die Diskontbank, das Akzepthaus

acceptance sampling   die Stichprobenprüfung

acceptor   der Akzeptant

accession rate   die Einstellungsquote

accident damage   der Unfallschaden

accommodation bill   der Gefälligkeitswechsel

accommodation credit   der Gefälligkeitskredit

accommodation endorsement das Gefälligkeitsindossament

accommodation paper das Gefälligkeitsakzept

accommodation parity die Gefälligkeitsparität

accommodation platform die Gefälligkeitsplattform

accompanied goods die begleiteten Waren

accord and satisfaction der aussergerichtliche Vergleich

account das Konto

account balance der Kontostand

account day der Abrechnungstag

account executive der Kundenbetreuer, der Wertpapierberater

account for (v) Rechenschaft ablegen

account number die Kontonummer

accountable rechenschaftspflichtig

accountant der Buchhalter

accountant, chief der Buchhaltungsleiter

accountant (CPA) der Wirtschaftsprüfer

accounting, cost die Kostenrechnung

accounting department die Buchhaltung

accounting, management das Rechnungswesen für Betriebsführungsbedürfnisse

accounting method die Buchungsmethode, das Buchungsverfahren

accounting period der Rechnungsabschnitt, der Buchungszeitraum

accounting principles die Bilanzierungsrichtlinien

accounts payable die kurz- und mittelfristigen Verbindlichkeiten, die Buchschulden

accounts receivable die ausstehenden Forderungen, die Buchforderungen

accretion der Zuwachs

accrual das Auflaufen

accrue (v) auflaufen, anwachsen

accrued assets die antizipativen Aktiva

accrued depreciation die entstandende Abschreibung

accrued expenses der antizipative Aufwand

accrued interest die aufgelaufenen Zinsen

accrued revenue   der antizipative Ertrag

accrued taxes   die aufgelaufenen Steuern, die Steuerschulden

accumulated depreciation   die Wertberichtigung auf das Anlagevermögen

acid-test ratio   der Barliquiditätsgrad, das Flüssigkeitsverhältnis

acknowledge (v)   bestätigen

acknowledgement of payment   die Zahlungsbestätigung

acoustic coupler   die akustische Koppelung

acquire (v)   erwerben, gewinnen

acquired rights   die erworbenen Rechte

acquisition   der Erwerb

acquisition profile   das Erwerbungsprofil

acreage allotment   die Parzellierung

acronym   das Akronym

across the board   generell, allgemein

act of God   die höhere Gewalt

action, legal   die Klage, der Prozeß

active account   das Aktivkonto

active assets   die Aktiva

active debts   die Außenstände

actual cash value   der effektive Geldwert, der Versicherungswert

actual costs   die Selbstkosten, die Istkosten

actual liability   die tatsächliche Haftpflicht

actual total loss   der tatsächliche Gesamtverlust

actuals   die Effektiveinnahmen

actuary   der Versicherungsmathematiker, der Versicherungsstatistiker

ad valorem duty   der Wertzoll

add-on sales   der Mehrumsatz

addendum   der Zusatz

address commission   die Provision des Verladers

adjudge (v)   gerichtlich entscheiden

adjudication   das Urteil

adjust (v)   anpassen, ausgleichen

adjust (v) (correct)   berichtigen

adjusted CIF price   der berichtigte cif-Preis

adjusted gross income das steuerpflichtige Bruttoeinkommen

adjusted rate der angepaßter Kurs, der Staffeltarif

adjusting entry die Berichtigungsbuchung

adjustment account das Berichtigungskonto

adjustment trigger der Regelungsauslöser

administration die Verwaltung

administrative verwaltungsmäßig

administrative expenses die Verwaltungskosten

administrator der Verwalter

advance (v) (money) vorschießen

advance (v) (promote) fördern

advance freight die vorausbezahlte Fracht

advance notice die Vorankündigung

advance payment die Vorauszahlung

advance refunding die Rückerstattung im voraus

adverse balance der Sollsaldo, der Verlustsaldo

advertisement die Reklame, die Werbung

advertising agency die Werbeagentur

advertising budget das Werbebudget, der Werbeetat

advertising campaign die Werbekampagne

advertising expenses die Werbekosten

advertising manager der Werbeleiter, der Publicitymanager

advertising media die Werbeträger

advertising rate der Anzeigentarif

advertising research die Werbeforschung

advice note das Benachrichtigungsschreiben

advise (v) beraten

advisory council der Beirat

advisory service der Beratungsdienst

affidavit die eidesstattliche Erklärung

affiliate die Tochtergesellschaft, die Konzerngesellschaft

affirmative action die Vorschriften über die Anstellung von Frauen und Minoritäten

affreightment der Schiffsfrachtvertrag

afloat (debt-free) schuldenfrei

afloat (in circulation) im Umlauf

after-hours trading die nachbörslichen Umsätze

after-sales service   der Kundendienst

after-sight   das nach Sicht Akzept

after-tax real rate of return   der Realgewinn nach Steuern

afterdate (v)   nachdatieren

against all risks   gegen alle Gefahren

agency   die Agentur, die Vertretung

agency fee   die Vertretungsgebühr

agenda   die Tagesordnung

agent   der Vertreter

aggregate demand   die Gesamtnachfrage

aggregate risk   das Gesamtrisiko

aggregate supply   das Gesamtangebot

agreement   die Übereinstimmung, die Vereinbarung

agreement (written)   der Vertrag

agricultural paper   das landwirtschaftliche Akzept

agricultural products   die landwirtschaftlichen Erzeugnisse

agriculture   die Landwirtschaft

air express   der Luftexpress, das Lufteilgut

air freight   die Luftfracht

air shipment   die Luftfrachtsendung

algorithm   der Algorithmus

alien corporation   die ausländische Gesellschaft

all in cost   der Gesamtpreis, die Gesamtkosten

all or none   alles oder nichts

allocation of costs   die Kostenzuteilung

allocation of responsibilities   die Verantwortungsverteilung

allocation, resource   die Mittelverwendung

allonge   der Verlängerungsabschnitt

allot (v)   verteilen, zuweisen

allotment   die Verteilung, die Zuweisung

allotment letter   der Zuteilungsschein

allow (v)   erlauben

allowance, depreciation   der Abschreibungsbetrag

allowance (discount)   der Rabatt

allowance (subsidy)   der Zuschuß

alongside   neben, daneben

alteration die Änderung

alternative order die Alternativbestellung

amalgamation die Vereinigung, die Fusion

amend (v) abändern, ändern

amendment die Abänderung, die Änderung

amortization die Tilgung, die Amortisation

amount der Betrag

amount due der Schuldbetrag

analog computer der Analogrechner, der Analog-computer

analysis die Analyse, die Untersuchung, die Studie

analysis, breakeven die Deckungsbeitragsrechnung

analysis, competitor die Konkurrenzstudie

analysis, cost die Kostenanalyse

analysis, cost-benefit die Kostennutzenanalyse

analysis, critical path die Analyse der Netzplan-technik

analysis, financial die Finanzanalyse

analysis, functional die Funktionsanalyse

analysis, input-output die Eingaben-Ausgaben Analyse

analysis, investment die Investitionsanalyse, die An-lagenanalyse

analysis, job die Arbeitsstudie, die Arbeitsplatzun-tersuchung

analysis, needs die Bedarfsanalyse

analysis, product die Warenanalyse

analysis, profitability die Rentabilitätsanalyse

analysis, risk die Risikoanalyse

analysis, sales die Absatzanalyse

analysis, systems die Systemanalyse

analyst der Analytiker

anchorage dues die Ankergebühr

ancillary operation der Nebenbetrieb

annual jährlich

annual accounts die Jahresabrechnung, der Jahres-abschluss

annual audit die Jahresprüfung

annual report der Jahresbericht

annuitant der Leibrentenempfänger

annuity die Jahresrente

antidumping duty der Antidumpingzoll

antique authenticity certificate die Echtheitsbescheinigung für Antiquitäten

antitrust laws die Kartellgesetze

apparel die Kleidung

application form das Antragsformular

applied proceeds swap der angewandte Erlöstausch

appointment (engagement) die Verabredung

appointment (nomination) die Ernennung

appraisal die Schätzung, die Bewertung

appraise (v) bewerten, abschätzen

appreciation die Wertsteigerung, der Wertzuwachs

apprentice der Lehrling

appropriation der Bereitstellungfonds

approval die Bewilligung, die Zustimmung

approve (v) billigen

approved securities die genehmigten Wertpapiere

arbitrage die Arbitrage

arbitration das Schiedsverfahren

arbitration agreement das Schiedsabkommen

arbitrator der Schiedsrichter

area manager der Gebietsleiter, der Bezirksleiter

arithmetic mean das arithmetische Mittel

armaments die Rüstung

arrears die Ruckstände

as is goods die Waren ohne Gewähr, die Ausschußware

as per advice laut Bericht

as soon as possible so schnell wie möglich, so bald wie möglich

asked price der Briefkurs

assay die Feinheitgehaltsbestimmung

assay (v) prüfen

assemble (v) (people) versammeln

assemble (v) (things) zustammenstellen, montieren

assembly die Versammlung, die Montage

assembly line die Montagebahn, das Fließband

assess (v) bewerten

assessed valuation   die steuerliche Veranlagung

assessment   die Veranlagung, die Besteuerung

asset   das Vermögensstück

asset turnover   der Vermögensumsatz

asset value   der Vermögenswert

assets, accrued   die antizipativen Aktiva

assets, current   das kurzfristige Umlaufvermögen

assets, fixed   die Sachanlagen

assets, intangible   die immateriellen Werte

assets, liquid   das Umlaufvermögen

assets, net   das Reinvermögen

assets, tangible   die Sachanlagevermögen, die greifbaren Vermögenswerte

assign (v)   übertragen, zuweisen

assignee   der Übernehmer

assignor   der Abtretende

assistant   der Assistent

assistant general manager   der stellvertretende Generaldirektor

assistant manager   der stellvertretende Geschäftsführer

associate company   die Tochtergesellschaft, das Konzernunternehmen

assumed liability   die übernommene Verpflichtung

at and from   zu und von

at best   bestens, bestenfalls

at or better   zum Bestkauf, bestens kaufen

at par   zu pari, zum Nennwert

at sight   bei Sicht

at the close   bei Börsenschluß

at the market   zum Marktpreis

at the opening   bei Börsenöffnung

attach (v) (affix, adhere)   anhängen, beifügen

attach (v) (seize)   beschlagnahmen

attache case   die Aktentasche, der Aktenkoffer

attachment (contract)   das Anhängsel

attended time   die Wartezeit, die Anwesenheitszeit

attestation   die Bescheinigung, das Attest

attorney   der Anwalt, der Rechtsanwalt

attorney, power of   die Vollmacht

attrition   die Abnutzung

audit (v)   prüfen

audit, internal   die innerbetriebliche Revision

audit trail   der Prüfungsweg

auditing balance sheet   die Bilanzprüfung

auditor   der Buchprüfer

autarchy   die wirtschaftliche Unabhängigkeit, die Autarkie

authority, to have (v)   berechtigt sein, die Vollmacht haben

authorize (v)   ermächtigen, genehmigen

authorized dealer   der bevollmächtigte Händler

authorized shares   die genehmigten Aktien

authorized signature   die autorisierte Unterschrift

automatic   automatisch

automation   die Automation

autonomous   selbständig

availability, subject to   vorbehaltlich der Verfügbarkeit

average   der Durchschnitt

average cost   die Durchschnittskosten

average life   die durchschnittliche Lebensdauer

average price   der Durchschnittspreis

average unit cost   die durchschnittlichen Einheitskosten

B

back date (v)   zurückdatieren

back order   der noch nicht erledigte Auftrag

back pay   der Lohnrückstand

back selling   das Rückverkaufen

back taxes   die Steuerrückstände

back-to-back credit   das Gegenakkreditiv

back-to-back loan   die völlig gedeckte Anleihe

backlog   der Rückstand

backup bonds   die Pfandbriefe

backwardation   der Deport

bad debt   die uneinbringliche Forderung

balance   die Bilanz

balance, bank   das Bankguthaben

balance, credit   der Kreditsaldo

balance of payments   die Zahlungsbilanz

balance of trade   die Handelsbilanz

balance sheet   die Bilanz

balanced budget   der ausgeglichene Haushalt

bale capacity   die Ballenkapazität

bale cargo   die Ballenladung

ballast bonus   der Ballastbonus

balloon payment (loan repayment)   die größte
Zahlung

bank   die Bank

bank acceptance   das Bankakzept

bank account   das Bankkonto

bank balance   das Bankguthaben

bank charges   die Bankgebühren

bank check   der Bankscheck

bank deposit   die Bankeinlage

bank draft   die Banktratte, der Wechsel

bank examiner   der Bankrevisor

bank exchange   der Bankwechsel

bank holiday   der Bankfeiertag

bank letter of credit   das Bankakkreditiv, der Bankkreditbrief

bank loan   das Bankdarlehen

bank money order   die Bankgeldanweisung

bank note   die Banknote

bank rate   der Bankzins

bank release   die Bankfreigabe

bank statement   der Kontoauszug

bankbook   das Bankbuch

bankruptcy   der Konkurs, der Bankrott

bar chart   das Säulendiagramm

bareboat charter   der Bootsverleih ohne Mannschaft
und Verpflegung

bargain   der Gelegenheitskauf

bargaining power   die Verhandlungsstärke

barratry   die vorsätzliche Ladungsbeschädigung, die
Anstiftung zum Prozessieren

barter   der Tauschhandel

barter (v)   tauschen

base currency   die Grundwährung

base price   der Grundpreis

base rate   der Grundtarif

base year   das Basisjahr, das Vergleichsjahr

basis point   der Basispunkt

batch processing   die Schubverarbeitung, die Stapel-verarbeitung

batch production   die Serienproduktion

batten fitted   mit Latten versehen

baud   das Baud

bear (v)   tragen

bear market   die Baissebörse

bearer   der Inhaber

bearer bond   die Inhaberobligation

bearer security   das Inhaberpapier

bell-shaped curve   die Glockenkurve

below par   unter pari

below the line   unter dem Strich, langfristig

beneficiary   der Begünstigte

bequest   das Vermächtnis

berth terms   die Stückgutfracht

bid and asked   Brief und Geld, Angebot und Nach-frage

bid price   der Geldkurs

bid, takeover   das Übernahmeangebot

bill broker   der Wechselmakler

bill (currency)   die Banknote, der Geldschein

bill (invoice)   die Rechnung

bill of exchange   der Wechsel

bill of lading   der Frachtbrief

bill of sale   die Verkaufsurkunde, der Kaufvertrag

bill of sight   der Sichtwechsel

billboard   die Anschlagetafel

binary notation   die binäre Zahlendarstellung, die Binärschreibung

binder   der Vorvertrag

black market   der Schwarzmarkt

blanket insurance   die Kollektivversicherung
blanket order   der Blankoauftrag
blockage of funds   die Geldsperre
blocked currency   die nicht frei konvertierbare Währung
blue-chip stock   das erstklassige Wertpapier
blue-collar worker   der Fabrikarbeiter
blueprint   die Blaupause
board, executive   der Vorstand
board meeting   die Vorstandssitzung
board of directors   der Vorstand
board of supervisors   der Aufsichtsrat
boardroom   der Sitzungsraum
bond   die Schuldverschreibung, die Obligation, die Anleihe
bond issue   die Anleiheausgabe, die Anleiheemission
bond power   die Schuldverschreibungsvollmacht
bond rating   die Anleihebewertung
bonded carrier   der versicherte Bote
bonded goods   die Waren unter Zollverschluß, die zollpflichtigen Waren
bonded warehouse   das Zollagerhaus, der Zollspeicher, das Transitlager
bonus (premium)   die Prämie, die Gratifikation
book inventory   das Buchinventar
book value   der Buchwert
book value per share   der Buchwert pro Aktie
bookkeeping   die Buchhaltung
boom   die Hochkonjunktur
border   die Grenze
border tax adjustment   die Grenzsteuerberichtigung
borrow (v)   borgen
boycott   der Boykott
branch office   die Filiale, das Zweiggeschäft, die Zweigstelle
brand   die Marke
brand acceptance   die Annahme als Markenartikel
brand image   das Markenimage
brand loyalty   die Markentreue

brand recognition   die Markenanerkennung

break even (v)   die Gewinnschwelle erreichen

break-even point   der Kostendeckungspunkt, die Gewinnschwelle

breakeven analysis   die Deckungsbeitragsrechnung

briefcase   die Aktentasche

broken stowage   die Staulücken

broker   der Makler

budget   das Budget, der Haushalt, der Etat

budget, advertising   das Werbebudget, der Werbeetat

budget appropriation   die Haushaltsmittelbereitstellung

budget, balanced   der ausgeglichene Haushalt

budget, capital   das Investitionsbudget

budget, cash   der Kassenvoranschlag, der Zahlungshaushalt

budget forecast   der Haushaltsvoranschlag

budget, investment   das Investitionsbudget

budget, marketing   das Absatzbudget

budget, sales   der Absatzplan

bug (computers)   der Fehler, die Störung

bull   der Haussespekulant

bull market   die Hausseelbörse

burden rate   der Gemeinkostensatz

bureaucrat   der Bürokrat

business activity   die Geschäftstätigkeit

business card   die Geschäftskarte

business cycle   der Konjunkturzyklus

business management   die Betriebsleitung

business plan   der Geschäftsplan

business policy   die Betriebspolitik

business strategy   die Geschäftsstrategie

buy at best (v)   bestens kaufen

buy back (v)   zurückkaufen

buy on close (v)   bei Börsenschluß kaufen

buy on opening (v)   bei Börsenöffnung kaufen

buyer   der Käufer, der Abnehmer

buyer's market   der Käufermarkt

buyer's option   die Käuferoption

buyer's premium   das Käuferaufgeld

buyer's responsibility   die Verantwortung des Käufers

buyout (takeover)   die Übernahme

by-laws   die Vorschriften, die Statuten, die Satzung

by-product   das Nebenprodukt

byte   das Byte

C

cable   das Kabel, das Telegramm

cable transfer   die telegraphische Überweisung, die Drahtüberweisung

calculator   der Rechner

call (v)   anrufen, einziehen, kündigen

call back (v)   abrufen, zurückrufen

call feature   die Kündigungsklausel

call loan   der vorzeitig kündbare Kredit

call money   das täglich kündbare Geld

call option   die Bezugsoption

call price   der Kündigungspreis

call protection   der Kündigungsschutz

call rate   der Kündigungstarif

call rule   die Kündigungsregel

campaign, advertising   die Werbekampagne

cancel (v)   abbestellen

cancelled check   der eingelöste Scheck

capacity   die Kapazität

capacity, manufacturing   die Produktionskapazität, die Herstellungskapazität

capacity, plant   die betriebliche Leitsungsfähigkeit

capacity utilization   die Kapazitätsausnutzung

capital   das Kapital

capital account   das Kapitalkonto

capital asset   das Anlagevermögen

capital budget   das Investitionsbudget

capital expenditure   die Investitionsausgabe, der Kapitalaufwand

capital exports   die Kapitalausfuhr

capital gain (loss)   der Kapitalertrag (der Kapitalverlust)

capital goods   die Investitionsgüter, die Anlagewerte

capital increase   die Kapitalerhöhung

capital-intensive   kapitalintensiv

capital market   der Kapitalmarkt

capital-output ratio   der Kapitalkoeffizient

capital, raising   die Kapitalaufnahme, die Kapital-aufbringung

capital, return on   die Kapitalrendite

capital, risk   das Risikokapital

capital spending   die Kapitalaufwendungen

capital stock   die Stammaktie

capital structure   die Kapitalstruktur

capital surplus   der Kapitalüberschuß

capital, working   das Betriebskapital, das Umlaufs-vermögen

capitalism   der Kapitalismus

capitalization   die Kapitalisierung

cargo   die Ladung, die Fracht

carload   die Wagenladung

carnet   das Zollpapier für vorübergehende zollfreie Einführ

carrier   der Spediteur, der Transportunternehmer

carrier's risk   die Transporthaftung

carry back (v)   zurückbringen, zurücktragen

carry forward (v)   übertragen, vortragen

carrying charges   die Betriebskosten, die Lagerkosten

carrying value   der Buchwert

carryover   der Verlustvortrag

cartel   das Kartell

cash   das Bargeld

cash-and-carry   der Verkauf gegen Barzahlung und Selbstabholung

cash-basis accounting   die Buchführung der bar durchgeführten Geschäfte

cash balance   der Kassenbestand, der Geldbestand

cash before delivery   die Barzahlung im voraus

cash book   das Kassabuch

cash budget   der Kassenvoranschlag, der Zahlungs-haushalt

cash delivery   die Bargeldzustellung

cash discount das Kassaskonto, der Barzahlungsrabatt

cash dividend die Bardividende

cash entry der Kasseneintrag

cash flow der Finanzfluß, der Cash-flow, die Liquidität

cash flow statement die Kapitalflußrechnung

cash in advance die Vorausbezahlung

cash management die Kassenhaltung

cash on delivery die Zahlung bei Lieferung, die Nachnahmesendung

cash surrender value der Rückkaufswert

cashier's check der Kassenscheck, der Bankscheck

cassette die Kassette

casualty insurance die Unfallversicherung

catalog der Katalog, das Preisverzeichnis

ceiling die Höchstgrenze

central bank die Zentralbank

central processing unit die Zentralrecheneinheit

central rate der Leitkurs

centralization die Zentralisierung

certificate die Bescheinigung, die Bestätigung, das Zeugnis

certificate of deposit das Depositenzertifikat, der Depositenschein

certificate of incorporation die Gründungsurkunde

certificate of origin das Ursprungszeugnis, die Herkunftsbescheinigung

certified check der bestätigte Scheck

certified public accountant der Wirtschaftsprüfer

chain of command die Befehlskette

chain store das Filialgeschäft

chain store group das Zweigstellenunternehmen

chairman of the board der Vorstandsvorsitzende

chamber of commerce die Handelskammer

channel of distribution der Absatzweg

charge account das Kreditkonto

charge off (v) abbuchen, abschreiben, absetzen

charges die Spesen, die Gebühren, die Auslagen

chart, bar das Säulendiagramm

chart, flow   das Schaubild

chart, management   die Geschäftsleitungstabelle, das Betriebsführungsschaubild

charter (mercantile lease)   die Befrachtung

charter (written instrument)   das Statut, die Satzung

chartered accountant   der Wirtschaftsprüfer

charterparty agent   der Frachtvertragsagent

chattel   die Fahrnis, die bewegliche Sache

chattel mortgage   die Mobiliarhypothek

cheap   billig

check   der Scheck

check in (v)   sich anmelden

checking account   das Scheckkonto, das Girokonto

checklist   die Kontrolliste, die Checkliste

chemical   chemisch

chief accountant   der Buchhaltungsleiter

chief buyer   der Haupteinkäufer

chief executive   der Vorstandsvorsitzende

chip   der Mikrochip

civil action   die Zivilklage

civil engineering   das Bauingenieurwesen

claim   der Anspruch, die Forderung

classified advertisement   die Kleinanzeige

clean document   die uneingeschränkte Urkunde

clearinghouse   die Girozentrale, die Abrechnungsstelle

closed account   das abgeschlossene Konto

closed-end fund   der Investmentfonds mit begrenzter Emissionshöhe

closely held corporation   die personenbezogene Aktiengesellschaft

closing entry   die Abschlußbuchung

closing price   der Schlußkurs

co-ownership   das Miteigentum

coal   die Kohle

codicil   das Kodizill, der Testamentsanhang

coffee break   die Kaffeepause

coinsurance   die Mitversicherung

cold call   der Überraschungsanruf

collateral   die Deckung, die Sicherheit

colleague   der Mitarbeiter, der Kollege

collect on delivery   die Nachnahme

collection period   die Einziehungszeit

collective agreement   der Mantelvertrag, der Tarifvertrag

collective bargaining   die Tarifverhandlungen

combination   die Vereinigung, das Kartell, der Konzern

commerce   der Handel

commercial bank   die Handelsbank

commercial (broadcasting)   die Werbesendung

commercial grade   die handelsübliche Qualität

commercial invoice   die Faktura, die Handelsrechnung

commission (agency)   der Ausschuß

commission (fee)   die Provision

commitment   die Verpflichtung

commodity   die Handelsware

commodity exchange   die Warenbörse

common carrier   das öffentliche Verkehrsunternehmen

common market   der gemeinsame Markt

common market (European Common Market)   die Europäische Wirtschaftsgemeinschaft

common stock   die Stammaktie

company   die Gesellschaft, die Firma

company goal   das Gesellschaftsziel

company policy   die Betriebspolitik, die Firmenpolitik

compensating balance   das Kontokorrentguthaben

compensation   die Vergütung, die Entschädigung

compensation (salary)   das Gehalt

compensation trade   der Kompensationshandel

competition   die Konkurrenz

competitive advantage   der Wettbewerbsvorteil

competitive price   der konkurrenzfähige Preis

competitive strategy   die Wettbewerbsstrategie

competitor   der Konkurrent

competitor analysis   die Konkurrenzstudie

complimentary copy   das freie Exemplar

component   der Bestandteil, der Bauteil

composite index   der Mischindex

compound interest   der Zinseszins

comptroller   der Rechnungsprüfer

computer   der Computer, die Rechenanlage

computer, analog   der Analogrechner, der Analogcomputer

computer center   die Datenverarbeitungszentrale

computer, digital   der Digitalrechner

computer input   die Computereingabe

computer language   die Computersprache

computer memory   der Speicher des Computers

computer output   das Computerergebnis

computer program   das Computerprogramm

computer storage   die Datenspeicherung

computer terminal   das Computerterminal

conditional acceptance   die bedingte Annahme, die Annahme mit Vorbehalt

conditional sales contract   der bedingte Verkaufsvertrag

conference room   der Sitzungssaal, der Konferenzraum

confidential   vertraulich

confirmation of order   die Auftragsbestätigung

conflict of interest   der Interessenkonflikt

conglomerate   der Mischkonzern, der Großkonzern

consideration (contract law)   die Gegenleistung, das Entgeld

consignee   der Empfänger

consignment   die Sendung

consignment note   der Frachtbrief

consolidated financial statement   der konsolidierte Finanzbericht

consolidation   der Konzernabschluß, die konsolidierte Bilanz

consortium   das Konsortium

consular invoice   die Konsulatsfaktura

consultant   der Berater

consultant, management   der Unternehmensberater

consumer   der Verbraucher

consumer acceptance   die Verbraucherannahme

consumer credit   der Konsumentenkredit, der Kundenkredit

consumer goods   die Konsumgüter

consumer price index   der Lebenshaltungsindex, der Verbraucherpreisindex

consumer research   die Verbraucherforschung

consumer satisfaction   die Verbraucherzufriedenstellung

container   der Behälter, der Container

contango   die Reportprämie

contingencies   die unvorhergesehenen Ausgaben

contingent fund   die außerordentliche Rücklage, der Reservefonds

contingent liability   die Eventuellverbindlichkeit

contract   der Vertrag

contract carrier   der vertragliche Frachtführer

contract month   der Vertragsmonat

controllable costs   die wechselnden Kosten

controller   der Leiter des Rechnungswesens

controlling interest   die Aktienmehrheit

convertible debentures   die Wandelobligationen, die konvertierbaren Obligationen

convertible preferred stock   die konvertierbare Vorzugsaktie

cooperation agreement   das Kooperationsabkommen

cooperative   die Genossenschaft

cooperative advertising   die Gemeinschaftswerbung

copy (advertising text)   der Werbetext, der Reklametext

copy testing   die Werbetextprüfung

copyright   das Urheberrecht

corporate growth   das Unternehmenswachstum

corporate image   das Gesellschaftsbild

corporate planning   die Gesellschaftsplanung

corporate structure   die Gesellschaftsstruktur

corporate tax   die Körperschaftssteuer

corporation   die Aktiengesellschaft, die Gesellschaft mit beschränkter Haftung (GmbH)

corpus   das Stammkapital

correspondence   der Briefwechsel, die Korrespondenz

correspondent bank   die Korrespondenzbank

cost   die Kosten

cost accounting   die Kostenrechnung

cost analysis   die Kostenanalyse

cost and freight   Kosten und Fracht

cost-benefit analysis   die Kostennutzenanalyse

cost control   die Kostenüberwachung

cost effective   kostenintensiv

cost factor   der Kostenfaktor

cost of capital   die Kapitalkosten

cost of goods sold   die Umsatzselbstkosten

cost of living   die Lebenshaltungskosten

cost-plus contract   der Auftrag auf Basis Selbstkosten plus Gewinn

cost-price squeeze   die Kostenpreisschere

cost reduction   die Kosteneinsparung

cotton   die Baumwolle

counter check   der Kassenscheck

counterfeit   die Fälschung, die Nachahmung

countervailing duty   der Ausgleichszoll

country of origin   das Ursprungsland

country of risk   das Risiko übernehmende Land

coupon (bond interest)   der Zinsabschnitt, der Zinskoupon

courier service   der Botendienst, der Kurier

covenant   der Zinsabschnitt, der Zinskoupon

courier service   der Botendienst, der Kurier

covenant (promises)   der Vertrag

cover charge   der Mindestbetrag, das Gedeck

cover letter   der Begleitbrief

cover ratio   das Deckungsverhältnis

coverage (insurance)   der Versicherungsschutz

credit   der Kredit

credit (v)   gutschreiben

credit balance   das Kreditsaldo

credit bank   die Kreditbank

credit bureau   die Kreditanstalt

credit buyer der Kreditkäufer

credit card die Kreditkarte

credit control die Kreditkontrolle

credit insurance die Kreditversicherung

credit line die Kreditlinie

credit management die Kreditverwaltung

credit note die Gutschriftsanzeige

credit rating die Krediteinschätzung, die Bonitätsprüfung

credit reference die Kreditreferenz

credit terms die Kreditbedingungen

credit union der Kreditverein

creditor der Gläubiger

critical path analysis die Analyse der Netzplantechnik

cross-licensing der Lizenzaustausch

cultural export permit die Ausfuhrlizenz für Kulturgüter

cultural property der Kulturbesitz

cum dividend mit Dividende

cumulative anhäufend, kumulativ

cumulative preferred stock die kumulative Vorzugsaktie

currency das Geld, die Währung

currency band die Währungsgruppe

currency clause die Währungsklausel

currency exchange der Geldwechsel

current assets das kurzfristige Umlaufvermögen

current liabilities die kurzfristige Verbindlichkeit

current ratio der Liquiditätsgrad

current yield die laufende Rendite

curriculum vitae der Lebenslauf

customer der Kunde

customer service der Kundendienst

customs der Zoll

customs broker der Zollagent, die Zollagentin

customs collector der Zolleinnehmer

customs duty die Zollgebühr, der Zoll

customs entry die Zollerklärung

customs union   der Zollverein
cutback   die Verminderung, die Einsparung

D

daily   täglich
dairy products   die Molkereiprodukte
damage   der Schaden
data   die Angaben, die Daten
data acquisition   der Datenerwerb
data bank   die Datenbank
data base   die Angabengrundlage
data processing   die Datenverarbeitung
date of delivery   der Liefertermin
day loan   das Maklerdarlehen, das Tagesgeld
day order   der Tagesauftrag
dead freight   die Leerfracht, die Faulfracht
dead rent   der feste Pachtzins, die Mindestpacht
deadline   der Stichtag, der letzte Termin, der Fristablauf
deadlock   der völlige Stillstand, die Pattsituation
deal (agreement)   das Abkommen, das Geschäft
deal (transaction)   der Handel
dealer   der Händler
dealership   die Handlung, die Franchise
debenture   die Schuldverschreibung, die Obligation
debit   das Soll
debit entry   der Debetposten, die Lastschrift
debit note   die Lastschriftanzeige
debt   die Schuld
debug (v) (computers)   einen Fehler beseitigen
deductible   abzugsfähig
deduction   der Abzug
deed   die Urkunde
deed of sale   der Kaufbrief
deed of transfer   die Übertragungsurkunde, die Auflassungsurkunde
deed of trust   der Treuhandvertrag
default (v)   zahlungsunfähig werden
defective   mangelhaft, fehlerhaft
deferred annuities   die aufgeschobenen Renten

deferred assets die zeitweilig nicht einlösbaren Aktiva

deferred charges die aktiven Rechnungsabgrenzungen, die gestundeten Zahlungen

deferred deliveries die aufgeschobenen Lieferungen

deferred income die im voraus eingegangenen Erträge

deferred liabilities die aufgeschobenen Schulden

deferred tax die zurückgestellte Steuerzahlung

deficit das Defizit

deficit financing die Defizitfinanzierung

deficit spending die Defizitspende

deflation die Deflation

delay der Aufschub, die Verzögerung

delinquent account das rückständige Konto, die unbezahlte Rechnung

delivered price der Lieferpreis

delivery die Lieferung, die Zustellung

delivery date der Liefertermin

delivery notice der Lieferschein

delivery points die Erfüllungsorte

delivery price der Lieferpreis

demand die Forderung, die Nachfrage

demand (v) verlangen

demand deposit die Sichteinlage, das tägliche Geld

demand line of credit die Kontokorrentkreditlinie

demographic demographisch

demotion die Zurückstufung

demurrage (fee for) das Liegegeld

demurrage (period of) die Überliegezeit

department die Abteilung

department store das Warenhaus, das Kaufhaus

depletion allowance die Abschreibung für Substanzverringerung

depletion control die Verringerungskontrolle

deposit die Einlage, die Kaution

deposit account das Depositenkonto

deposit, bank die Bankeinlage

depository das Depot

depreciation die Abschreibung

draft   die Tratte, der Entwurf

drawback (disadvantage)   die Nachteil

drawback (export premium)   die Erstattung, die Ausfuhrprämie

drawback (money)   die Rückerstattung

drawdown   herabziehen

drawee   der Akzeptant, der Bezogene

drawer   der Aussteller

drayage   das Rollgeld

drop shipment   die direkte Verschiffung, die Auftragssendung

dry cargo   die Trockenladung

dry goods   die Textilien, die Schnittwaren

dumping (goods in foreign market)   die Schleuderausfuhr, das Dumping

dun (v)   mahnenzur Zahlung drängen, die Garnierung

duopoly   das Duopol

durable goods   die langlebigen Gebrauchsgüter, die dauerhaften Verbrauchsgüter

duress   der Zwang

duty (customs)   der Zoll

duty (free)   die Gebühr

duty (obligation)   die Pflicht

duty (tax)   die Steuer

dutyfree   zollfrei

E

earmark (v)   bestimmen, kennzeichnen

earnings   die Einnahmen

earnings on assets   der Aktivenertrag

earnings per share   der Gewinn pro Aktie

earnings performance   die Ertragsleistung, die Ertragskraft

earnings report   der Gewinnbericht

earnings yield   das Ertragsergebnis

earnings, retained   die thesaurierten Gewinne

econometrics   die Ökonometrie

economic   wirtschaftlich

economic indicators   die Konjunkturindikatoren

economic life die wirtschaftliche Nutzungsdauer, die wirtschaftliche Lebensdauer

economics die Wirtschaftslehre, die Volkswirtschaftslehre

economy of scale die Kostenherabsetzung bei Betriebsvergrößerung

effective yield die Effektivverzinsung

efficiency die Leistungsfähigkeit, die Effizienz

elasticity (of supply or demand) die Elastizität von Angebot und Nachfrage

electrical engineering die Elektrotechnik

electronic whiteboard das elektronische Weißbrett

embargo die Handelssperre

embezzlement die Unterschlagung

employee der Angestellte

employee counseling die Angestelltenberatung

employee relations die innerbetrieblichen Beziehungen

employment agency das Stellenvermittlungsbüro

encumbrance die Belastung, die Hypothekenschulden

end of period der Rechnungsschluß

end product das Fertigprodukt, das Enderzeugnis

end-use certificate der Zweck-Gebrauch Schein

endorsee der Girat

endorsement das Indossament, das Giro

endorsement (approval) die Zustimmung

endowment die Dotation, die Stiftung

engineering das Ingenieurwesen

enlarge (v) vergrößern

enterprise das Unternehmen

entrepreneur der Unternehmer

entry permit die Einreisebewilligung, der Passierschein

equal pay for equal work der gleiche Lohn für die gleiche Arbeit

equipment die Ausrüstung

equipment leasing das Ausrüstungsleasing

equity das Eigenkapital

equity investments die Beteiligung an Kapitalgesellschaften

equity share der Eigenkapitalanteil

ergonomics   die Ergonomie, die Arbeitsplatzanalyse
error   der Irrtum, der Fehler
escalator clause   die Steigerungsklausel
escape clause   die Ausweichklausel, die Rücktrittsklausel
escheat   der Heimfall einer Erbschaft an den Staat
escrow   der Treuhandvertrag
escrow account   das Treuhandkonto
estate   die Erbschaft
estate (landed)   das Gut
estate (testamentary)   der Nachlaß
estate agent   der Grundstücksverwalter
estate tax   die Nachlaßsteuer
estimate   die Schätzung, die Bewertung
estimate (v)   schätzen
estimated price   der Schätzwert, der Schätzpreis
estimated time of arrival   die voraussichtliche Ankunft
estimated time of departure   die voraussichtliche Abfahrt
Eurobond   die Euroanleihe
Eurocurrency   das Guthaben in konvertierbarer
Währung
Eurodollar   der Eurodollar
evaluation   die Bewertung
ex dividend   ohne Dividende, dividendlos
ex dock   ab Dock
ex factory   ab Fabrik
ex mill   ab Betrieb
ex mine   ab Grube
ex rights   ohne Rechte
ex ship   ab Schiff
ex warehouse   ab Lager
ex works   ab Werk
exchange (commodity)   die Warenbörse
exchange (stock)   die Börse
exchange (v)   tauschen
exchange control   die Devisenkontrolle
exchange discount   der Wechseldiskont
exchange loss   der Kursverlust

exchange rate   der Wechselkurs
exchange risk   das Währungsrisiko
exchange value   der Tauschwert
exchange value (on stock exchange)   der Börsenwert
excise duty   die Verbrauchsabgabe
excise license   die Schankkonzession
excise tax   die Verbrauchssteuer, die Gewerbesteuer
executive   der leitende Angestellte
executive board   der Vorstand
executive committee   das geschäftsführende Vorstand
executive compensation   die Vergütung für leitende Angestellte
executive director   der Geschäftsführer
executive search   die Suche von Führungskräften
executor (of an estate)   der Testamentsvollstrecker
exemption   die Befreiung
exemption (tax exemption)   der Steuerfreibetrag
expectations, up to our   unseren Erwartungen entsprechend
expected result   das erwünschte Ergebnis
expenditure   der Aufwand, die Ausgabe
expense account   das Spesenkonto, die Auslagenabrechnung
expenses   die Auslagen
expiry date   der Verfalltag
export (v)   ausführen
export agent   der Ausfuhragent
export credit   der Ausfuhrkredit
export duty   der Ausfuhrzoll
export entry   die Ausfuhrzollerklärung
export house   das Exportgeschäft
export manager   der Leiter der Exportabteilung
export middleman   der Exportmakler
export permit   die Ausfuhrbewilligung
export quota   die Ausfuhrquote
export regulation   die Ausfuhrbestimmung
export sales contract   der Exportverkaufsvertrag
export tax   die Ausfuhrsteuer
Export-Import bank   die Export-Import Bank
expropriation   die Enteignung
extra dividend   die Zusatzdividende

F

face value   der Nennwert

facilities (means of production)   die Produktionsmittel

facilities (possibilities)   die Möglichkeiten

factor (agent)   der Kommissionär

factor (component, element)   der Faktor

factor analysis   die Faktorenanalyse

factor rating   die Faktorenbewertung

factoring   das Faktoring, der Ankauf offener Buchforderungen

factory   die Fabrik

factory overhead   die Fertigungsgemeinkosten

fail (v)   mißlingen

fail (v) (go bankrupt)   Bankrott machen

failure   der Konkurs, der Misserfolg

fair market value   der angemessene Marktpreis

fair return   der angemessene Ertrag

fair trade   die Lauterkeit des Wettbewerbs, die Preisbindung

farm out (v)   verpachten

feed ratio   das Zuführungsverhältnis

feedback   die Rückwirkung, das Feedback

fidelity bond   die Betriebstreuhandversicherung

fiduciary   der Treuhänder, der Betraute

fiduciary issue   die Notenausgabe ohne Deckung

fiduciary loan   das treuhänderische Darlehen

field warehousing   die Lagerung sicherungsübereig-
neter Waren

file (v)   ablegen

file (v) (papers)   zu den Akten legen

file (v) (submit forms)   einreichen, vorlegen

finalize (v)   abschließen, fertigmachen

finance (v)   finanzieren

finance company   die Finanzierungsgesellschaft

financial analysis   die Finanzanalyse

financial appraisal   die Finanzbewertung

financial control   die Finanzkontrolle

financial director   der Finanzdirektor

financial highlights   finanzielle Höhepunkte

financial incentive   der finanzielle Anreiz

financial management   die Finanzverwaltung

financial pages, newspaper   der Wirtschaftsteil

financial period   die Bilanzperiode

financial planning   die Finanzplanung

financial services   die Finanzdienstleistungen

financial statement   der Finanzstatus, der Bilanz-abschluß

financial year   das Haushaltsjahr, das Geschäftsjahr, das Betriebsjahr

fine (penalty)   die Geldstrafe

finished goods inventory   der Bestand an Fertigwaren

fire (v)   feuern, herauswerfen

firm   die Firma

first in-first out (FIFO)   die Zurstentnahme der älteren Vorräte und deren Bilanzierung zum Buchwert

first preferred stock   die Vorzugsaktien erster Ausgabe

fiscal agent   die Zahlstelle, der Vertreter des Fiskus

fiscal drag   die Steuerbremse

fiscal year   das Rechnungsjahr, das Geschäftsjahr

fishyback service   der Land-Seewegverkehr

fixed assets   die Sachanlagen

fixed capital   das Anlagekapital

fixed charges   die Generalkosten, die Festkosten

fixed costs   die Fixkosten

fixed expenses   die laufenden Ausgaben

fixed income security   das festverzinsliche Wertpapier

fixed investment   die festverzinsliche Anlage

fixed liability   die langfristige Verbindlichkeit

fixed rate of exchange   der feste Wechselkurs

fixed term   die bestimmte Zeitdauer, die festgelegte Frist

fixture   das Inventarstück, die feste Anglage

flat bond   die Obligation ohne aufgelaufene Zinsen

flat rate   der einheitliche Satz, die Pauschale

flat yield   der Pauschalbetrag

flatcar   der offene Güterwagen

fleet policy   die Kraftfahrzeugsammelpolice, die Gruppenpolice

flexible tariff   der Staffeltarif, der dehnbare Zolltarif

float (outstanding checks)   die im Einzug befindlichen Schecks

float (v) (currency)   floaten

float (v) (issue stock)   eine Emission begeben

floater   die Pauschalversicherung

floating assets   das kurzfristige Umlaufvermögen

floating charge   die schwebende Belastung

floating debt   die schwebende Schuld, die unfundierte Schuld

floating exchange rate   der gleitende Wechselkurs

floating rate   der freie Kurs

floor (stock exchange)   der Börsensaal

floppy disk   die Diskette

flow chart   das Schaubild

follow-up order   der Anschlußauftrag

follow up (v)   verfolgen, nachfassen

foodstuffs   die Nahrungsmittel, die Lebensmittel

footing (accounting)   die Addition

for export   zur Ausfuhr

forecast   die Vorschau, die Prognose, voraussagen

foreign bill of exchange   der Fremdwährungswechsel

foreign corporation   die ausländische Gesellschaft

foreign currency   die Devisen, die Auslandswährung

foreign debt   die Auslandsverschuldung

foreign exchange   die Devisen

foreign security   das ausländische Wertpapier

foreign tax credit   die Auslandssteuergutschrift

foreign trade   der Außenhandel, die Außenwirtschaft

foreman   der Vorarbeiter, der Werkmeister, der Gruppenführer

forgery   die Fälschung

form letter   der Musterbrief, der Standardbrief

format   das Format

forward (v)   befördern, nachsenden

forward contract   der Terminabschluß

forward cover   die Kurssicherung

forward margin   die Termindeckung

forward market   der Terminmarkt

forward purchase   der Terminkauf
forward shipment   die Terminsendung
forwarding agent   der Spediteur
foul bill of lading   das unreine Konnossement
franchise   der Konzessionsbetrieb, der Lizenzbetrieb
fraud   der Betrug
free alongside ship   frei längsseite Schiff
free and clear (debt free) schuldenfrei
free and clear (unencumbered)   lastenfrei
free and clear (unmortgaged)   hypothekenfrei
free enterprise   die Privatwirtschaft, die freie Marktwirtschaft
free list   die Freiliste
free market   der freie Markt
free of particular average   frei von besonderer Havarie
free on board (fob)   frei Schiff, franko Bord, fob
free on rail   frei Eisenbahn
free port   der Freihafen
free time   die Freizeit
free trade   der Freihandel
free trade zone   die Freihandelszone
freelance writer   der freischaffende Schriftsteller
freight   die Fracht
freight all kinds   der Frachtbetrieb
freight allowed   Frachtkostenrückerstattung möglich
freight collect   die Fracht gegen Nachnahme
freight forwarder   der Frachtführer
freight included   Fracht inbegriffen
freight prepaid   vorausbezahlte Fracht
frequency curve   die Frequenzkurve
fringe benefits   die Zusatzleistungen, die Nebenvergütungen
fringe market   der Randmarkt
front-end fee (front-end load)   die Anfangsprovision
front-end financing   die Vorausbezahlung der Finanzierungskosten, die Gründungsfinanzierung
frozen assets   die eingefrorenen Guthaben
functional analysis   die Funktionsanalyse
fund   die Kasse, der Fonds, die Mittel

fund, contingent die außerordentliche Rücklage, der Reservefonds

fund, sinking der Tilgungsfonds

fund, trust der Treuhandfonds

funded debt die verbriefte Schuld

funds, public die öffentlichen Mittel

funds, working die Betriebsmittel

fungible vertretbar, ersetzbar

futures die Termingeschäfte

futures option die Terminoption

G

garnishment die Beschlagnahme

gas das Gas

gasoline das Benzin

gearing der festverzinsliche Anteil am Gesamtkapital

gearless die Kapitalanlage ohne geborgte Mittel

general acceptance das Blankoakzept, das unbeschränkte Akzept

general average loss der Schaden aus allgemeiner Havarie

general manager der Generaldirektor

general meeting die Generalversammlung

general partnership die offene Handelsgesellschaft

general strike der Generalstreik

gentleman's agreement die Vereinbarung auf Treu und Glauben, das Gentleman's Agreement

gilt-edged investment die mündelsichere Anlage

glut das Überangebot, die Schwemme

go around (v) herumgehen

go public (v) umwandeln in eine Aktiengesellschaft

godown das Lager

going concern value der Ertragswert, der Teilwert

going rate (going price) der übliche Satz

gold clause die Goldklausel

gold price der Goldpreis

gold reserves die Goldbestände

good delivery die einwandfreie Überbringung

goods die Waren, die Güter

goodwill   das Ansehen einer Firma, der Goodwill

government   die Regierung

government agency   die Regierungstelle, die Verwaltungsbehörde

government bank   die Staatsbank, die Nationalbank, die Zentralbank

government bonds   die Staatspapiere, die Staatsanleihen

grace period   die tilgungsfreie Zeit, die Freiperiode

graduated tax   die gestaffelte Steuer

graft   die Bestechung

grain   das Getreide, das Korn

graph   das Diagramm, die graphische Darstellung

gratuity   die Gratifikation, die Vergütung, die Abfindung

gray market   der graue Markt

grievance procedure   das Schlichtungsverfahren

gross domestic product   das Bruttosozialprodukt

gross income   das Bruttoeinkommen

gross investment   die Bruttoanlageninvestition

gross loss   der Bruttoverlust

gross margin   die Bruttogewinnspanne

gross national product   das Bruttosozialprodukt

gross price   der Bruttopreis

gross profit   der Bruttogewinn, der Rohgewinn

gross receipts   die Bruttoeinnahmen

gross sales   der Bruttoumsatz

gross spread   der Bruttopreisunterschied

gross weight   das Rohgewicht

gross yield   der Bruttoertrag

group account   der Konzernabschluß

group dynamics   die Gruppendynamik

group insurance   die Gruppenversicherung

growth   das Wachstum

growth area   das Wachstumsgebiet

growth index   der Wachstumsindex

growth industry   die Wachstumsindustrie

growth potential   das Wachstumspotential

growth rate   die Zuwachsrate

growth stock   die Wachstumsaktie

guarantee   die Garantie, die Bürgschaft

guaranty bond   die gesicherte Obligation, der Garantieschein

guaranty company   die Kautionsversicherungsgesellschaft

guesstimate (v)   vermuten, ungefähr schätzen

guideline   die Richtlinie

H

half-life   das Halbleben

handicap   der Nachteil

handling   die Abwicklung, die Beförderung

harbor dues   die Hafengebühren

hard copy   der Klartext, der geschriebene Text

hard currency   die Hartwährung

hard sell   die aggressive Verkaufspolitik, die Holzhammermethode

hardware   die Mettalwaren, die Eisenwaren

hardware (computer)   die Hardware

head office   das Hauptbüro, die Zentrale

headhunter   der Kopfjäger, der Jäger auf Nachwuchskräfte

headquarters   der Hauptsitz, die Zentrale

heavy industry   die Schwerindustrie

heavy lift charge   der Schwergutaufschlag

hedge (v)   sich gegen Verluste sichern

hidden asset   die stille Reserve

highest bidder   der Meistbietende

hire (v)   anstellen

hoard (v)   hamstern, horten, thesaurieren

holder   der Inhaber, der Besitzer

holder in due course   der ausgewiesene Inhaber, der rechtmäßige Inhaber

holding company   die Dachgesellschaft, die Holdinggesellschaft

holding period   die Besitzdauer, die Haltezeit

holiday   der Ruhetag, der arbeitsfreie Tag

home market   der Binnenmarkt

hot money   das heiße Geld

hourly earnings der Stundenlohn
house-to-house selling der Direktverkauf an der Haustür
housing authority (construction) die Baubehörde
housing authority (residential) das Wohnungsamt
human resources das Angestelltenpotential
hybrid computer der Hybridrechner
hyphenate (v) mit Bindestrich schreiben
hypothecation die Verpfändung, die Beleihung

I

idle capacity die ungenutzte Kapazität
illegal gesetzwidrig
illegal shipments die gesetzwidrigen Sendungen
imitation die Nachahmung
impact on (v) wirken auf
impending change die bevorstehende Änderung
implication (conclusion) die Folgerung
implication (involvement) die Verwicklung
implied agreement die stillschweigend verstandene Zustimmung, die stillschweigende Vereinbarung
import die Einfuhr, der Import
import (v) einführen, importieren
import declaration die Einfuhrerklärung
import deposits die Einfuhrdepots
import duty der Einfuhrzoll
import entry die Einfuhrdeklaration
import license die Einfuhrerlaubnis, die Importlizenz
import quota die Einfuhrquote
import regulations die Einfuhrvorschriften
import tariff der Einfuhrzoll
import tax die Einfuhrsteuer
importer of record der protokollierte Importeur
impound (v) beschlagnehmen
improve upon (v) verbessern
improvement die Verbesserung
impulse purchase der Impulskauf, der Spontankauf
imputed zugeschrieben

in the red   im Debet

in transit   unterwegs

inadequate   unzulänglich

incentive   der Ansporn, der Anreiz

inchoate interest   das Anwartschaftsrecht

incidental expenses   die Nebenausgaben

income   das Einkommen

income account   das Ertragskonto

income bonds   die Gewinnobligationen

income bracket   die Einkommensgruppe

income statement   die Gewinn- und Verlustrechnung

income tax   die Einkommensteuer

income, gross   das Bruttoeinkommen

income, net   das Nettoeinkommen

incorporate (v)   gesellschaftlich organisieren und gründen

increase   die Vermehrung, der Aufschlag, die Erhöhung

increase (v)   vermehren

increased costs   die gestiegenen Kosten

incremental cash flow   der Geldumlaufzuwachs

incremental costs   die Grenzkosten

indebtedness   die Verschuldung

indemnity   die Entschädigung

indenture   die Vertragsurkunde

index   der Index

index (v)   registrieren, verzeichnen

index option   die Indexoption

indexing   die Indexierung

indirect claim   der indirekte Anspruch

indirect costs   die Gemeinkosten

indirect expenses   die Fertigungsgemeinkosten

indirect labor   die Gemeinkostenlöhne

indirect tax   die indirekte Steuer

industrial accident   der Arbeitsunfall

industrial arbitration   die gewerbliche Schiedsgerichtbarkeit

industrial engineering   die Gewerbetechnik, die Fertigungssteuerung

industrial goods   die Investitionsgüter, die Industrieprodukte

industrial insurance   die Betriebsversicherung

industrial planning   die Industrieplanung

industrial relations   die Arbeitsbeziehungen

industrial union   die Industriegewerkschaft

industry   die Industrie

industrywide   die gesamte Industrie betreffend

inefficient   ineffizient, wirkungslos

inelastic demand   starre Nachfrage

inelastic supply   starres Angebot

infant industry   die schutzzollbedürftige Industrie

inflation   die Inflation

inflationary   inflationär

infrastructure   die Infrastruktur

inheritance tax   die Nachlaßsteuer, die Erbschaftssteuer

injunction   die gerichtliche Anordnung, die richterliche Verfügung

inland bill of lading   der inländische Frachtbrief

innovation   die Neuerung

input   die Eingabe

input-output analysis   die Eingaben-Ausgaben
Analyse

insolvent   zahlungsunfähig, insolvent

inspection   die Prüfung, die Untersuchung, die Inspektion

inspector   der Inspektor, der Prüfungsbeamte

instability   die Unbeständigkeit

installment credit   der Teilzahlungskredit

installment plan   der Teilzahlungsplan

institutional advertising   die Firmenwerbung

institutional investor   der institutionelle Investor

instruct (v) (order)   anordnen

instruct (v) (teach)   unterrichten

instrument (document)   die Urkunde

instrumental capital   das Produktivkapital

insufficient assets   die unzureichende Aktiva

insurance   die Versicherung

insurance broker   der Versicherungsmakler

insurance company   die Versicherungsgesellschaft

insurance fund   die Versicherungskasse

insurance policy   die Versicherungspolice

insurance premium   die Versicherungsprämie, der Versicherungsbeitrag

insurance underwriter   der Versicherer

intangible assets   die immateriellen Werte

integrated management system   das eingegliederte Führungssystem

interact (v)   aufeinander wirken, sich gegenseitig beeinflußen

interbank   zwischen Banken

interest   das Interesse (general)

interest (return on capital)   der Zins, die Verzinsung

interest (share)   der Anteil

interest arbitrage   die Zinsarbitrage

interest expenses   die Zinsaufwendungen

interest income   der Zinsertrag

interest parity   der Interessenausgleich

interest period   der Verzinsungszeitraum

interest rate   der Zinssatz, der Zinsfuß

interim   einstweilig, zwischenzeitlich, interimistisch

interim budget   der Zwischenhaushalt

interim statement   die Zwischenbilanz, der Zwischenabschluß

interlocking directorate   der Schachtelaufsichtsrat

intermediary   der Vermittler

intermediary goods   die Zwischenwaren

internal   inner, intern

internal audit   die innerbetriebliche Revision

internal funding   die Innenfinanzierung

internal rate of return   die interne Rendite

internal revenue tax   die inländischen Steuern und Abgaben

International Date Line   die internationale Datumsgrenze

International Development Agency   Die Internationale Entwicklungsstelle

International Monetary Fund   Der Weltwährungsfonds

interstate commerce   der zwischenstaatliche Handel

intervene (v)   dazwischentreten, sich einmischen

interview das Interview, die Unterredung

intestate ohne Testament

intrinsic value der innere Wert

invalidate (v) ungültig machen

inventory das Inventar, der Vorrat, der Bestand

inventory control die Bestandsüberwachung

inventory turnover der Lagerumschlag

inverted market der umgekehrte Markt

invest (v) anlegen, investieren

invested capital das angelegte Kapital

investment die Kapitalanlage, die Investition

investment adviser der Finanzberater, der Anlage-berater

investment analysis die Investitionsanalyse, die An-lagenanalyse

investment bank die Emissionsbank

investment budget das Investitionsbudget

investment company die Investmentgesellschaft

investment credit der Anlagekredit

investment criteria die Investitionskriterien

investment grade die Investitionseinstufung und Be-wertung

investment letter der Anlagebrief

investment policy die Investitionspolitik

investment program das Investitionsprogramm

investment strategy die Investitionstaktik, die In-vestitionsstrategie

investment trust die Investmenttreuhandgesellschaft

investor relations die Beziehungen zu den Anlegern

invisible unsichtbar

invitation to bid die Ausschreibung, die Auffor-derung zur Einreichung von Angeboten

invoice die Rechnung, die Faktura

invoice cost der Fakturenpreis, der Bruttoeinkaufs-preis

issue (v) ausgeben, emittieren

issue price der Ausgabekurs

issue, stock die Ausgabe

issue stock die Emission

issued shares die ausgegebenen Aktien

item   der Artikel, der Eintrag, der Posten

itemize (v)   aufgliedern, einzeln aufführen

itemized account   die spezifizierte Rechnung

J

Jason clause   die Jasonsklausel

jawbone (v)   gründlich besprechen, lange diskutieren

jet lag   die Müdigkeit nach dem Flug, die Nachflugerschöpfung

job   die Arbeit

job analysis   die Arbeitsstudie, die Arbeitsplatzuntersuchung

job description   die Arbeitsbeschreibung, die Stellenbeschreibung

job evaluation   die Arbeitsbewertung

job hopper   der häufige Stellenwechsler

job lot   der Restposten, die Partieware, die Ramschwaren

job performance   die Arbeitsleistung

job security   die Arbeitsplatzsicherheit

job shop   der Einzelfertigungsbetrieb

jobber   der Grossist, der Unterlieferant, der Börsenmakler

jobber's turn   der Lagerumschlag des Grossisten

joint account   das gemeinschaftliche Konto, die gemeinsame Rechnung

joint cost   die Umlagekosten

joint estate   der gemeinsame Besitz

joint liability   die gesamtschuldnerische Haftung

joint owner   der Miteigentümer

joint stock company   die Aktiengesellschaft

joint venture   das gemeinschaftliche Unternehmen, das Joint-venture

journal   das Geschäftstagebuch, das Journal

journeyman   der Geselle

joystick   der Steuerknüppel

junior partner   der Juniorpartner

junior security   das Wertpapier nachgeordneter Sicherheit

jurisdiction   der Amtsbereich, der Gerichtsbezirk

K

keep posted (v)   auf dem laufenden halten

key exports   die Hauptausfuhrwaren

key man insurance   die Versicherung für Personen in Schlüsselstellungen

Keynesian economics   die Keynessche Wirtschaftslehre

keypuncher   der Locher

kickback   das Schmiergeld

kiting   die Wechselreiterei

knot   (nautical) die Seemeile

know-how   das Können, die Erfahrung, das Wissen

L

labor   die Arbeiterschaft

labor code   die Arbeitsverfassung

labor dispute   die Tarifstreitigkeit

labor force   die Arbeitskräfte, die Belegschaft

labor-intensive   lohnintensiv, arbeitsintensiv

labor law   das Arbeitsrecht

labor leader   der Arbeiterführer, der Gewerkschaftsführer

labor market   der Arbeitsmarkt

labor relations   das Arbeitgeber-Arbeitnehmerverhältnis

labor-saving   arbeitsparend

labor turnover   der Personalwechsel

labor union   die Gewerkschaft

laborer   der Arbeiter

lagging indicator   der nachhängende Konjunkturindikator

laissez-faire   der freie Wettbewerb

land   das Land

land grant   die Landzuteilung

land reform   die Bodenreform

land tax   die Grundsteuer

landed cost   die Gesamtkosten für importierte Waren

landing certificate   der Löschschein

landing charges   die Landungsgebühren

landing costs   die Löschkosten

landowner   der Grundbesitzer

large-scale   großangelegt

last in-first out (LIFO)   die Zuerstentnahme der neuen Vorräte

law   das Gesetz, das Statut

law of diminishing returns   das Gesetz vom abnehmenden Ertrag

lawsuit   der Prozeß, die Klage

lawyer   der Rechtsanwalt

lay off (v)   entlassen

lay time   die Liegezeit

lay up (v)   ein Schiff außer Dienst stellen

laydays   die Liegetage, die Löschzeit

layout   die Gestaltungsskizze, das Arbeitsschema, (of premises) die Anlage

lead time   die Vorlaufzeit

leader   der Leiter, der Chef, der Führer, der Lockartikel

leading indicator   der Vorindikator

leads and lags   gut und schlecht verkaufte Artikel

leakage   die Leckage

learning curve   die Lernkurve

lease   der Mietvertrag, die Pacht

lease (v)   mieten, pachten, leasen

leased department   die gemietete Abteilung

leave of absence   der Urlaub

ledger   das Hauptbuch

ledger account   das Hauptbuchkonto

ledger entry   die Hauptbucheintragung

legacy   das Vermächtnis

legal action   die Klage, der Prozeß

legal capital   das festgesetzte Eigenkapital

legal entity   die juristische Person

legal holiday   der gesetzliche Feiertag

legal list (fiduciary investments)   die Investitionsliste

legal monopoly   das gesetzliche Monopol

legal reserve (banking)   die gesetzliche Rücklage

legal tender   das gesetzliche Zahlungsmittel

lending margin   die Kreditsicherungsgrenze

less-than-carload   die Stückgutsendung

lessee   der Mieter, der Pächter

lessor   der Vermieter

letter   der Brief

letter of credit   der Kreditbrief, das Akkreditiv

letter of guaranty   der Mietsvertrag

letter of indemnity   die Kannossementsgarantie

letter of introduction   das Empfehlungsschreiben

letterhead   der Geschäftsbogen

level out (v)   ausgleichen, abflachen

leverage   die Hebelwirkung, der Einfluß

leveraged lease   der Mietsvertrag mit Bestimmungen für Einrichtungsfinanzierung und eventuellem Ankauf

levy taxes (v)   Steuern erheben

liability   die Haftung

liability, actual   die tatsächliche Haftpflicht

liability, assumed   die übernommene Verpflichtung

liability, contingent   die Eventuellverbindlichkeit

liability, current   die kurzfristige Verbindlichkeit

liability, fixed   die langfristige Verbindlichkeit

liability insurance   die Haftpflichtversicherung

liability, secured   die gesicherte Haftung

liability, unsecured   die ungesicherte Haftung

liable for tax   steuerpflichtig

liable to (responsible)   verantwortlich

liaison   die Verbindung

libel   die Verleumdung

license   die Erlaubnis, die Lizenz

license fees   die Lizenzgebühren

licensed warehouse   das genehmigte Lagerhaus

lien   das Pfandrecht

life cycle   die Lebensdauer, die Nutzungsdauer

life insurance policy   die Lebensversicherungspolice

life member   das Mitglied auf Lebenszeit

life of a patent   die Dauer eines Patentes

lighterage   der Schutentransport

limit order (stock market)   die limitierte Börsenorder

limited liability   die beschränkte Haftung

limited partnership   die Kommanditgesellschaft
line executive   der Liniendirektor
line management   das Linienmanagement
line of business   der Geschäftsbereich, die Branche
lineal estimation   die lineare Schätzung
linear   gradlinig
linear programming   die lineare Programmierung
linear terms   die linearen Bedingungen
liquid assets   das Umlaufvermögen
liquidation   die Auflösung
liquidation value   der Auflösungswert
liquidity   die Liquidität
liquidity preference   die Liquiditätsbevorzugung
liquidity ratio   der Liquiditätsgrad
list price   der Listenpreis
listed securities   die amtlich notierten Werte
listing   die Verzeichnung, die Katalogisierung
litigation   der Rechtsstreit
living trust   das Treuhandverhältnis unter Lebenden
load (sales charge)   die Verkaufsgebühr
load factor   der Kapazitätsausnutzungsgrad
loan   die Anleihe, das Darlehn
loan agreement   der Darlehnsvertrag
loan value   der Beleihungswert, der Lombardwert
lobbying   die Meinungsbeeinflussung der Abgeordneten durch Interessengruppen
local customs   die Ortsgebräuche
local tax   die Kommunalsteuer, die Gemeindesteuer
lock in   Kapital blockieren
lock out (v)   aussperren
logistics   die Logistik
logo   das Firmenschild, das Firmenzeichen
long hedge   der langfristige Terminkauf
long interest   die langfristige Verzinsung
long ton   die englische Tonne
long-range planning   die langfristige Planung
long-term capital account   das langfristige Kapitalkonto

long-term debt   die langfristige Schuld

loss   der Verlust

loss, gross   der Bruttoverlust

loss leader   der Zugartikel, der Lockartikel, das Lockvogelangebot

loss-loss ratio   das Gesamtverlustverhältnis

loss, net   der Reinverlust

loss, total   der Totalverlust

lot   das Los, der Posten

low income   die niedrige Einkommensstufe

low-interest loans   die niedrigverzinslichen Darlehen

low-yield bonds   die niedrigverzinslichen Schuldverschreibungen

lump sum   der Pauschalbetrag, die einmalige Summe

luxury goods   die Luxuswaren

luxury tax   die Luxussteuer

M

machinery   der Maschinenpark

macroeconomics   die Makroökonomie

magnetic memory   der Magnetspeicher

magnetic tape   das Magnetband

mail order   der Versandhandel, der Postversand

mail-order sales   der Verkauf durch Versandgeschäft

mailing list   die Adressenkartei, die Postversandliste

mainframe computer   der Hauptrechner

maintenance   die Instandhaltung, die Wartung

maintenance contract   der Instandhaltungsvertrag, der Wartungsvertrag

maintenance margin   die Erhaltungsspanne

maize   der Mais, der Kukuruz

majority interest   die Anteilmehrheit

make available (v)   zur Verfügung stellen

make-or-buy decision   die Entscheidung über Eigenfertigung oder Ankauf

make-ready   die Zurichtung

makeshift   der Notbehelf

man (gal) Friday   der treue Gehilfe (die treue Gehilfin)

man hours   die Arbeitsstunden

manage (v)   (administrate) verwalten

manage (control)   kontrollieren

manage (direct)   führen, leiten, dirigieren

managed costs   die kontrollierten Kosten

managed economy   die Planwirtschaft, die gelenkte Wirtschaft

managed float   der kontrollierte Kassenvorschuß

management   das Management, die Verwaltung, die Leitung, die Betriebsführung

management accounting   das Rechnungswesen für Betriebsführungsbedürfnisse

management by objectives   die Betriebsführung durch Zielvorgabe

management chart   die Geschäftsleitungstabelle, das Betriebsführungsschaubild

management consultant   der Unternehmensberater

management fee   die Verwaltungsgebühr

management group   die Führungsgruppe

management team   die Leitungsschicht

management, business   die Betriebsleitung

management, credit   die Kreditverwaltung

management, financial   die Finanzverwaltung

management, line   das Linienmanagement

management, market   die Marktleitung

management, office   die Büroleitung

management, personnel   die Personalleitung

management, product   das Produktmanagement

management, sales   die Vertriebsleitung

management, sales   die Absatzleitung

management, systems   die Systemsteuerung

management, top   die oberste Führungsschicht, das Topmanagement

manager   der Leiter, der Geschäftsführer, der Manager

mandate   der Befehl, das Mandat

mandatory redemption   die Zwangseinziehung

manifest   die Frachtliste

manmade   die synthetischen Stoffe, die Kunststoffe

manmade fibers   die künstlichen Fasern
manpower   die Arbeitskräfte, der Personalbestand
manual worker   der Schwerarbeiter, der Handarbeiter
manufacturer   der Hersteller
manufacturer's agent   der Herstellervertreter
manufacturer's representative   der Handlungs-
   reisende
manufacturing capacity   die Herstellungskapazität
manufacturing   die Produktionskapazität
manufacturing control   die Fertigungssteuerung
margin   der Mindesteinzahlungsbetrag, die Verdienstspanne
margin call   die Kreditkündigung mit Geldforderung
margin, gross   die Bruttogewinnspanne
margin, net   die Nettogewinnspanne
margin of safety   die Sicherheitskoeffizient
margin, profit   die Gewinnspanne
margin requirements   der Mindesteinschuß
marginal account   das Einschußkonto
marginal cost   die Grenzkosten
marginal pricing   die marginale Preisfestsetzung
marginal productivity   die Grenzproduktivität
marginal revenue   der Grenzertrag
marine cargo insurance   die Seetransportversicherung
marine underwriter   der Seeversicherer
maritime contract   der Schiffahrtsvertrag
markdown   die Preissenkung, die Preisherabsetzung
market   der Markt
market (v)   vertreiben, absetzen, verkaufen
market access   der Marktzugang
market appraisal   die Markteinschätzung
market concentration   die Marktkonzentration
market dynamics   die Marktdynamik
market forces   die Marktkräfte
market forecast   die Marktprognose
market index   der Börsenindex
market letter   der Börsenbrief
market-maker   der Börsenmakler, der Kursfestsetzer

market management   die Marktleitung
market penetration   die Marktdurchdringung
market plan   der Marktplan
market planner   der Absatzplan
market position   die Marktlage, die Absatzposition
market potential   das Marktpotential
market price   der Marktpreis
market rating   die Börsenmarkteinstufung
market report   der Marktbericht, der Börsenbericht
market research   die Marktforschung
market saturation   die Marktsättigung
market share   der Marktanteil
market, stock   die börse
market survey   die Marktstudie, die Marktübersicht
market trends   die Markttendenzen
market value (general)   der Marktwert
market value (stocks)   der Kurswert
marketable securities   die börsengängigen Werte
marketing   der Absatz, der Vertrieb, der Verkauf, das Marketing
marketing budget   das Absatzbudget
marketing concept   das Absatzkonzept
marketing plan   der Absatzplan
marketplace   der Marktplatz
markup   der Preisaufschlag, der Aufschlag
mass communications   die Massenkommunikation, die Massenmedien
mass marketing   der Massenabsatz, der Großvertrieb
mass media   die Massenmedien, die Informationswege, die Werbeträger
mass production   die Massenproduktion
master agreement   das Manteltarifabkommen
matched samples   die abgestimmten Vergleichsproben
materials   die Materialien, die Werkstoffe
maternity leave   der Mutterschaftsurlaub
mathematical model   das mathematische Modell
matrix management   die Matrizenüberwachung
maturity   die Reife
maturity (due debts)   die Fälligkeit, der Verfall

maturity date   der Verfalltag

maximize (v)   steigern, aufs Höchstmaß bringen

mean (average)   der Durchschnitt

measure (v)   messen

mechanical engineering   der Maschinenbau

mechanic's lien   das Zurückbehaltungsrecht des Handwerkers

media   die Medien, die Werbeträger

median   der Zentralwert

mediation   die Vermittlung

medium of exchange   das Tauschmittel

medium term   mittelfristig

meet the price (v)   dem Preis entsprechen, einen konkurrenzfähigen Preis festsetzen können

meeting   die Tagung, die Sitzung, die Versammlung

member firm   die Mitgliedsfirma, im Börsenhandel eingetragener Verein

member of a firm   das Firmenmitglied

memorandum   das Rundschreiben

mercantile   kaufmännisch, handelsbezogen

mercantile agency   die Handelsagentur

mercantile law (in general)   das Handelsrecht

mercantile law (a specific law)   das Handelgesetz

merchandise   die Waren, die Güter

merchandising   die Absatztätigkeiten

merchant   der Kaufmann, der Händler, der Ladenbesitzer, der Krämer

merchant bank   die Handelsbank

merchant guild   die Handelskammer, die Kaufmannsinnung

merger   die Vereinigung, die Fusion

metals   die Metalle

method   die Methode, das Verfahren

metrification   die Anpassung an das Dezimalsystem, die Metrifikation

microchip   der Mikrochip

microcomputer   der Mikrocomputer

microfiche   das Mikrofiche

microfilm   der Mikrofilm

microprocessor   der Mikroprozessor

middle management   die mittlere Führungsschicht, das Mittelmanagement

middleman   der Zwischenhändler, der Vermittler, der Mittelmann

miller   die Müllerei

minicomputer   der Minicomputer

minimum reserves   die Mindestreserven

minimum wage   der Mindestlohn

minority interest   der Minderheitsanteil

mint   die Münzstätte, das Münzamt

miscalculation   der Rechenfehler

miscellaneous   Verschiedenes, Vermischtes

misleading   irreführend

misunderstanding   das Mißverständnis

mixed costs   die Mischkosten

mixed sampling   die ungleichartige Stichprobenauswahl

mobility of labor   die Beweglichkeit der Arbeitskräfte

mock-up   das Lehrmodell, das Anschauungsmodell

mode   die Art, die Weise

model   das Muster, das Modell, das Vorbild

modem   der Modem

modular production   die Vorfertigung

monetary base   die Geldmenge

monetary credits   die Währungskredite, die Devisengelder

monetary policy   die Geldpolitik

monetary standard   die Währungseinheit

money   das Geld

money broker   der Geldmakler

money manager   der Geldverwalter

money market   der Geldmarkt

money order   die Geldanweisung, die Zahlungsanweisung, die Postanweisung

money shop   der "Geldlader", die Wechselstube, die Bank

money supply   die Geldversorgung, der Geldbestand

monitor   der Abhörer

monopoly   das Monopol

monopsony   die Monopsonie

Monte Carlo technique   die Monte Carlo Methode

moonlighting   die Ausübung einer Zusatzbeschäftigung, der Doppelverdienst

morale   die Arbeitsmoral

moratorium   das Moratorium, der Zahlungsaufschub, die Stundung

mortgage   die Hypothek

mortgage bank   die Hypothekenbank

mortgage bond   der Hypothekenbrief

mortgage certificate   der Hypothekenschein

mortgage debenture   der Hypothekenpfandbrief

most-favored nation   das meistbegünstigte Land

motion   die Bewegung

motion (parliamentary)   der Antrag

motivation study   die Motivationsstudie

movement of goods   der Gütertransport

moving average   der gleitende Durchschnitt

moving expenses   die Umzugskosten

moving parity   die veränderliche Parität

multicurrency   die Multiwährung

multilateral agreement   das mehrseitige Abkommen

multilateral trade   der mehrseitige Handel

multinational corporation   die multinationale Gesellschaft

multiple exchange rate   die gespaltenen Wechselkurse

multiple taxation   die Mehrfachbesteuerung

multiples   die Preis-Gewinn Verhältnisse

multiplier   der Multiplikator

multiprogramming   die Mehrprogrammverarbeitung

municipal bond   die Kommunalobligation

mutual   der Investmentfonds

mutual fund   die Investmentgesellschaft

mutual savings bank   die Sparkasse

mutually exclusive classes   die gegenseitig sich ausschließenden Gattungen

N

named point of destination   der genannte Bestimmungsort

named point of exportation   der genannte Ausfuhrort

named point of origin   der genannte Ursprungsort

named port of importation   der genannte Einfuhrhafen

named port of shipment   der genannte Versandhafen

national bank   die Staatsbank, die Zentralbank

national debt   die Staatsverschuldung

nationalism   der Nationalismus

nationalism (economic)   der Staatssozialismus

nationalization   die Verstaatlichung

native produce   das Inlandserzeugnis

natural gas   das Erdgas

natural resources   die Naturschätze, die Bodenschätze

near money   die geldähnliche Forderung

needs analysis   die Bedarfsanalyse

negative cash flow   der negative Zahlungsstrom

negative pledge   das Unterlassungsversprechen

negligent   nachlässig

negotiable (v)   verhandeln

negotiable (convertible transferable)   übertragbar

negotiable securities   die übertragbaren Wertpapiere

negotiable (subject to discussion)   verhandlungsfähig

negotiated sale   der getätigte Verkauf

negotiation   die Verhandlung

net asset value   der Reinvermögenswert

net asset worth   das Eigenkapital

net assets   das Reinvermögen

net borrowed reserves   die Nettofremdkapitalreserven

net cash flow   der Nettobargeldstrom

net change   die Nettoänderung

net equity assets   das Nettoeigenkapital

net income   das Nettoeinkommen

net investment   die Nettoinvestition

net loss   der Reinverlust

net margin   die Nettogewinnspanne

net position of a trader   der Nettostand eines Maklers

net present value   der Nettobarwert

net profit   der Reingewinn, der Nettogewinn

net sales   der Nettoumsatz

net working capital   das Nettobetriebskapital

net worth   das Eigenkapital, der Nettowert

network   das Netz

new issue   die Neubegebung, die Neuausgabe, die Neuemission

new money   das neue Geld

new product development   die Entwicklung eines neuen Produkts

night depository   das Nachtdepot

no-load fund   der gebührenfreie Investmentfonds

no par value   die nennwertlose Aktie

no problem   kein Problem

nominal price   der Nominelpreis

nominal yield   der Nennertrag

noncumulative preferred stock   die nichtkumulative Vorzugsaktie

noncurrent assets   die langfristigen Vermögenswerte

nondurable goods   die Verbrauchsgüter

nonfeasance   die pflichtwidrige Unterlassung, die Nichterfüllung

nonmember   das Nichtmitglied

nonprofit (not-for-profit)   gemiennützig, nicht auf Gewinn ausgerichtet

nonresident   der Devisenausländer, der Gebietsfremde

nonvoting stock   die Aktien ohne Stimmberechtigung

norm   die Norm

not otherwise indexed by name   nicht sonst im Namenregister verzeichnet

notary   der Notar

note, credit   die Gutschriftsanzeige

note, debit   die Lastschriftanzeige

note, promissory   der Eigenwechsel, der Schuldschein

note receivable   der Besitzwechsel

novation   die Novation, die Schuldübernahme

null and void   null und nichtig

nullify (v)   aufheben

numerical control   die zahlenmäßige Steuerung

O

obligation die Verpflichtung

obsolescence das Veralten, die Überalterung

occupation der Beruf

occupational hazard das Berufsrisiko

odd lot die ungerade Menge

odd lot broker der Börsenmakler in kleinen Mengen

off line in unabhängiger Datenverarbeitung, nicht an die Zentrale gekoppelt

off-the-books ohne Geschäftsbucheintragung

offer (v) bieten

offer for sale zum Verkauf anbieten, feilhalten

offered price der Angebotspreis

offered rate der Briefkurs

office das Büro, das Amt

office, branch die Filiale, das Zweiggeschäft, die Zweigstelle

office, head die Zentrale, das Hauptbüro

office management die Büroleitung

offset printing der Offsetdruck

offshore company die offshore Gesellschaft

oligopoly das Oligopol

oligopsony die Oligopsonie

omit (v) auslassen

on account auf Ziel, auf Rechnung

on consignment in Kommission, kommissionsweise

on cost die laufenden Ausgaben

on demand auf Verlangen

on line (computer) mit der Datenverarbeitung verbunden, on line

on-sale date der Verkaufstermin

on-the-job training die Ausbildung am Arbeitsplatz

open account das laufende Konto, das Kontokorrentkonto

open cover die Generalversicherung, die Pauschalversicherung

open door policy die Politik der offenen Tür

open market der Freiverkehr, der Offenmarkt

open market operations die Offenmarktpolitik der Notenbank

open order die unbefristete Order

open shop der gewerkschaftsfreie Betrieb

opening balance der Anfangsbestand

opening price der Eröffnungskurs, der Anfangskurs

operating budget das Betriebsbudget

operating expenses die Betriebskosten

operating income das Betriebsergebnis, das Betriebseinkommen

operating loss der Betriebsverlust

operating profit der Betriebsgewinn

operating statement die Betriebsergebnisrechnung

operating unit die Betriebseinheit

operations audit die Betriebstätigkeitsprüfung

operations headquarters die Betriebszentrale

operations management die Betriebsführung

opportunity cost die Opportunitätskosten, die alternativen Kosten, die Wartekosten

option die Option

option (put or call options) das Börsentermingeschäft

optional beliebig optional freigestellt

order die Bestellung, der Auftrag

order (command) der Befehl, bestellen

order form der Bestellschein

order number die Bestellnummer

order of the day die Tagesbestellung

order, to place an (v) einen Auftrag erteilen

ordinary capital das Stammkapital

organization die Organisation

organization chart der Organisationsplan, das Organisationsschema

original cost die Anschaffungskosten, die Erwerbskosten

original entry die Grundbuchung

original maturity die ursprüngliche Fälligkeit

other assets (other liabilities) das sonstige Vermögen (die sonstigen Verbindlichkeiten)

out-of-pocket expenses die Barauslagen

outbid (v) überbieten

outlay   die Auslage
outlet   der Absatz, die Verkaufsstelle
outlook   die Aussicht
outlook (philosophy)   die Anschauung
output   die Arbeitsleistung, die Erzeugung
outsized articles   die übergroßen Artikel
outstanding contract   der noch rechtskräftige Vertrag
outstanding debt   die Außenstände, die ausstehenden
  Forderungen
outstanding stock   die ausstehenden Aktien
outturn   der Ausstoß
outturner   der Ertrag
over the counter   freihändig
over-the-counter quotation   der freihändige Kurs
overage   der Überbetrag
overbought   zu stark gekauft
overcapitalized   überkapitalisiert
overcharge   zuviel fordern
overcharge (v)   überfordern
overdraft   die Überziehung, die Kreditüberschreitung
overdue   überfällig
overhang   überhängen
overhead   die Generalkosten, die Gemeinkosten
overlap   überlangen, überlappen, übergreifen
overnight   über Nacht
overpayment   die Überzahlung
overseas common point   der Gemeinpunkt in Übersee
oversold   zu stark verkauft
overstock   der Überfluß
oversubscribe (v)   überzeichnen
oversupply   das Überangebot
overtime   die Überstunden
overvalue (v)   überbewerten
owner   der Besitzer, der Inhaber
owner's equity   das Eigenkapital
ownership   das Eigentum, der Besitz

P

package deal   das Kopplungsgeschäft

package deals das Verhandlungspaket
packaging die Verpackung
packing case die Packkiste
packing list der Packzettel
paid holiday der bezahlte Feiertag
paid in full voll bezahlt
paid-in surplus der nicht entnommene Gewinn
paid up capital das voll eingezahlte Kapital
paid up shares die eingezahlten Anteile
pallet die Palette
palletized freight die palettierte Ladung
paper das Papier
paper profit der Buchgewinn, der Scheingewinn
paper tape der Lochstreifen
par value der Nennwert, der Pariwert
par, above über pari
par, below unter pari
parcel post die Paketpost
parent company die Muttergesellschaft, die Dachgesellschaft
parity die Parität, die Gleichheit
parity income ratio das Paritätseinkommenverhältnis
parity price der Paritätspreis
part der Teil, das Stück
part cargo die Teilladung, die Teilfracht
partial payment die Teilzahlung
participation fee die Beteiligungsgebühr
participation loan die Beteiligungsanleihe
particular average loss der Schaden in besonderer Havarie
partner der Teilhaber, der Beteiligte
partnership die Personengesellschaft, die Teilhaberschaft
party (contract) die Vertragspartei, der Kontrahent
pass (written permit) der Personalausweis
passbook das Bankbuch, das Sparbuch
passed dividend die nicht ausgeschüttete Dividende
past due überfällig
patent das Patent

patent application die Patentanmeldung
patent infringement die Patentverletzung
patent law das Patentrecht
patent pending das angemeldete Patent
patent royalty die Patentabgabe
patented process das patentierte Verfahren
pattern das Muster
pay (v) zahlen
pay off (v) tilgen
pay up (v) vollständig bezahlen
payable on demand zahlbar bei Sicht
payable to bearer an den Inhaber zahlbar
payable to order an Order zahlbar
payback period der Zurückzahlungszeitraum
payee der Zahlungsempfänger
payer der Zahler
payload die Nutzlast
paymaster der Zahlungsmeister, der Kassierer für Auszahlungen
payment die Zahlung
payment in full die volle Zahlung
payment in kind die Sachleistung
payment, refused die verweigerte Zahlung
payout period die Kapitalrückflußdauer
payroll die Gehälterliste, die Lohnliste
payroll tax die Lohnsteuer
peak load die Spitzenbelastung
pegged price der Stützpreis, der Stützkurs
pegging die Kursstützung, die Preisstützung
penalty clause die Strafklausel
penalty-fraud action das Strafverfahren wegen Unterschlagung
penny stock die Kleinaktie
pension fund die Pensionskasse
per capita pro Kopf
per diem pro Tag
per share pro Anteil
percent das Prozent
percentage earnings die Provisionseinkünfte

percentage of profit   der Gewinnanteilprozentsatz

percentage point   der Prozentpunkt

performance bond   die Gewährleistungsgarantie, die Submissionsgarantie

period   die Periode

period (time)   der Zeitraum

periodic inventory   die periodische Bestandsaufnahme

peripherals   die Randmaschinen

perks   die Nebeneinkünfte

permit   der Zulassungsschein, die Erlaubnis

perpetual inventory   die permanente Buchinventur

personal deduction   der persönliche Abzug

personal exemption   der persönliche Freibetrag

personal income tax   die persönliche Einkommensteuer

personal liability   die persönliche Haftpflicht

personal property   das Privateigentum

personality test   die Persönlichkeitsprüfung

personnel   das Personal, die Belegschaft

personnel department   die Personalabteilung

personnel management   die Personalleitung

petrochemical   petrochemisch

petrodollars   die Erdöldollars, die Petrodollars

petroleum   das Erdöl, das Petroleum

phase in (v)   stufenweise einführen

phase out (v)   stufenweise einstellen, allmählich abschaffen

physical inventory   die körperliche Inventur

picket line   die Streikpostenkette

pickup and delivery   die Abholung und Lieferung

pie chart   das Kreisdiagramm

piecework   die Stückarbeit, die Akkordarbeit

piggyback service   der Huckepackverkehr

pilferage   der kleinediebstahl, die dieberei

pilotage   das Lotsengeld

pipage   das Röhrensystem, die Gebühr für, die Leitung durch Röhren

place an order (v)   einen Auftrag erteilen

place of business   das Geschäftslokal

placement (personnel) die Stellenvermittlung

plan der Plan, (action) der Handlungsplan

plan, market der Marktplan

plan der Absatzplan

planned obsolescence die geplante Überalterung

plant capacity die betriebliche Leistungsfähigkeit

plant location die Fabriklage

plant manager der Werkleiter, der Betriebsleiter

pledge das Pfand

plenary meeting die Vollversammlung, die Plenarsitzung

plow back earnings (v) selbstfinanzieren, den Geschäftsgewinn wieder anlegen

plus accrued interest zuzüglich aufgelaufener Zinsen

point, breakeven der Kostendeckungspunkt

point, breaker die Gewinnschwelle

point of order die Verfahrensfrage, der Tagesordnungspunkt

point of sale der Verkaufspunkt

point, percentage der Prozentpunkt

policy (action) die Politik

policy (insurance) die Police

policy (principle) der Grundsatz

policyholder der Policeinhaber

pool (v) zusammenlegen

pool of funds der Sammelfonds

pooling of interests eine Interessengemeinschaft bilden

portfolio das Portefeuille

portfolio management die Portefeuilleverwaltung, die Vermögensverwaltung

portfolio theory die Portfeuilletheorie

position limit das Orderlimit

positive cash flow der positive Zahlungsstrom

post (v) (bookkeeping) verbuchen

postdated nachdatiert

postpone (v) aufschieben

potential buyer der potentielle Kunde, der Kaufinteressent

potential sales der potentielle Umsatz, die Absatzmöglichkeiten

power consumption der Stromverbrauch

power of attorney die Vollmacht

practical praktisch, zweckmäßig

practice die Praktik, die Gewohnheit

preemptive das Bezugsrecht

preemptive right das Vorkaufsrecht

prefabricated house das Fertighaus

prefabrication die Vorfertigung

preferential debts die bevorrechtigten Forderungen

preferential tariff der Vorzugszoll, der Begünstigungstarif

preferred stock die Vorzugsaktie

preliminary prospectus der Vorprospekt

premises das Grundstück

premium, insurance die Versicherungsprämie, der Versicherungsbeitrag

premium offer das Zugabenangebot

premium payment die Prämienzahlung

premium pricing die Spitzenpreisansetzung

prepaid expenses (balance sheet) die vorausgezahlten Aufwendungen, die aktiven Rechnungsabgrenzungsposten

prepay (v) vorauszahlen

president der Präsident, der Vorsitzende, der Generaldirektor

preventive maintenance die vorbeugende Instandhaltung

price der Preis, einen Preis ansetzen

price (v) auspreisen

price abatement der Preisnachlaß

price cutting die Preissenkung

price differential der Preisunterschied

price/earnings (p/e) ratio das Preis-Einnahmen Verhältnis, das Kurs-Ertrags Verhältnis

price elasticity die Preiselastizität

price fixing die Preisbindung

price freeze der Preisstop

price increase die Preiserhöhung

price index der Preisindex

price limit die Preisgrenze

price list die Preisliste, das Preisverzeichnis

price range   die Preislage, die Preisskala
price support   die Subvention, die Preisstützung
price tag   der Preiszettel
price war   der Preiskrieg
primary market   der Hauptmarkt
primary reserve   die Primärreserven
primary reserves   die Kassenreserven
prime costs   die Selbstkosten, die Gestehungskosten
prime rate   der Leitzinssatz
prime time   die Hauptsendezeit
principal (capital)   das Grundkapital
principal (employer of an agent)   der Auftraggeber
printed matter   die Drucksache
printout   der Computerausdruck
priority   der Vorrang, die Priorität, das Vorzugsrecht
private fleet   der eigene Wagenpark, die Privatflotte
private label (or brand)   die Privatmarke
private placement (finance)   die Privatplazierung, die direktplazierung
pro forma statement   die fiktive Bilanz
probate   die Testamentseröffnung und Bestätigung
problem   das Problem
problem analysis   die Problemanalyse
problem solving   die Problemlösung
proceeds   die Erlöse
process (v)   bearbeiten process verarbeiten
processing error   der Bearbeitungsfehler
procurement   die Beschaffung
product   das Erzeugnis, das Produkt
product analysis   die Warenanalyse
product design   die Produktgestaltung
product development   die Produktentwicklung
product dynamics   die Produktdynamik
product group   die Produktgruppe
product life   die Lebensdauer, das Produktsortiment
product management   das Produktmanagement
product profitability   die Produktrentabilität
production   die Herstellung, die Produktion, die Fertigung

production control   die Fertigungssteuerung, die Produktionslenkung

production costs   die Fertigungskosten, der Produktionsaufwand

production line   die Produktion am laufenden Band

production process   das Fertigungsverfahren

production schedule   der Fertigungsplan

productivity   die Produktivität

profession   der Beruf

professional   der Fachmann

profit   der Gewinn, der Verdienst

profit-and-loss account   das Gewinn- und Verlustkonto

profit-and-loss statement   die Gewinn- und Verlustrechnung

profit factor   der Gewinnfaktor

profit, gross   der Rohgewinn, der Bruttogewinn

profit impact   die Gewinnwirkung

profit margin   die Gewinnspanne, die Verdienstspanne

profit, net   der Reingewinn, der Nettogewinn

profit projection   die Gewinnnprognose

profit sharing   die Gewinnbeteiligung

profit-taking   die Gewinnrealisierung, die Gewinnsicherung

profitability   die Rentabilität

profitability analysis   die Rentabilitätsanalyse

pro forma invoice   die Proformarechnung

program   das Programm

program (v)   programmieren

prohibited goods   die Schmuggelwaren

project   das Vorhaben

project (v)   planen, vermuten

project planning   die Projektplanung

promissory note   der Eigenwechsel, der Schuldschein

promotion   die Förderung, die Beförderung

promotion, sales   die Verkaufsförderung

proof of loss   der Schadennachweis

property   der Besitz, das Eigentum

proprietary   gesetzlich geschützt, der Inhaber

proprietor der Eigentümer

prospectus der Prospekt, das Zeichnungsangebot

protectionism das Schutzzollsystem, der Protektionismus

protest (banking, law) der Wechselprotest

proxy die Bevollmächtigung, die Stimmrechtsermächtigung

proxy statement das Vollmachtsformular

public auction die öffentliche Versteigerung

public company die Aktiengesellschaft

public domain das Gemeingut, der staatliche Grundbesitz

public funds die öffentlichen Mittel

public offering das öffentliche Angebot

public opinion poll die Meinungsforschung

public property das Staatseigentum, das Eigentum, der öffentlichen Hand

public relations die Öffentlichkeitsarbeit, die offentliche Meinungspflege

public sale der öffentliche Verkauf

public sector der Regierungssektor, der öffentliche Bereich

public utility der Versorgungsbetrieb

public works die öffentlichen Arbeiten

publicity die Publizität

pump priming die Konjunkturspritze

punch card die Lochkarte

purchase (v) kaufen

purchase money mortgage die Restkaufgeldhypothek

purchase order der Kaufauftrag, die Bestellung

purchase price der Kaufpreis

purchasing agent der Einkaufsleiter, der Zwischenhändler

purchasing manager der Einkaufsleiter

purchasing power die Kaufkraft

pure risk das reine Risiko

put and call das Stellagegeschäft

put in a bid (v) ein Angebot machen

put option die Verkaufsoption

pyramid selling   das Schneeballverkaufssystem
pyramiding   die Nutzung noch nicht realisierter Gewinne

Q

qualification   die Qualifikation, die Befähigung
qualified acceptance endorsement   das eingeschränkte Indossament
quality control   die Qualitätskontrolle
quality goods   die Qualitätswaren
quantity   die Menge, die Quantität
quantity discount   der Mengenrabatt
quasi-public company   der quasi-öffentliche Betrieb
quick assets   die flüssige Anlagen
quit claim deed   der Grundstückkaufvertrag
quorum   die beschlußfähige Anzahl, die Beschlußfähigkeit
quota   die Quote, das Kontingent
quota (export)   die Ausfuhrquote
quota (import)   die Einfuhrquote
quota (sales)   die Verkaufsquote
quota system   das Kontingentierungssystem
quotation (stock exchange)   die Notierung

R

rack jobber   der Großlieferant
rail shipment   die Bahnsendung
railroad   die Eisenbahn, die Bahn
rain check   die Gültigkeitsverlängerung
raising capital   die Kapitalaufnahme, die Kapitalaufbringung
rally   die Erholung, der Aufschwung
rally (v)   sich sammeln
random access memory   der direkte Speicherzugriff
random sample   die Stichprobe
rate   der Kurs, die Rate
rate of growth   die Wachstumsrate
rate of increase   die Zuwachsrate
rate of interest   der Zinsfuß, der Zinssatz
rate of return   die Rentabilitätsrate, der Zinssatz

rating (credit)   die Krediteinschätzung, Bonitätsprüfung

rating (market)   die Börsenmarkteinstufung

ratio   das Verhältnis, das Maß

rationing   die Rationierung

raw materials   die Rohstoffe

ready cash   das verfügbare Bargeld

real assets   das Grundvermögen

real estate   der Grundbesitz

real income   das Realeinkommen

real investment   die Realinvestition

real price   der Effektivpreis

real time   die Echtzeit, die Realzeit

real wages   die Reallöhne

reasonable care   die angemessene Sorgfalt

rebate   der Preisnachlaß

recapitalization   die Neufinanzierung

receipt (paper)   die Quittung

receipt (reception)   der Empfang

recession   der Rückgang, die Rezession

reciprocal training   die gegenseitige Ausbildung

record date   das Protokolldatum

recourse   der Rückgriff

recovery   die Wiedererlangung, der Aufschwung

recovery of expenses   die Ausgabenvergütung, die Kostendeckung

red tape   der Amtsschimmel, die Bürokratie

redeemable bond   die kündbare Obligation

redemption allowance   die Einlösungsvergütung

redemption fund   der Tilgungsfonds, der Ablösungsfonds

redemption premium   die Einlösungsprämie

rediscount rate   der Rediskontsatz

reexport (v)   wieder ausführen

reference, credit   die Kreditreferenz

reference number   das Aktienzeichen, die Geschäftsnummer

refinancing   die Refinanzierung

reflation   die Reflation

refund   die Rückzahlung, die Rückerstattung

refuse acceptance (v)   die Annahme verweigern

refuse payment (v)   die Zahlung verweigern

registered check   der eingetragene Scheck, der Namensscheck

registered mail   die Einschreibepost

registered representative   der eingetragene Vertreter, der Börsenmakler

registered security   das Namenspapier

registered trademark   das eingetragene Warenzeichen

regression analysis   die Regressionsanalyse

regressive tax   die rückwirkende Steuer

regular warehouse   das eingetragene Lagerhaus, der öffentliche Lagerbetrieb

regulation   die Vorschrift

reimburse (v)   entschädigen, zurückzahlen

reinsurer   der Rückversicherer

reliable source   die zuverlässige Quelle

remainder   der Rest, das Übrige

remedy (law)   das Rechtsmittel, der Rechtsbehelf, die gesetzliche Abhilfe

remission of a customs duty   der Zollerlaß, der Gebührennachlaß

remission of a tax   der Steuernachlaß

remuneration   die Vergütung

renegotiate (v)   neu verhandeln, modifizieren, abändern

renew (v)   erneuern

rent   die Miete

rent (v) (rent from)   mieten

rent (v) (rent to)   vermieten

reorder (v)   nachbestellen, neubestellen

reorganization   die Umorganisierung, die Neugestaltung

repay (v)   zurückzahlen

repeat order   die Nachbestellung, die Neubestellung, der Wiederholungsauftrag

replacement cost   die Wiederbeschaffungskosten

replacement parts   die Ersatzteile

reply (v)   beantworten

report der Bericht, die Meldung, die Nachricht
repossession die Wiederinbesitznahme
representative der Vertreter
reproduction die Wiederherstellung, die Reproduktion
request for bid die Ausschreibung, die Angebotsaufforderung
requirement die Anforderung
resale der Wiederverkauf, der Weiterverkauf
research die Forschung
research and development die Forschung und Entwicklung
reserve die Rücklage
resident buyer der ansässige Einkäufer
resolution der Beschluß, die Resolution
resource allocation die Mittelverwendung
restore (v) restaurieren
restrictions on export (import) die Ausfuhrbeschränkungen (die Einfuhrbeschränkungen)
restructure (v) umschichten, umstrukturieren
resume (v) wiederaufnehmen
retail der Einzelhandel, der Einzelverkauf, das detailgeschäft
retail bank die Handelsbank, die Geschäftsbank
retail merchandise die Einzelhandelswaren
retail outlet die Einzelhandelsverkaufsstelle
retail price der Einzelhandelspreis
retail sales tax die Einzelhandelsumsatzsteuer
retail trade der Einzelhandel, der Detailverkauf
retained earnings die thesaurierten Gewinne
retained profits die zurückbehaltenen Gewinne
retirement der Ruhestand
retirement (debt) die Schuldentilgung
retroactive rückwirkend
return on assets managed die Anlagenrendite
return on capital die Kapitalrendite
return on investment die Kapitalverzinsung
return on sales die Umsatzrendite
return, rate of die Rentabilitätsrate, der Zinssatz
revaluation die Umwertung, die Neubewertung

revenue   die Einnahme

revenue bond   die Ertragsobligation, die Einkommensobligation

reverse stock split   die Aktienzusammenlegung

revocable trust   das widerrufliche Treuhandverhältnis

revolving credit   der revolvierende Kredit

revolving fund   die rückzahlbare Staatsubvention

revolving letter of credit   das revolvierende Akkreditiv

reward   die Belohnung

rider (contracts)   die Zusatzklausel

right of recourse   das Regreßrecht, der Rückgriffsanspruch

right of way   die Vorfahrt

risk   die Gefahr, das Risiko

risk analysis   die Risikoanalyse

risk assessment   die Risikoeinschätzung

risk capital   das Risikokapital

rollback   die Preissenkung

rolling stock   die Eisenbahnbetriebsmittel, der Wagenpark

rollover   die automatische Erneuerung

rough draft   der Vorentwurf

rough estimate   die Überschlagsrechnung, der Voranschlag

round lot   das Hundertaktienpaket, der Börsenschluß

routine   der Programmablauf, die Routine

royalty   der Autorenanteil

royalty (book)   das Autorenhonorar

royalty (patent)   die Lizenzgebühr

running expenses   die laufenden Unkosten

rush order   der Eilauftrag

S

safe deposit box   das Bankfach, die Stahlkammer, der Panzerkasten

safeguard (v)   schützen

salary   das Gehalt

sales   der Umsatz

sales analysis   die Absatzanalyse

sales budget   der Absatzplan

sales estimate   die Umsatzschätzung, die Absatzkalkulation

sales force   das Verkaufspersonal

sales forecast   die Verkaufsprognose

sales management   die Absatzleitung, die Vertriebsleitung

sales promotion   die Verkaufsförderung

sales quota   die Verkaufsquote

sales tax   die Umsatzsteuer

sales territory   das Absatzgebiet

sales turnover   der Warenumsatz

sales volume   das Verkaufsvolumen

salvage (v)   bergen, retten

salvage charges   die Bergungskosten

salvage value (junk, scrap)   der Schrottwert

salvage value (recovery)   der Bergungswert

sample   die Probe

sample (v)   probieren

sample line   die Musterkollektion, die Auswahl

sample size   der Stichprobenumfang, die Auswahlgroße

savings   die Ersparnisse

savings account   das Sparkonto

savings bank   die Sparkasse

savings bond   die Staatsschuldverschreibung

scalper   der Weiterverkaufsgewinner, der Speculativhändler

schedule   der Zeitplan

schedule (v)   ansetzen

screen (v)   sieben

script   das Drehbuch, das Manuskript

sealed bid   das versiegelte Angebot

seasonal   jahreszeitlich, saisonal, saisonbedingt

second mortgage   die zweite Hypothek, die nachrangige Hypothek

second position   zweitstellig

second rate   zweitrangig, minderwertig

secondary market (securities)   der Wertpapierhandel

secretary   die Sekretärin, der Schriftführer

secured accounts die gesicherte Konten
secured liability die gesicherte Haftung
securities die Effekten, die Wertpapiere
security die Sicherheit
self-appraisal die Selbstschätzung
self-employed selbständig
self-service die Selbstbedienung
sell (v) verkaufen
sell and lease back verkaufen und anschließend mieten, die Nachkaufsmietung
sell direct (v) direkt verkaufen
semivariable costs die Sprungkosten
senior issue die mit Vorrechten ausgestattete Wertpapieremission
seniority das dienstalter
separation die Trennung
serial bonds die Serienanleihen
serial storage die Serienspeicherung
service (v) versorgen, instandhalten
service, advisory der Beratungsdienst
service contract der dienstvertrag, der Instandhaltungsvertrag
service, customer der Kundendienst
set-up costs die Rüstkosten, die Aufstellungskosten
settlement die Regelung, der Ausgleich, die Vereinbarung
settlement in full der vollständige Ausgleich
severance pay die Entlassungsabfindung
shareholder der Aktionär, der Teilhaber
shareholders' equity das Eigenkapital
shareholders' meeting die Aktionärsversammlung
shares die Aktien
shift (working hours) die Schicht
shipment die Sendung
shipper der Versender
shipping agent der Spediteur, der Versender
shipping charges die Versandkosten
shipping container der Versandbehälter
shipping expenses die Verladekosten

shipping instructions   die Versandanweisungen

shopping center   das Geschäftszentrum

short delivery   die Minderlieferung

short of cash   knapp bei Kasse

short position   die Leerverkaufsposition

short sale   der Leerverkauf

short shipment   die Mindersendung, die Minderlieferung

short supply   die Unterversorgung, die Knappheit

short-term capital account   das kurzfristiges Kapitalkonto

short-term debt   die kurzfristige Verschuldung

short-term financing   die kurzfristige Finanzierung

shortage   der Mangel

sick leave   die Krankheitsabwesenheit

sight draft   der Sichtwechsel

signature   die Unterschrift

silent partner   der stille Gesellschafter

simulate (v)   vorgeben, simulieren

sinking fund   der Tilgungsfonds

skilled labor   die gelernte Arbeitskräfte, die Facharbeiter

sliding parity   die veränderliche Parität

sliding price scale   die bewegliche Preisskala

slump   die Flaute, die Baisse, der Rückgang

small business   der Kleinbetrieb, der Mittelstand

soft currency   die weiche Währung

soft goods   die Textilien

soft loan   das zinsbegünstigte Darlehen

soft sell   die weiche Verkaufstour

software   die Software, das Computerprogramm

sole agent   der Alleinvertreter

sole proprietorship   die Einzelfirma

sole rights   das Alleinrecht

solvency   die Zahlungsfähigkeit

specialist (stock exchange)   der Börsenspezialist

specialty goods   die Spezialerzeugnisse

specific duty   der Stückzoll

speculator   der Spekulant

speed up (v)   beschleunigen

spin off   die Vermögemsübertragung gegen Aktien

split, stock   die Aktienaufteilung, der Aktiensplit

spoilage   der Verderb, der Ausschuß

sponsor (of a fund or partnership)   der Förderer, der Schirmherr

spot delivery   die Platzlieferung

spot market   der Kassamarkt

spread   die Spanne, die Differenz, die Marge

spreadsheet   die Matrixbilanz, der Verteilungsbogen

staff   der Stab

staff and line   Stab und Linie

staff assistant   der Stabsassistent

staff organization   die Stabsorganisation

stagflation   die Stagflation

stale check   der veralteter Scheck

stand-alone word processor   der alleinstehender Datenverarbeiter

stand-alone workstation   der unabhängiger Arbeitsplatz

stand in line (v)   Schlange stehen

standard costs   die Plankosten

standard deviation   die Standardabweichung

standard of living   der Lebensstandard

standard practice   das übliches Verfahren

standard time   die Normalzeit

standardization   die Normung, die Vereinheitlichung

standing charges   die laufende Kosten

standing costs   die Fixkosten

standing order   der Dauerauftrag

start-up costs   die Anfangskosten

statement   die Angabe

statement, financial   der Finanzstatuz, der Bilanzabschluß

statement of account   der Kontoauszug

statement, pro forma   die fiktive Bilanz

statement, profit-and-loss   die Gewinn- und Verlustrechnung

statistics   die Statistik

statute   die Satzung

statute of limitations   die gesetezliche Verjährungs-schriften

stock (inventory)   der Vorrat

stock (share)   die Aktie

stock-in-trade   de Warenbestand

stock certificate   das Aktienzertifikat

stock exchange   die Börse

stock index   der Börsenindex

stock issue   die Ausgabe, die Emission

stock market   der Aktienmarkt, die Effektenbörse

stock option   das Aktienbezugsrecht

stock portfolio   das Aktienportefeuille

stock power   die Börsenvollmacht

stock profit   der Aktiengewinn

stock purchase   der Vorratskauf, der Aktienkauf

stock split   die Aktienaufteilung, der Aktiensplit

stock takeover   der Erwerb der Aktienmehrheit

stock turnover   der Lagerumschlag

stockbroker   der Börsenmakler

stockholder   der Aktionär

stockholders' equity   das Aktienkapital

stop-loss order   der limitierter Börsenauftrag

storage   die Aufbewahrung, die Lagerung

storaged (computer)   die Speicherung

store   der Laden, das Geschäft

store (v)   aufbewahren

store (computer)   speichern

stowage   die Verstauung

stowage charges   der Stauerlohn

straddle   die Stellage

strapping   die Ladungsriemen

strategic articles   die strategischen Artikel

streamline (v)   rationalisieren, modernisieren

stress management   die Streßbewältigung

strike (v)   streiken

strike, wildcat   der wilde Streik, der Spontanstreik

strikebreaker   der Streikbrecher

stuffing   das Füllmaterial, die Füllung

subcontract der Nebenvertrag, der Zulieferant, der Subunternehmer

subject to availability vorbehaltlich der Verfügbarkeit

sublease die Untervermietung, die Unterpacht

subscription price (periodicals) der Bezugspreis

subscription price (securities) der Zeichnungspreis

subsidiary die Konzerngesellschaft, die Tochtergesellschaft

subsidy die Subvention

substandard unter der Norm

sum-of-the-years digits die digitale Jahressummenabschreibung

supersede (v) aufheben, verdrängen

supervisor die Aufsichtsperson

supplier der Lieferant

supply and demand (das) Angebot und (die) Nachfrage

support activities die Unterstützungstätigkeiten

surcharge der Aufschlag

surety company die Kautionsversicherungsgesellschaft

surplus capital der Kapitalüberschuß

surplus goods der Warenüberschuß

surtax die Zusatzsteuer, der Steuerzuschlag

suspend payment (v) die Zahlungen einstellen

swear vereidigen

swear (v) schwören

switching charges die Rangiergebühren

syndicate das Syndikat, das Konsortium

systems analysis die Systemanalyse

systems design die Systemgestaltung

systems engineering die Systemerarbeitung

systems management die Systemsteuerung

T

table of contents das Inhaltsverzeichnis, die Disposition

take down (v) aufschreiben, notieren

take-home pay das Nettogehalt

take off (v) abziehen, starten

take out (v) herausnehmen
take out (v) (insurance) abschließen
take out (v) (patent) erwirken
takeover die Übernahme
takeover bid das Übernahmeangebot
tangible assets das Sachanlagevermögen, die greifbaren Vermögenswerte
tanker der Tanker
target price der Richtpreis
tariff der Tarif, der Zoll
tariff adjustment die Zollangleichung
tariff barriers die Zollschranken
tariff charge die Zollgebühr
tariff classification die Zolleinstufung
tariff commodity die Zollware
tariff differential der Zollunterschied
tariff war der Zollkrieg
task force der Arbeitsausschuß, der Arbeitsstab
tax die Steuer, die Abgabe
tax abatement der Steuernachlaß
tax allowance der Steuerfreibetrag, die Steuervergünstigung
tax base die Besteuerungsgrundlage
tax burden die Steuerlast
tax collector der Steuereinnehmer, der Steuererheber
tax deduction der Steuerabzug
tax evasion die Steuerhinterziehung
tax, excise die Verbrauchssteuer, die Gewerbesteuer
tax-free steuerfrei
tax-free income das steuerfreie Einkommen
tax haven die Steueroase
tax relief die Steuervergünstigung
tax, sales die Umsatzsteuer
tax shelter die steuerbegünstigte Anlagemöglichkeit
taxation die Besteuerung
taxpayer der Steuerzahler
team management das Gruppenmanagement
technical technisch, fachgemäß
technology die Technologie

telecommunications die Telekommunikation, die Fernmeldetechnologie

telegram das Telegramm

telemarketing der Fernvertrieb

telephone der Fernsprecher, das Telefon

television das Fernsehen

television, cable das Kabelfernsehen

telex der Fernschreiber, das Telex

teller der Schalterbeamter

temporary vorläufig, zeitweilig, vorübergehend

tenant der Mieter, der Pächter

tender offer das Lieferungsangebot

term bond die Festobligation

term insurance die Kurzversicherung, die Versicherung auf Zeit

terminal das Terminal

terminate (v) beenden

terminate (v) (employment) kündigen

terms of sale die Verkaufsbedingungen

terms of trade die Handelsbedingungen

territorial waters das Hoheitsgewässer

territory das Gebiet

thin market der schwache Markt, der lustlose Markt

third-party exporter der Drittexporteur

through bill of lading das Transitkonnossement

throughput der Durchsatz, die Verarbeitungsmenge

ticker (stock prices) der Börsenfernschreiber

ticker tape das Papierband

tied aid die gebundene Hilfe

tied loan die zweckgebundene Anleihe

tight market die angespannte Marktlage

time and motion study die Zeit- und Bewegungsstudie

time bill of exchange der Zeitwechsel

time deposit die befristete Einlage

time order der zeitlich bestimmte limitierte Börsenauftrag

time sharing die gemeinschaftliche Computerbenutzung

time zone die Zeitzone

timetable (airplanes)   der Flugplan

timetable (schedule)   der Zeitplan

timetable (trains)   der Fahrplan

tip (inside information)   der Wink, der Börsentip

title   der Rechtstitel, der Eigentumstitel

title insurance   die Rechtsmängelversicherung

tombstone advertisement   die Wertpapieremissions-anzeige

tonnage   die Tonnage, die Ladungsfähigkeit

tools   die Werkzeuge

top management   die oberste Führungsschicht, das Topmanagement

top price   der Höchstpreis

top quality   die Spitzenqualität

tort   die Delikthandlung, das Zivilunrecht, die Straftat

total loss   der Totalverlust

tourism   der Fremdenverkehr

trade   der Handel

trade (v)   handeln

trade acceptance   das Handelsakzept, der Waren-wechsel

trade agreement   das Handelsabkommen, der Han-delsvertrag

trade association   der Handelsverband, die Industrie-genossenschaft

trade barrier   die Handelsschranke

trade commission   die Handelskommission

trade credit   der Handelskredit

trade date   das Handelsdatum

trade discount   der Händlerrabatt

trade fair   die Gewerbeausstellung

trade house   das Gewerbehaus, das Handelshaus

trade union   die Gewerkschaft

trademark   die Schutzmarke, die Handelsmarke

trader   der Händler

trader (stocks)   der Börsenmakler

trading company   die Handelsgesellschaft

trading limit   die Handelsgrenze

trainee   der Voluntär, der Praktikant

tranche   die Tranche, der Abschnitt

transaction   das Geschäft

transfer   der Übertrag, die Umschreibstelle für Effekten

transfer (v)   übertragen, überweisen

transfer agent   der Effektenüberträger

transit, in   unterwegs

translator   der Übersetzer

transportation   der Transport, das Verkehrswesen

travel agency   das Reisebüro

traveler's check   der Reisescheck

treasurer   der Schatzmeister, der Leiter der Finanzabteilung

treasury bills   die Schatzwechsel

treasury bonds   die Staatsanleihen

treasury notes   die Staatsobligationen

treasury stock   die Vorratsaktien

treaty   der Vertrag

trend   die Tendenz, die Entwicklungsrichtung

trial balance   die Probebilanz, die Vorbilanz

troubleshoot (v)   Störungen auffinden und beseitigen

truckload   die Lastwagenladung, die LKW-Ladung

trust   das Treuhandverhältnis

trust company   die Treuhandgesellschaft

trust fund   der Treuhandfonds

trust receipt   der Hinterlegungsschein

trustee   der Treuhänder, der Vermögensverwalter

turn-key contract   der schlüsselfertiger Vertrag

turnover   der Umschlag, der Geschäftsumsatz

two-tiered market   der zweistufiger Markt, der gespaltener Markt

typist   der Maschinenschreiber

U

ultra vires act   die Vollmachtsüberschreitung

unaccompanied goods   die unbegleitete Waren

uncollectible accounts   die uneinbringliche Forderungen

undercapitalized   unterkapitalisiert

undercut (v)   unterbieten

underdeveloped nations   die Entwicklungsländer
underestimate (v)   unterschätzen
underpaid   schlecht bezahlt, unterbezahlt
undersigned   unterzeichnet
understanding (agreement)   das Übereinkommen
undertake (v)   unternehmen
undervalue (v)   unterbewerten
underwriter   der Versichererder, der Anleihegarant
underwriter (securities)   die Emissionsbank
undeveloped   unentwickelt
unearned increment   der nicht verdiente Wertzuwachs
unearned revenue   die transitorischen Passiva
unemployment   die Arbeitslosigkeit
unemployment compensation   die Arbeitslosenunterstützung
unfair competition   der unlautere Wettbewerb
unfavorable   ungünstig, unvorteilhaft
unfeasible   undurchführbar
union contract   der Tarifvertrag
union label   das Gewerkschaftsetikett
union, labor   die Gewerkschaft
unit costs   die Stückkosten
unit load discount   der Rabatt je Verladeeinheit
unit price   der Stückpreis
unlisted   nicht eingetragen, nicht verzeichnet
unload (v)   entladen
unsecured liability   die ungesicherte Haftung
unsecured loan   die ungesicherte Anleihe
unskilled labor   die ungelernten Arbeitskräfte
up to our expectations   unseren Erwartungen entsprechend
upmarket   der Haussemarkt
upturn   der Aufschwung, die Aufwärtsbewegung
urban renewal   die Stadterneuerung
urban sprawl   die Stadtausbreitung
urgent   dringend
use tax   die Gebrauchssteuer
useful life   die Nutzungsdauer

user-friendly ergonomisch, benutzerfreundlich

usury der Wucher

utility der Versorgungsbetrieb

V

valid gültig

validate (v) validieren

valuation die Bewertung

value der Wert

value-added tax (VAT) die Mehrwertssteuer

value, asset der Vermögenswert

value, book der Buchwert

value engineer die Wertplanungstechnik

value engineering die Wertanalyse

value, face der Nennwert

value for duty der Zollwert

value, market (general) der Marktwert

value, market (stocks) der Kurswert

variable annuity die veränderliche Jahresrente

variable costs die veränderlichen Kosten

variable import levy die schwankende Einfuhrabschöpfung

variable margin der variable Erlösüberschuß

variable rate der schwankende Kurs

variable rate mortgage die Staffelhypothek

variance die Abweichung, die Veränderung

velocity of money die Geldumlaufgeschwindigkeit

vendor der Verkäufer

vendor's lien das Eigentumsvorbehalt des Verkaufers

venture capital das Risikokapital, das Wagniskapital

vertical integration die vertikale Verflechtung

vested interests die wohlerworbene Rechte

vested rights die verbriefte Rechte

veto der Einspruch, das Veto

vice-president der Vizepräsident

video cassette recorder die Fernsehbandaufnahme

visible balance of trade die sichtbare Handelsbilanz

voice-activated stimmaktiviert

voiced check der mündlich bestätigter Scheck

void   ungültig, nichtig
volatile market   die sprunghafte Börsenmarktlage
volume   der Umfang, das Volumen
volume discount   der Mengenrabatt
voluntary   freiwillig
voting right   das Stimmrecht
voucher   der Beleg

W

wage   der Lohn
wage differential   der Lohnunterschied
wage dispute   der Lohnstreit
wage drift   die Lohnrichtung
wage earner   der Lohnempfänger
wage freeze   der Lohnstopp
wage level   das Lohnniveau
wage-price spiral   die Lohn-Preis-Spirale
wage scale   die Lohnskala
wage structure   die Lohnstruktur
wages   die Löhne
waiver clause   die Verzichtsklausel
walkout   die Arbeitsniederlegung
want-ad   die Kleinanzeige, die Suchanzeige
warehouse   das Lagerhaus
warehousekeeper   der Lageraufseher
warrant (guarantee)   die Gewähr, die Garantie, die
  Bürgschaft
warranty   die Gewähr
wasting asset   das kurzlebige Wirtschaftsgut
waybill   der Frachtbrief, der Frachtzettel
wealth   der Reichtum, das Vermögen
wear and tear   der Verschleiß, die Gebrauchsabnutzung
weight   das Gewicht
weighted average   der gewogene Durchschnitt
wharf   der Kai, die Anlegstelle
wharfage   die Löschungskosten
wharfage charges   die Kaigebühren
when issued   zur Emissionszeit

white-collar worker der Büroangestellte
wholesale market der Großhandel
wholesale price der Großhandelspreis
wholesale trade der Großhandel
wholesaler der Großhändler
wildcat strike der wilder Streik, der Spontanstreik
will der Wille, das Testament
windfall profit der unerwarteter Gewinn
window dressing die Schaufensterdekoration, die Bilanzverschleierung
wire transfer die telegraphische Überweisung
with average mit Durchschnittsberechnung
with regard to betreffs
withdrawal die Zurücknahme, die Abhebung
withholding tax die Quellensteuer
witness der Zeuge
witness (v) bezeugen
word processor das Textverarbeitungsgerät
work (v) arbeiten
work by contract vertragsgemäß arbeiten
work cycle der Arbeitsgang
work day der Arbeitstag
work in progress die Arbeit im Gang, die Halbfabrikate
work load die Arbeitsbelastung
work order der Arbeitsauftrag, die Arbeitsfolge
work station die Arbeitsstätte
workforce die Arbeitskräfte
working assets das Betriebsvermögen
working balance die Betriebsbilanz
working capital das Betriebskapital, das Umlaufsvermögen
working class die Arbeiterklasse
working funds die Betriebsmittel
working hours die Arbeitszeit
working papers die Arbeitspapiere
working tools die Arbeitsmittel
workplace der Arbeitsplatz
workshop die Werkstatt

World Bank Die Internationale Wiederaufbaubank, Die Weltbank

worth, net das Eigenkapital, der Nettowert

worthless wertlos

writ der Gerichtsbefehl

write off (v) abschreiben, abbuchen

write-off die Abschreibung, die Abbuchung

writedown die Herabsetzung

written agreement der schriftlicher Vertrag, die schriftliche Vereinbarung

Y

yardstick der Maßstab

year das Jahr

year-end das Jahresende, der Jahresabschluß

year, fiscal das Geschäftsjahr, das Rechnungsjahr

yield der Ertrag, die Rendite

yield to maturity die Effektivverzinsung

Z

zero coupon die Anleihe ohne Zinskoupon

ZIP code die Postleitzahl

zone das Gebiet

zone die Zone

zoning law die Wohn- und Industriebaubestimmungen

GERMAN TO ENGLISH

A

ab Betrieb ex mill

ab Fabrik ex factory

ab Grube ex mine

ab Lager ex warehouse

ab Schiff ex ship

ab Werk ex works

abändern amend (v), renegotiate (v)

Abänderung (f) amendment

abandonnieren abandon (v)

abbestellen cancel (v)

abbuchen charge off (v), write off (v)

Abbuchung (f) write-off

Abfindung (f) gratuity

abflachen level out (v)

Abgabe (f) tax

Abgeordnetenbeeinflussung durch Interessengruppen (pl) lobbying

abgeschlossenes Konto (n) closed account

abgestimmte Vergleichsproben (pl) matched samples

Abhebung (f) withdrawal

Abholung und Lieferung (f) pickup and delivery

Abhörer (m) monitor

ablegen file (v)

ablösen discharge (v) (obligation)

Ablösungsfonds (m) redemption fund

Abnehmer (m) buyer

Abnutzung (f) attrition

Abrechnungstag (m) account day

Abrechnungstelle (f) clearinghouse

abrufen call back (v)

Absatz (m) marketing, outlet

Absatzanalyse (f) sales analysis

Absatzbudget (n) marketing budget

Absatzgebiet (n) sales territory

Absatzkalkulation (f) sales estimate

Absatzkonzept (n) marketing concept
Absatzleitung (f) sales management
Absatzmöglichkeiten (pl) potential sales
Absatzplan (m) marketing plan, sales budget
Absatzposition (f) market position
Absatztätigkeiten (pl) merchandising
Absatzweg (m) channel of distribution
abschätzen appraise (v)
Abschlag (m) abatement (reduction)
abschließen finalize (v)
abschließen (insurance) take out (v)
Abschlußbuchung (f) closing entry
Abschnitt (m) tranche
abschreiben charge off (v), write off (v)
Abschreibung (f) depreciation, write-off
Abschreibung für Substanzverringerung (f) depletion allowance
Abschreibungsbetrag (m) depreciation allowance
Absendung (f) dispatch
absetzen charge off (v), market
absorbieren absorb (v)
Abteilung (f) department
Abtretende (m) assignor
Abweichung (f) variance
Abwertung (f) devaluation
Abwesenheit (f) absenteeism
Abwicklung (f) handling
abziehen take off (v)
Abzug (m) deduction
abzugsfähig deductible
Addition (f) footing (accounting)
Adressenkartei (f) mailing list
Agentur (f) agency
aggressive Verkaufspolitik (f) hard sell
Akkordarbeit (f) piecework
Akkreditiv (n) letter of credit
Akronym (n) acronym
Aktenkoffer (m) attache case
Aktentasche (f) attache case, briefcase

KEY TO PRONUNCIATION
VOWELS

	SOUND IN ENGLISH	EXAMPLE
a	aa (long; far)	haben (HAA-ben)
	ah (short: hot)	hatte (HAH-teh)
ä	ay (long; way)	Bäder (BAY-duh)
	eh (short; met)	Gepäck (geh-PEHK)
e	ay (long; hay)	leben (LAY-ben)
	eh (short; end)	helfen (HEHL-fen)
	e (unstressed syllables ending in -n, -l, and -t	lieben (LEE-ben)
	uh (unstressed syllables ending in -er, mother)	Ritter (RIT-uh)
i	ee (long; fleet)	Ihnen (EE-nen)
	i (short; wit)	wissen (VIss-en)
ie	ee (always long; martini)	Liebe (LEE-beh)
o	oh (long; rose)	Rose (ROH-zeh)
	o (short; love)	komm (kom)
ö	er (like her, but sounded with the lips forward and rounded)	hören (HER-en)
u	oo (long; bloom)	Schuh (shoo)
	u (short; bull)	Bulle (BUL-eh)
ü	ew (like dream, but with lips forward and rounded)	Bruder (BREW-duh)
y	ew (like the German ü)	lyrisch (LEW-rish)

DIPHTHONGS

ai, ay	eye (eye)	schreiben (SHREYE-ben)
ei, ey		
au	ow (brown)	braun (brown)
äu, eu	oy (joy)	treu (troy)

CONSONANTS

f, h, k, l, m, n, p, t, x	usually pronounced as in English	
b	p (between vowel and consonant or at end of word: map)	Leib (leyep)
	b (elsewhere as in English)	bin (bin)
c	ts (before e, i, ö, and ä: wits)	Cäsar (TSAY-zahr)
	k (elsewhere; cold)	Coburg (KOH-boork)
ch	kh (strongly aspirated (breathy) sound; "Hugh")	durch (doorkh)
chs	k (sometimes: kind)	Lachs (lahks)
d	t (between vowel and consonant and at end of word; cat)	Hund (hunt)
	d (otherwise: dollar)	Dank (dank)
g	g (hard; gods)	Geist (geyest)
	k (at end of word; backpack)	Tag (taak)
	kh (words ending in ig; happy or whisky)	windig (VIN-dikh)
j	y (year)	Jahr (yaar)
qu	kv (k, followed by v)	Quell (kvehl)
r	r (rolled in the throat)	Reise (REYE-zeh)
s	z (preceding vowels or between them; zap)	See (zay)
	sh (at beginning of syllable, before p and t: shell)	spielen (SHPEE-len)
	s, ss (elsewhere: sing)	Was ist das? (vahs ist dahs)
ß, ss	s, ss (always: sell)	weiß (veyes)
sch	sh (show)	schlau (shlow)
tsch	ch (cheer)	Kitsch (kich)
tz	ts (wits)	Katze (KAH-tseh)
v	f (father)	Vater (FAA-tuh)
	v (violin)	Violine (vee-o-LEE-neh)
w	v (vest)	Wasser (VAH-suh)
z	ts (grits)	Zeit (tseyet)

Barron's Bilingual Business Guides
Talking Business in German
© Copyright 1987 by Barron's Educational Series, Inc.

allmählich abschaffen   phase out (v)
Alternativbestellung (f)   alternative order
alternative Kosten (pl)   opportunity cost
Amortisation (f)   amortization
Amt (n)   office (official)
amtlich notierte Werte (pl)   listed securities
Amtsbereich (m)   jurisdiction
Amtsschimmel (m)   red tape
an den Inhaber zahlbar   payable to bearer
an Order zahlbar   payable to order
Analogcomputer (m)   analog computer
Analogrechner (m)   analog computer
Analyse (f)   analysis
Analyse der Netzplantechnik (f)   critical path analysis
Analytiker (m)   analyst
ändern   amend (v)
Änderung (f)   alteration, amendment
Anfangsbestand (m)   opening balance
Anfangskosten (pl)   start-up costs
Anfangskurs (m)   opening price
Anfangsprovision (f)   front-end fee (front-end load)
Anforderung (f)   requirement
Angabe (f)   statement, data
Angabengrundlage (f)   data base
Angebot (n)   supply and demand
Angebot und Nachfrage   bid and asked
Angebotsaufforderung (f)   request for bid
Angebotspreis (m)   offered price
angelegtes Kapital (n)   invested capital
angemeldetes Patent (n)   patent pending
angemessener Ertrag (m)   fair return
angemessener Marktpreis (m)   fair market value
angemessene Sorgfalt (f)   reasonable care
angepasster Kurs (m)   adjusted rate
angespannte Marktlage (f)   tight market
Angestellter (m)   employee
Angestelltenberatung (f)   employee counseling
Angestelltenpotential (n)   human resources

angewandter Erlöstausch (m)   applied proceeds swap
anhängen   attach (v) (affix, adhere)
Anhängsel (n)   attachment (contract)
anhäufend   cumulative
Ankauf (m)   leveraged lease
Ankauf offener Buchforderungen (m)   factoring
Ankergebühr (f)   anchorage dues
Anlage (f)   layout (of premises)
Anlageberater (m)   investment adviser
Anlagebrief (m)   investment letter
Anlagekapital (n)   fixed capital
Anlagekredit (m)   investment credit
Anlagenanalyse (f)   investment analysis
Anlagenrendite (f)   return on assets managed
Anlagevermögen (n)   capital asset
Anlagewerte (pl)   capital goods
anlegen   invest (v)
Anlegestelle (f)   wharf
Anleihe (f)   bond, loan
Anleihe ohne Zinskoupon (f)   zero coupon
Anleiheausgabe (f)   bond issue
Anleihebewertung (f)   bond rating
Anleiheemission (f)   bond issue
Anleihegarant (m)   underwriter
Annahme (f)   acceptance (agreement)
Annahme als Markenartikel (f)   brand acceptance
Annahme mit Vorbehalt (f)   conditional acceptance
Annahme verweigern (f)   refuse acceptance (v)
Annahmevertrag (m)   acceptance agreement
annehmbares Qualittäsniveau (n)   acceptable quality level
annehmen   accept (v)
anordnen   instruct (v) (order)
anpassen   adjust (v)
Anpassung an (f)   metrification
Anreiz (m)   incentive
anrufen   call (v)
ansässiger Einkäufer (m)   resident buyer
Anschaffungskosten (f)   original cost

Anschauung (f) outlook (philosophy)
Anschauungsmodell (n) mock-up
Anschlagetafel (f) billboard
Anschlussauftrag (m) follow-up order
Ansehen einer Firma (n) goodwill
ansetzen schedule (v)
Ansporn (m) incentive
Anspruch (m) claim
anstellen hire (v)
Anstiftung (f) zum Prozessieren barratry
Anteil (share) (m) interest
Anteilmehrheit (f) majority interest
Antidumpingzoll (m) antidumping duty
antizipative Aufwand (m) accrued expenses
antizipativer Aufwand (m) accrued expenses
antizipativer Ertrag (m) accrued revenue
antizipative Aktiva (pl) accrued assets
Antragsformular (n) application form
anwachsen accrue (v)
Anwalt (m) attorney
Anwartschaftsrecht (n) inchoate interest
Anwesenheitszeit (f) attended time
Anzahlung (f) down payment
Anzeigentarif (m) advertising rate
Arbeit (f) job
Arbeit im Gang (f) work in progress
arbeiten work (v)
Arbeiter (m) laborer
Arbeiterführer (m) labor leader
Arbeiterklasse (f) working class
Arbeiterschaft (f) labor
Arbeitgeber-Arbeitnehmerverhältnis (n) labor relations
Arbeitsauftrag (m) work order
Arbeitsausschuß (m) task force
Arbeitsbelastung (f) work load
Arbeitsbeschreibung (f) job description
Arbeitsbewertung (f) job evaluation
Arbeitsbeziehungen (f) industrial relations

Arbeitsfolge (f) work order (sequence)
arbeitsfreier Tag (m) holiday
Arbeitsgang (m) work cycle
arbeitsintensiv labor-intensive
Arbeitskräfte (pl) labor force, manpower, workforce
Arbeitsleistung (f) job performance, output
Arbeitslosenunterstützung (f) unemployment compensation
Arbeitslosigkeit (f) unemployment
Arbeitsmarkt (m) labor market
Arbeitsmittel (f) working tools
Arbeitsmoral (f) morale
Arbeitsniederlegung (f) walkout
Arbeitspapiere (pl) working papers
arbeitsparend labor-saving
Arbeitsplatz (m) workplace
Arbeitsplatzanalyse (f) ergonomics
Arbeitsplatzsicherheit (f) job security
Arbeitsplatzuntersuchung (f) job analysis
Arbeitsrecht (n) labor law
Arbeitsschema (n) layout
Arbeitsstab (m) task force
Arbeitsstätte (f) work station
Arbeitsstudie (f) job analysis
Arbeitsstunden (pl) man hours
Arbeitstag (m) work day
Arbeitsteilung (f) division of labor
Arbeitsunfall (m) industrial accident
Arbeitsverfassung (f) labor code
Arbeitszeit (f) working hours
Arbitrage (f) arbitrage
arithmetische Mittel (n) arithmetic mean
Art (f) mode
Artikel (m) item
Assistent (m) assistant
Attest (n) attestation
auf dem laufenden halten keep posted (v)
auf der ganzen Linie down the line
auf Rechnung on account

auf Verlangen on demand

auf Ziel on account

aufbewahren store (v)

Aufbewahrung (f) storage

aufeinander wirken interact (v)

Aufforderung zur Einreichung von Angeboten (f) invitation to bid

aufgeben abandon (v)

aufgelaufene Steuern (pl) accrued taxes

aufgelaufene Zinsen (pl) accrued interest

aufgeschobene Lieferungen (pl) deferred deliveries

aufgeschobene Renten (pl) deferred annuities

aufgeschobene Schulden (pl) deferred liabilities

aufgliedern itemize (v)

aufheben nullify (v), supersede (v)

Auflassungsurkunde (f) deed of transfer

auflaufen accrue (v)

Auflaufen (n) accrual

Auflösung (f) liquidation

Auflösungswert (m) liquidation value

aufs Höchstmaß bringen maximize

aufschieben postpone (v)

Aufschlag (m) increase, markup, surcharge

aufschreiben take down (v)

Aufschub (m) delay

Aufschwung (m) rally, recovery, upturn

Aufsichtsperson (f) supervisor

Aufsichtsrat (m) board of supervisors

Aufstellungskosten (pl) set-up costs

Auftrag (m) order

Auftrag auf Basis Selbstkosten plus Gewinn (m) cost-plus contract

Auftraggeber (m) principal (employer of an agent)

Auftragsbestätigung (f) confirmation of order

Auftragssendung (f) drop shipment

Aufwand (m) expenditure

Aufwärtsbewegung (f) upturn

Ausbildung am Arbeitsplatz (f) on-the-job training

ausbuchen abandon (v)

Ausbuchung (f) abandonment

ausfahren export (v)

Ausfallzeit einer Maschine (f) downtime of a machine

Ausfuhragent (m) export agent

Ausfuhrbeschränkungen (die Einfuhrbeschränkungen) (pl) restrictions on export (import)

Ausfuhrbestimmung (f) export regulation

Ausfuhrbewilligung (f) export permit

Ausfuhrkredit (m) export credit

Ausfuhrlizenz für Kulturgüter (f) cultural export permit

Ausfuhrprämie (export premium) (f) drawback

Ausfuhrquote (f) export quota

Ausfuhrsteuer (f) export tax

Ausfuhrzoll (m) export duty

Ausfuhrzollerklärung (f) export entry

Ausgabe (f) expenditure, stock issue

Ausgabekurs (m) issue price

Ausgabenvergütung (f) recovery of expenses

ausgeben issue (v)

ausgegebene Aktien (pl) issued shares

ausgeglichener Haushalt (m) balanced budget

ausgewiesener Inhaber (m) holder in due course

Ausgleich (m) settlement

ausgleichen adjust (v), level out (v)

Ausgleichszoll (m) countervailing duty

Auslage (f) disbursement, outlay

Auslagen (pl) charges, expenses

Auslagenabrechnung (f) expense account

ausländische Gesellschaft (f) alien corporation, foreign corporation

ausländisches Wertpapier (n) foreign security

Auslandssteuergutschrift (f) foreign tax credit

Auslandsverschuldung (f) foreign debt

Auslandswährung (f) foreign currency

auslassen omit (v)

auspreisen price (v)

Ausrüstung (f) equipment

Ausrüstungsmietung (f) equipment leasing

Ausschreibung (f)   invitation to bid, request for bid

Ausschuß (m)   commission (agency), spoilage

Ausschußware (pl)   as is goods

Außenhandel (m)   foreign trade

Außenstände (f)   active debts, outstanding debt

Außenwirtschaft (f)   foreign trade

außergerichtlicher Vergleich (m)   accord and satisfaction

außerordentliche Rücklage (f)   contingent fund

Aussicht (f)   outlook

aussperren   lock out (v)

ausstehende Aktien (pl)   outstanding stock

ausstehende Forderungen (pl)   accounts receivable, outstanding debt

Aussteller (m)   drawer

Ausstoß (m)   outturn

Ausübung einer Zusatzbeschäftigung (f)   moonlighting

Auswahl (f)   sample line

Auswahlgrösse (f)   sample size

Ausweichklausel (f)   escape clause

Autarkie (f)   autarky

Automation (f)   automation

automatisch   automatic

automatische Erneuerung (f)   rollover

Autorenanteil (m)   royalty

Autorenhonorar (n)   royalty (book)

autorisierte Unterschrift (f)   authorized signature

B

Bahn (f)   railroad

Bahnsendung (f)   rail shipment

Baisse (f)   down period, slump

Baissebewegung (f)   downturn

Baissebörse (f)   bear market

Ballastbonus (m)   ballast bonus

Ballenkapazität (f)   bale capacity

Ballenladung (f)   bale cargo

Bank (f)   bank, money shop

Bankakkreditiv (n)   bank letter of credit

Bankakzept (n)   bank acceptance
Bankbuch (n)   bankbook, passbook
Bankdarlehen (n)   bank loan
Bankeinlage (f)   bank deposit
Bankfach (n)   safe deposit box
Bankfeiertag (m)   bank holiday
Bankfreigabe (f)   bank release
Bankgebühren (pl)   bank charges
Bankgeldanweisung (f)   bank money order
Bankguthaben (n)   bank balance
Bankkonto (n)   bank account
Bankkreditbrief (m)   bank letter of credit
Banknote (f)   bank note, bill (currency)
Bankrevisor (m)   bank examiner
Bankrott (m)   bankruptcy
Bankrott machen (v)   fail (go bankrupt)
Bankscheck (m)   bank check, cashier's check
Banktratte (f)   bank draft
Bankwechsel (m)   bank exchange
Bankzins (m)   bank rate
Barauslagen (pl)   out-of-pocket expenses
Bardividende (f)   cash dividend
Bargeld (n)   cash
Bargeldzustellung (f)   cash delivery
Barliquiditätsgrad (m)   acid-test ratio
Barzahlung im voraus (f)   cash before delivery
Barzahlungsrabatt (m)   cash discount
Basisjahr (n)   base year
Basispunkt (m)   basis point
Baubehörde (f)   housing authority (construction)
Baud (n)   baud
Bauingenieurwesen (n)   civil engineering
Baumwolle (f)   cotton
Bauteil (m)   component
beantworten   reply (v)
bearbeiten   process (v)
Bearbeitungsfehler (m)   processing error
Bedarfsanalyse (f)   needs analysis
bedingte Annahme (f)   conditional acceptance

bedingter Verkaufsvertrag (m)   conditional sales contract

beenden   terminate (v)

Befähigung (f)   qualification

Befehl (m)   mandate, order (command)

Befehlskette (f)   chain of command

befördern   forward (v)

Beförderung (f)   handling, promotion

Befrachtung (f)   charter (mercantile lease)

Befreiung (f)   exemption

befristete Einlage (f)   time deposit

Begleitbrief (m)   cover letter

begleitete Waren (pl)   accompanied goods

Begünstigter (m)   beneficiary

Begünstigungstarif (m)   preferential tariff

Behälter (m)   container

bei Börsenöffnung   at the opening

bei Börsenöffnung kaufen   buy on opening (v)

bei Börsenschluß   at the close

bei Börsenschluß kaufen   buy on close (v)

bei Sicht   at sight

beifügen   attach (v) (affix, adhere)

Beirat (m)   advisory council

Belastung (f)   encumbrance

Beleg (m)   voucher

Belegschaft (f)   labor force, personnel

Beleihung (f)   hypothecation

Beleihungswert (m)   loan value

beliebig   optional

Belohnung (f)   reward

Benachrichtigungsschreiben (n)   advice note

benutzerfreundlich   user-friendly

Benzin (n)   gasoline

beraten   advise (v)

Berater (m)   consultant

Beratungsdienst (m)   advisory service

berechtigt sein   authority, to have (v)

Bereitstellungfonds (m)   appropriation

bergen   salvage (v)

Bergungskosten (pl)   salvage charges
Bergungswert (m)   salvage value (recovery)
Bericht (m)   report
berichtigen   adjust (v) (correct)
berichtigter cif-Preis (m)   adjusted CIF price
Berichtigungsbuchung (f)   adjusting entry
Berichtigungskonto (n)   adjustment account
Beruf (m)   occupation, profession
Berufsrisiko (n)   occupational hazard
Beschaffung (f)   procurement
Bescheinigung (f)   attestation, certificate
Beschlagnahme (f)   garnishment
beschlagnahmen   attach (v) (seize), impound (v)
beschleunigen   speed up (v)
Beschluß (m)   resolution
beschlußfähige Anzahl (f)   quorum
Beschlußfähigkeit (f)   quorum
beschränkte Haftung (f)   limited liability
Besitz (m)   ownership, property
Besitzdauer (f)   holding period
Besitzer (m)   holder, owner
Besitzwechsel (m)   note receivable
Bestand (m)   inventory
Bestand an Fertigwaren (m)   finished goods inventory
Bestandsüberwachung (f)   inventory control
Bestandteil (m)   component
bestätigen   acknowledge (v)
bestätigter Scheck (m)   certified check
Bestätigung (f)   certificate
Bestechung (f)   graft
bestellen   order (v)
Bestellnummer (f)   order number
Bestellschein (m)   order form
Bestellung (f)   order, purchase order
bestenfalls   at best
bestens   at best
bestens kaufen   at or better, buy at best (v)
Besteuerung (f)   assessment, taxation

Besteuerungsgrundlage (f)   tax base

bestimmen   earmark (v)

bestimmte Zeitdauer (f)   fixed term

Beteiligter (m)   partner

Beteiligung an Kapitalgesellschaften (f)   equity investments

Beteiligungsanleihe (f)   participation loan

Beteiligungsgebühr (f)   participation fee

Betrag (m)   amount

Betrauter (m)   fiduciary

betreffs   with regard to

betriebliche Leistungsfähigkeit (f)   plant capacity

Betriebsbilanz (f)   working balance

Betriebsbudget (n)   operating budget

Betriebseinheit (f)   operating unit

Betriebseinkommen (n)   operating income

Betriebsergebnis (n)   operating income

Betriebsergebnisrechnung (f)   operating statement

Betriebsführung (f)   management, operations management

Betriebsführung durch Zielvorgabe (f)   management by objectives

Betriebsführungsschaubild (n)   management chart

Betriebsgewinn (m)   operating profit

Betriebsjahr (n)   financial year

Betriebskapital (n)   working capital

Betriebskosten (pl)   carrying charges, operating expenses

Betriebsleiter (m)   plant manager

Betriebsleitung (f)   business management

Betriebsmittel (pl)   working funds

Betriebspolitik (f)   business policy, company policy

Betriebstätigkeitsprüfung (f)   operations audit

Betriebstreuhandversicherung (f)   fidelity bond

Betriebsvergrößerung   economy of scale

Betriebsverlust (m)   operating loss

Betriebsvermögen (n)   working assets

Betriebsversicherung (f)   industrial insurance

Betriebszentrale (f)   operations headquarters

Betrug (m)   fraud

Betrügerei (f) double dealing
bevollmächtigter Händler (m) authorized dealer
Bevollmächtigung (f) proxy
bevorrechtigte Forderungen (pl) preferential debts
bevorstehende Änderung (f) impending change
bewegliche Preisskala (f) sliding price scale
bewegliche Sache (f) chattel
Beweglichkeit (f) mobility of labor
Bewegung (f) motion
bewerten appraise (v), assess (v)
Bewertung (f) appraisal, estimate, evaluation
Bewilligung (f) approval
bezahlter Feiertag (m) paid holiday
Bezahlung (f) disbursement
bezeugen witness (v)
Beziehungen zu den Anlegern (pl) investor relations
Bezirksleiter (m) area manager
Bezogener (m) drawee
Bezugsoption (f) call option
Bezugspreis (m) subscription price (periodicals)
Bezugsrecht (n) preemptive right
bieten offer (v)
Bilanz (f) balance, balance sheet
Bilanzabschluß (m) financial statement
Bilanzierungsrichtlinien (pl) accounting principles
Bilanzperiode (f) financial period
Bilanzprüfung (f) auditing balance sheet
Bilanzverschleierung (f) window dressing (balance
  sheet)
billig cheap
billigen approve (v)
binäre Zahlendarstellung (f) binary notation
Binärschreibung (f) binary notation
Binnenmarkt (m) home market
Blankoakzept (n) general acceptance
Blankoauftrag (m) blanket order
Blaupause (f) blueprint
Bodenreform (f) land reform
Bodenschätze (pl) natural resources

Bonitätsprüfung (f) credit rating

Bootsverleih ohne Mannschaft und Verpflegung (m) bareboat charter

borgen borrow (v)

Börse (f) market (stock market), stock exchange

Börsenbericht (m) market report

Börsenbrief (m) market letter

börsenfähige Effekten (pl) negotiable securities

Börsenfernschreiber (m) ticker (stock prices)

börsengängige Werte (pl) marketable securities

Börsenindex (m) market index, stock index

Börsenmakler (m) jobber, market-maker, registered representative, stockbroker

Börsenmakler (m) trader (stocks)

Börsenmakler in kleinen Mengen (m) odd lot broker

Börsenmarkteinstufung (f) market rating

Börsensaal (m) floor (stock exchange)

Börsenschluß (m) market closing

Börsenspezialist (m) specialist (stock exchange)

Börsentermingeschäft (n) option (put or call options)

Börsentip (m) tip (inside information)

Börsenvollmacht (f) stock power

Börsenwert (m) exchange value (on stock exchange)

Botendienst (m) courier service

Boykott (m) boycott

Branche (f) line of business

Brief (m) letter

Brief und Geld bid and asked

Briefkurs (m) asked price, offered rate

Briefwechsel (m) correspondence

Bruttoanlageninvestition (f) gross investment

Bruttoeinkaufspreis (m) invoice cost

Bruttoeinkommen (n) gross income

Bruttoeinnahmen (pl) gross receipts

Bruttoertrag (m) gross yield

Bruttogewinn (m) gross profit

Bruttogewinnspanne (f) gross margin

Bruttopreis (m) gross price

Bruttopreisunterschied (m) gross spread

Bruttosozialprodukt (n)   gross domestic product
Bruttosozialprodukt (n)   gross national product
Bruttoumsatz (m)   gross sales
Bruttoverlust (m)   gross loss
Buchforderungen (pl)   accounts receivable
Buchführung der bar durchgeführten Geschäfte (f)   cash-basis accounting
Buchgewinn (m)   paper profit
Buchhalter (m)   accountant
Buchhaltung (f)   accounting department, book-keeping
Buchhaltungsleiter (m)   chief accountant
Buchinventar (n)   book inventory
Buchprüfer (m)   auditor
Buchschulden (f)   accounts payable
Buchungsmethode (f)   accounting method
Buchungsverfahren (n)   accounting method
Buchungszeitraum (m)   accounting period
Buchwert (m)   book value, carrying value
Buchwert pro Aktie (m)   book value per share
Budget (n)   budget
Bürgschaft (f)   guanrantee, warrant (surety)
Büro (n)   office
Büroangestellter (m)   white-collar worker
Bürokrat (m)   bureaucrat
Bürokratie (f)   red tape
Büroleitung (f)   office management
Byte (n)   byte

C

chemisch   chemical
Computer (m)   computer
Computerausdruck (m)   printout
Computereingabe (f)   computer input
Computerergebnis (n)   computer output
Computerprogramm (n)   computer program, software
Computersprache (f)   computer language
Computerterminal (n)   computer terminal
Container (m)   container

D

Dachgesellschaft (f)   holding company, parent company

daneben   alongside

Darlehn (n)   loan

Darlehnsvertrag (m)   loan agreement

Daten (pl)   data

Datenbank (f)   data bank

Datenerwerb (m)   data acquisition

Datenspeicherung (f)   computer storage

Datenverarbeitung (f)   data processing

Datenverarbeitung verbunden (m)   on line

Datenverarbeitungszentrale (f)   computer center

Dauer eines Patentes (f)   life of a patent

Dauerauftrag (m)   standing order

dauerhafte Verbrauchsgüter (pl)   durable goods

dazwischentreten   intervene (v)

Debetposten (m)   debit entry

Deckung (f)   collateral

Deckungsbeitragsrechnung (f)   breakeven analysis

Deckungsverhältnis (n)   cover ratio

Defizit (n)   deficit

Defizitfinanzierung (f)   deficit financing

Defizitspende (f)   deficit spending

Deflation (f)   deflation

dehnbarer Zolltarif (m)   flexible tariff

Delikthandlung (f)   tort

dem Preis entsprechen   meet the price (v)

demographisch   demographic

den Geschäftsgewinn wieder anlegen   plow back earnings (v)

den Verlust auffangen   absorb the loss (v)

Deport (m)   backwardation

Depositenkonto (n)   deposit account

Depositenschein (m)   certificate of deposit

Depositenzertifikat (n)   certificate of deposit

Depot (n)   depository

Depression (f) depression
Desinvestition (f) divestment
Detailgeschäft (n) retail
Detailverkauf (m) retail trade
Devisen (f) foreign currency, foreign exchange
Devisenausländer (m) nonresident
Devisengelder (pl) monetary credits
Devisenkontrolle (f) exchange control
Dezimalsystem (n) metrification
Diagramm (n) graph
Dieberei (f) pilferage
Dienstalter (n) seniority
Dienstvertrag (m) service contract
Differenz (f) spread
digital digital
digitale Jahressummenabschreibung (f) sum-of-the-years digits
Digitalrechner (m) digital computer
direkt verkaufen sell direct (v)
Direktabsatz (m) direct selling
direkte Kursnotierung (f) direct quotation (stocks)
direkte Preisangabe (f) direct quotation
direkter Speicherzugriff (m) random access memory
direkte Verschiffung (f) drop shipment
direkte Auslagen (pl) direct expenses
direkte Kosten (pl) direct cost
Direktinvestition (f) direct investment
Direktor (m) director, management
Direktplazierung (f) private placement
Direktverkauf (m) direct selling
Direktverkauf an der Haustür (m) house-to-house selling
dirigieren manage (v)
Diskette (f) floppy disk
Diskont (m) discount
Diskontbank (f) acceptance house
Diskontierung (f) discounting
Diskontsatz (m) discount rate
Diskontwertpapiere (pl) discount securities

Disposition (f)   table of contents
Diversifikation (f)   diversification
Dividende (f)   dividend
Dividendenertrag (m)   dividend yield
dividendlos   ex dividend
Dockempfangsschein (m)   dock (ship's) receipt
Dockgebühren (pl)   dock handling charges
Docklagerschein (m)   dock (ship's) receipt
Dokument (n)   document
Doppelbesteuerung (f)   double taxation
doppelte Buchführung (f)   double-entry bookkeeping
Doppelverdienst (m)   moolinging
Doppelzüngigkeit (f)   double dealing
Dotation (f)   endowment
Drahtüberweisung (f)   cable transfer
Drehbuch (n)   script
dringend   urgent
Drittexporteur (m)   third-party exporter
Drucksache (f)   printed matter
Dumping (n)   dumping (goods in foreign market)
Duopol (n)   duopoly
Durchsatz (m)   throughput
Durchschnitt (m)   mean, average
durchschnittliche Einheitskosten (pl)   average unit cost
durchschnittliche Lebensdauer (f)   average life
Durchschnittskosten (pl)   average cost
Durchschnittspreis (m)   average price

E

Echtheitsbescheinigung für Antiquitäten (f)   antique authenticity certificate
Echtzeit (f)   real time
Effekten (pl)   securities
Effektenbörse (f)   stock market
Effektenüberträger (m)   transfer agent
effektiver Geldwert (m)   actual cash value
Effektiveinnahmen (pl)   actuals
Effektivpreis (m)   real price

Effektivverzinsung (f) effective yield, yield to maturity

Effizienz (f) efficiency

eidesstattliche Erklärung (f) affidavit

eigener Wagenpark (m) private fleet

Eigenkapital (n) equity, net asset worth, net worth

Eigenkapitalanteil (m) equity share

Eigenkapitalverwässerung (f) dilution of equity

Eigentum (n) ownership, property, public property

Eigentum der öffentlichen Hand (m) public property

Eigentümer (m) proprietor

Eigentümer ohne Leitungsfunktion (m) absentee owner

Eigentumstitel (m) title

Eigentumsvorbehalt des Verkäufers (m) vendor's lien

Eigenwechsel (m) promissory note

Eilauftrag (m) rush order

ein Angebot machen put in a bid (v)

ein Schiff außer Dienst stellen lay up (v)

eine Emission begeben float (v) (issue stock)

eine Interessengemeinschaft bilden pooling of interests

einen Auftrag erteilen place an order (v)

einen Fehler beseitigen debug (v) (computers)

einen konkurrenzfähigen Preis festsetzen können meet the price

einen Preis ansetzen price

Einfluss (m) leverage

Einfuhr (f) import

Einfuhrdeklaration (f) import entry

Einfuhrdepots (pl) import deposits

einführen import (v)

Einfuhrerklärung (f) import declaration

Einfuhrerlaubnis (f) import license

Einfuhrquote (f) import quota

Einfuhrsteuer (f) import tax

Einfuhrvorschriften (pl) import regulations

Einfuhrzoll (m) import duty, import tariff

Eingabe (f)   input

Eingaben-Ausgaben Analyse (f)   input-output analysis

eingefrorene Guthaben (pl)   frozen assets

eingegliedertes Führungssystem (n)   integrated management system

eingelöster Scheck (m)   cancelled check

eingeschränktes Indossament (n)   qualified acceptance endorsement

eingetragenes Lagerhaus (n)   regular warehouse

eingetragener Scheck (m)   registered check

eingetragener Vertreter (m)   registered representative

eingetragenes Warenzeichen (n)   registered trademark

eingezahlter Anteile (pl)   paid up shares

einheitlicher Satz (m)   flat rate

Einkaufsleiter (m)   purchasing agent, purchasing manager

Einkommen (n)   income

Einkommensstufe (f)   income bracket

Einkommensobligation (f)   revenue bond

Einkommensteuer (f)   income tax

Einlage (f)   deposit

Einlösungsprämie (f)   redemption premium

Einlösungsvergütung (f)   redemption allowance

einmalige Summe (f)   lump sum

Einnahme (f)   revenue, earnings

einreichen   file (v) (submit forms)

Einreisebewilligung (f)   entry permit

Einschreibepost (f)   registered mail

Einschußkonto (n)   marginal account

Einsparung (f)   cutback

Einspruch (m)   veto

Einstellung (f)   abatement (suspension)

Einstellung ungelernter Arbeitskräfte (f)   dilution of labor

Einstellungsquote (f)   accession rate

einstweilig   interim

Eintrag (m)   item

einwandfreie Überbringung (f)   good delivery

Einzelfertigungsbetrieb (m)   job shop

Einzelfirma (f) sole proprietorship

Einzelhandel (m) retail, retail trade

Einzelhandelspreis (m) retail price

Einzelhandelsumsatzsteuer (f) retail sales tax

Einzelhandelsverkaufsstelle (f) retail outlet

Einzelhandelswaren (pl) retail merchandise

Einzelkosten (pl) direct cost

einzeln aufführen itemize (v)

Einzelverkauf (m) retail

einziehen call (v)

Einziehungszeit (f) collection period

Eisenbahn (f) railroad

Eisenbahnbetriebsmittel (pl) rolling stock

Eisenwaren (pl) hardware

Elastizität (f) von Angebot (n) elasticity

elektronisches Weissbrett (n) electronic whiteboard

Elektrotechnik (f) electrical engineering

Emission (f) stock issue

Emissionsbank (f) investment bank, underwriter (securities)

emittieren issue (v)

Empfang (m) receipt (reception)

Empfänger (m) consignee

Empfehlungsschreiben (n) letter of introduction

Enderzeugnis (n) end product

englische Tonne (f) long ton

Enteignung (f) expropriation

Entgeld (n) consideration (contract law)

entladen unload (v)

entlassen discharge (v), fire, lay off (v)

Entlassungsabfindung (f) severance pay

entmutigender Faktor (m) disincentive

entschädigen reimburse (v)

Entschädigung (f) compensation, indemnity

entstandende Abschreibung (f) accrued depreciation

Entwicklung eines neuen Produkts (f) new product development

Entwicklungsländer (pl) underdeveloped nations

Entwicklungsrichtung (f) trend

Entwurf (m)   design, draft
Erbschaft (f)   estate
Erbschaftssteuer (f)   inheritance tax
Erdgas (n)   natural gas
Erdöl (n)   petroleum
Erdöldollars (pl)   petrodollars
Erfahrung (f)   know-how
Erfüllungsorte (pl)   delivery points
Ergonomie (f)   ergonomics
ergonomisch   user-friendly
Erhaltungsspanne (f)   maintenance margin
erhöhte Abschreibung (f)   accelerated depreciation
Erhöhung (f)   increase
Erholung (f)   rally
Erlös (m)   proceeds
erlauben   allow (v)
Erlaubnis (f)   license, permit
ermächtigen   authorize (v)
Ernennung (f)   appointment (nomination)
erneuern   renew (v)
Eröffnungskurs (m)   opening price
Ersatzteile (pl)   replacement parts
ersetzbar   fungible
Ersparnisse (pl)   savings
erstklassiges Wertpapier (n)   blue-chip stock
Ertrag (m)   outturner, yield
Ertragsergebnis (n)   earnings yield
Ertragskonto (n)   income account
Ertragskraft (f)   earnings performance
Ertragsleistung (f)   earnings performance
Ertragsobligation (f)   revenue bond
Ertragswert (m)   going concern value
Erwerb (m)   acquisition
Erwerb der Aktienmehrheit (m)   stock takeover
erwerben   acquire (v)
Erwerbskosten (f)   original cost
Erwerbungsprofil (n)   acquisition profile
erwirken (patent)   take out (v)
erworbene Rechte (pl)   acquired rights

erwünschtes Ergebnis (n) expected result

Erzeugnis (n) product, output

Etat (m) budget

Euroanleihe (f) Eurobond

Eurodollar (m) Eurodollar

Europäische Wirtschaftsgemeinschaft (f) common market (European Common Market)

Eventuellverbindlichkeit (f) contingent liability

Eventuellverbindlichkeit (f) liability, contingent

Export-Import Bank (f) Export-Import bank

Exportgeschäft (n) export house

Exportmakler (m) export middleman

Exportverkaufsvertrag (m) export sales contract

F

Fabrik (f) factory

Fabrikarbeiter (m) blue-collar worker

Fabriklage (f) plant location

Facharbeiter (f) skilled labor

fachgemäß technical

Fachmann (m) professional

Fahrnis (f) chattel

Fahrplan (trains) (m) timetable

Faktor (m) factor (component, element)

Faktorenanalyse (f) factor analysis

Faktorenbewertung (f) factor rating

Faktoring (n) factoring

Faktura (f) invoice

Fakturenpreis (m) invoice cost

Fälligkeit (f) maturity

Fälligkeitsklausel (f) acceleration clause

Fälschung (f) counterfeit, forgery

Faulfracht (f) dead freight

Feedback (n) feedback

Fehler (m) bug (computers), error

fehlerhaft defective

feilhalten offer for sale

Feinheitgehaltsbestimmung (f) assay

Fernmeldetechnologie (f) telecommunications

Fernschreiber (m)   telex
Fernsehbandaufnahme (f)   video cassette recorder
Fernsehen (n)   television
Fernsprecher (m)   telephone
Fernvertrieb (m)   telemarketing
Fertighaus (n)   prefabricated house
fertigmachen   finalize (v)
Fertigprodukt (n)   end product
Fertigung (f)   production
Fertigungsgemeinkosten (pl)   factory overhead, indirect expenses
Fertigungskosten (pl)   production costs
Fertigungslöhne (pl)   direct labor cost
Fertigungslohnkosten (pl)   direct labor
Fertigungsplan (m)   production schedule
Fertigungssteuerung (f)   industrial engineering, production control
Fertigungsverfahren (n)   production process
feste Anlage (f)   fixture
fester Pachtzins (m)   dead rent
fester Wechselkurs (m)   fixed rate of exchange
festgelegte Frist (f)   fixed term
festgesetztes Eigenkapital (n)   legal capital
Festkosten (pl)   fixed charges
Festobligation (f)   term bond
festverzinsliches Wertpapier (n)   fixed income security
feuern   fire (v)
fiktive Bilanz (f)   pro forma statement
Filiale (f)   branch office
Filialgeschäft (n)   chain store
Finanzanalyse (f)   financial analysis
Finanzberater (m)   investment adviser
Finanzbewertung (f)   financial appraisal
Finanzdienstleistungen (pl)   financial services
Finanzdirektor (m)   financial director
Finanzfluß (m)   cash flow
finanzieller Anreiz (m)   financial incentive
finanzielle Höhepunkte (pl)   financial highlights

finanzieren finance (v)
Finanzierungsgesellschaft (f) finance company
Finanzierungskosten (pl) front-end financing
Finanzkontrolle (f) financial control
Finanzplanung (f) financial planning
Finanzstatus (m) financial statement
Finanzverwaltung (f) financial management
Firma (f) company, firm
Firmenmitglied (n) member of a firm
Firmenpolitik (f) company policy
Firmenschild (n) logo
Firmenwerbung (f) institutional advertising
Firmenzeichen (n) logo
Fixkosten (pl) fixed costs, standing costs
Flaute (f) downswing, downturn, slump
Fließband (n) assembly line
Flugplan (airplanes) (m) timetable
flüssige Anlagen (pl) quick assets
Flüssigkeitsverhältnis (n) acid-test ratio
Folgerung (f) implication (conclusion)
Fonds (m) fund
Förderer (m) sponsor (of a fund or partnership)
fördern advance (v) (promote)
Förderung (f) promotion
Forderung (f) claim, demand
Format (n) format
Forschung (f) research
Forschung und Entwicklung (f) research and development
Frachtliste (f) manifest
Fracht (f) cargo, freight
Fracht gegen Nachnahme (f) freight collect
Fracht inbegriffen freight included
Frachtbetrieb (m) freight all kinds
Frachtbrief (m) bill of lading, consignment note, waybill
Frachtführer (m) freight forwarder
Frachtkostenrückerstattung möglich freight allowed
Frachtvertragsagent (m) charterparty agent

Frachtzettel (m) waybill
Franchise (f) dealership
franko Bord, fob free on board (fob)
frei Eisenbahn free on rail
frei längsseite Schiff free alongside ship
frei Schiff free on board (fob)
frei von besonderer Havarie free of particular average
freies Exemplar (n) complimentary copy
freier Kurs (m) floating rate
freier Markt (m) free market
freie Marktwirtschaft (f) free enterprise
freier Wettbewerb (m) laissez-faire
freigestellt optional
Freihafen (m) free port
Freihandel (m) free trade
Freihandelszone (f) free trade zone
freihändig over the counter
freihändiger Kurs (m) over-the-counter quotation
Freiliste (f) free list
Freiperiode (f) grace period
freischaffender Schriftsteller (m) freelance writer
Freiverkehr (m) open market
freiwillig voluntary
Freizeit (f) free time
Fremdenverkehr (m) tourism
Fremdwährungswechsel (m) foreign bill of exchange
Frequenzkurve (f) frequency curve
Fristablauf (m) deadline
führen manage (v) (direct)
Führer (m) leader
Führungsgruppe (f) management group
Füllmaterial (n) stuffing
Füllung (f) stuffing
Funktionsanalyse (f) functional analysis
Fusion (f) amalgamation, merger

G

Garantie (f) guarantee, warrant (guarantee)
Garantieschein (m) guaranty bond

Garnierung (f)   dun

Gas (n)   gas

Gebiet (n)   territory, zone

Gebietsfremder (m)   nonresident

Gebietsleiter (m)   area manager

Gebrauchsabnutzung (f)   wear and tear

Gebrauchssteuer (f)   use tax

Gebühr (f)   duty (fee)

Gebühren (pl)   charges

gebührenfreier Investmentfonds (m)   no-load fund

Gebührennachlaß (m)   remission of a customs duty

gebundene Hilfe (f)   tied aid

Gedeck (n)   cover charge

Gefahr (f)   risk

Gefälligkeitsakzept (n)   accommodation paper

Gefälligkeitsindossament (n)   accommodation endorsement

Gefälligkeitskredit (m)   accommodation credit

Gefälligkeitsparität (f)   accommodation parity

Gefälligkeitsplattform (f)   accommodation platform

Gefälligkeitswechsel (m)   accommodation bill

gegen alle Gefahren   against all risks

Gegenakkreditiv (n)   back-to-back credit

Gegenleistung (f)   consideration (contract law)

gegenseitig sich ausschließende Gattungen (pl)   mutually exclusive classes

gegenseitige Ausbildung (f)   reciprocal training

Gehalt (n)   compensation, salary

Gehälterliste (f)   payroll

Geld (n)   currency, money

geldähnliche Forderung (f)   near money

Geldanweisung (f)   money order

Geldbestand (m)   cash balance, money supply

Geldentwertung (f)   depreciation of currency

Geldkurs (m)   bid price

Geldladen (m)   money shop

Geldmakler (m)   money broker

Geldmarkt (m)   money market

Geldmenge (f)   monetary base

Geldpolitik (f)   monetary policy
Geldschein (m)   bill (currency)
Geldsperre (f)   blockage of funds
Geldstrafe (f)   fine (penalty)
Geldumlaufgeschwindigkeit (f)   velocity of money
Geldumlaufzuwachs (m)   incremental cash flow
Geldversorgung (f)   money supply
Geldverwalter (m)   money manager
Geldwechsel (m)   currency exchange
Gelegenheitskauf (m)   bargain
gelenkte Wirtschaft (f)   managed economy
gelernte Arbeitskräfte (pl)   skilled labor
Gemeindesteuer (f)   local tax
Gemeingut (n)   public domain
Gemeinkosten (pl)   indirect costs, overhead
Gemeinkostenlöhne (pl)   indirect labor
Gemeinkostensatz (m)   burden rate
Gemeinpunkt in Übersee (m)   overseas common point
gemeinsamer Besitz (m)   joint estate
gemeinsamer Markt (m)   common market
gemeinsame Rechnung (f)   joint account
gemeinschaftliche Computerbenutzung (f)   time sharing
gemeinschaftliches Konto (n)   joint account
gemeinschaftliches Unternehmen (n)   joint venture
Gemeinschaftswerbung (f)   cooperative advertising
gemeinnützig   nonprofit (not-for-profit)
gemietete Abteilung (f)   leased department
genannter Ausfuhrort (m)   named point of exportation
genannter Bestimmungsort (m)   named point of destination
genannter Einfuhrhafen (m)   named port of importation
genannter Ursprungsort (m)   named point of origin
genannter Versandhafen (m)   named port of shipment
genehmigen   authorize (v)
genehmigtes Lagerhaus (n)   licensed warehouse
genehmigte Aktien (pl)   authorized shares

genehmigte Wertpapiere (pl) approved securities
Generaldirektor (m) general manager, president
Generalkosten (pl) fixed charges, overhead
Generalstreik (m) general strike
Generalversammlung (f) general meeting
Generalversicherung (f) open cover
generell across the board
Genossenschaft (f) cooperative
geplante Überalterung (f) planned obsolescence
gerichtlich entscheiden adjudge (v)
gerichtliche Anordnung (f) injunction
Gerichtsbefehl (m) writ
Gerichtsbezirk (m) jurisdiction
Gesamtangebot (n) aggregate supply
gesamte Industrie (f) betreffend industrywide
Gesamtkapital gearing
Gesamtkosten (f) all in cost
Gesamtkosten für importierte Waren (pl) landed
  cost
Gesamtnachfrage (f) aggregate demand
Gesamtpreis (m) all in cost
Gesamtrisiko (n) aggregate risk
gesamtschuldnerische Haftung (f) joint liability
Gesamtverlustverhältnis (n) loss-loss ratio
Geschäft (n) store, transaction
Geschäftsbank (f) retail bank
Geschäftsbereich (m) line of business
Geschäftsbogen (m) letterhead
geschäftsführender Vorstand (m) executive committee
Geschäftsführer (m) director, executive director,
  management
Geschäftsjahr (n) financial year, fiscal year
Geschäftskarte (f) business card
Geschäftsleitungstabelle (f) management chart
Geschäftslokal (n) place of business
Geschäftsnummer (f) reference number
Geschäftsplan (m) business plan
Geschäftsstrategie (f) business strategy
Geschäftstagebuch (n) journal
Geschäftstätigkeit (f) business activity

Geschäftsumsatz (m)   turnover
Geschäftszentrum (n)   shopping center
geschriebener Text (m)   hard copy
Geselle (m)   journeyman
Gesellschaft (f)   company
Gesellschaft mit beschränkter Haftung (GmbH) (f)   corporation
gesellschaftlich organisieren   incorporate (v)
Gesellschaftsbild (n)   corporate image
Gesellschaftsplanung (f)   corporate planning
Gesellschaftsstruktur (f)   corporate structure
Gesellschaftsziel (n)   company goal
Gesetz (n)   law
Gesetz vom abnehmenden Ertrag (n)   law of diminishing returns
gesetzlich geschützt   proprietary
gesetzliche Abhilfe (f)   remedy (law)
gesetzlicher Feiertag (m)   legal holiday
gesetzliches Monopol (n)   legal monopoly
gesetzliche Rücklage (f)   legal reserve (banking)
gesetzliches Zahlungsmittel (n)   legal tender
gesetzwidrig   illegal
gesetzwidrige Sendungen (pl)   illegal shipments
gesicherte Haftung (f)   secured liability
gesicherte Obligation (f)   guaranty bond
gesicherte Konten (pl)   secured accounts
gespaltener Markt (m)   two-tiered market
gespaltene Wechselkurse (pl)   multiple exchange rate
gestaffelte Steuer (f)   graduated tax
Gestaltungsskizze (f)   layout
Gestehungskosten (f)   prime costs
gestezliche Verjährungsschriften (pl)   statute of limitations
gestiegene Kosten (pl)   increased costs
gestundete Zahlungen (pl)   deferred charges
getätigter Verkauf (m)   negotiated sale
Getreide (n)   grain
Gewähr (f)   warrant (guarantee), warranty
Gewährleistungsgarantie (f)   performance bond

Gewerbeausstellung (f)   trade fair

Gewerbehaus (n)   trade house

Gewerbesteuer (f)   excise tax

Gewerbetechnik (f)   industrial engineering

gewerbliche Schiedsgerichtsbarkeit (f)   industrial arbitration

Gewerkschaft (f)   labor union, trade union

Gewerkschaftsetikett (n)   union label

gewerkschaftsfreier Betrieb (m)   open shop

Gewerkschaftsführer (m)   labor leader

Gewicht (n)   weight

Gewinn (m)   profit

Gewinn pro Aktie (m)   earnings per share

Gewinn- und Verlustrechnung (f)   income statement, profit-and-loss statement

Gewinnanteilprozentsatz (m)   percentage of profit

Gewinnbericht (m)   earnings report

Gewinnbeteiligung (f)   profit sharing

gewinnen   acquire (v)

Gewinnfaktor (m)   profit factor

Gewinnnprognose (f)   profit projection

Gewinnobligationen (pl)   income bonds

Gewinnrealisierung (f)   profit-taking

Gewinnschwelle (f)   break-even point

Gewinnschwelle erreichen (f)   break even (v)

Gewinnsicherung (f)   profit-taking

Gewinnspanne (f)   profit margin

Gewinnwirkung (f)   profit impact

gewogener Durchschnitt (m)   weighted average

Gewohnheit (f)   practice

gezogener Wechsel (m)   direct paper

Girat (m)   endorsee

Giro (n)   endorsement

Girokonto (n)   checking account

Girozentrale (f)   clearinghouse

Gläubiger (m)   creditor

gleicher Lohn für die gleiche Arbeit (m)   equal pay for equal work

Gleichheit (f)   parity

gleitender Durchschnitt (m) moving average
gleitender Wechselkurs (m) floating exchange rate

Glockenkurve (f) bell-shaped curve
Goldbestände (f) gold reserves
Goldklausel (f) gold clause
Goldpreis (m) gold price
gradlinig linear
graphische Darstellung (f) graph
Gratifikation (f) gratuity

grauer Markt (m) gray market
greifbare Vermögenswerte (pl) tangible assets
Grenze (f) border
Grenzertrag (m) marginal revenue
Grenzkosten (pl) incremental costs, marginal cost
Grenzproduktivität (f) marginal productivity
Grenzsteuerberichtigung (f) border tax adjustment
großangelegt large-scale
Großhandel (m) wholesale market, wholesale trade
Großhandelspreis (m) wholesale price
Großhändler (m) wholesaler, distributor
Grossist (m) jobber
Großkonzern (m) conglomerate
Großlieferant (m) rack jobber
größte Zahlung (f) balloon payment (loan repayment)
Großvertrieb (m) mass marketing

Grundbesitz (m) real estate
Grundbesitzer (m) landowner
Grundbuchung (f) original entry
gründen incorporate (v)
Grundkapital (n) principal (capital)
gründlich besprechen jawbone (v)
Grundpreis (m) base price
Grundsatz (m) policy (principle)
Grundsteuer (f) land tax
Grundstück (n) premises
Grundstückkaufvertrag (m) quit claim deed
Grundstücksverwalter (m) estate agent

Grundtarif (m) base rate
Gründungsfinanzierung (f) front-end financing
Gründungsurkunde (f) certificate of incorporation
Grundvermögen (n) real assets
Grundwährung (f) base currency
Gruppendynamik (f) group dynamics
Gruppenführer (m) foreman
Gruppenmanagement (n) team management
Gruppenpolice (f) fleet policy
Gruppenversicherung (f) group insurance
gültig valid
Gültigkeitsverlängerung (f) rain check
Gut (n) estate (landed)
gut und schlecht verkaufte Artikel leads and lags
Güter (pl) goods, merchandise
Gütertransport (m) movement of goods
Guthaben in konvertierbarer Währung (n) Eurocurrency
gutschreiben credit (v)
Gutschriftsanzeige (f) credit note

H

Hafengebühren (pl) harbor dues
Haftpflichtversicherung (f) liability insurance
Haftung (f) liability
Halbfabrikate (pl) work in progress
Halbleben (n) half-life
Haltezeit (f) holding period
hamstern hoard (v)
Handarbeiter (m) manual worker
Handel (m) commerce, deal (transaction), trade
handeln trade (v)
Handelsabkommen (n) trade agreement
Handelsagentur (f) mercantile agency
Handelsakzept (n) trade acceptance
Handelsbank (f) commercial bank, merchant bank, retail bank
Handelsbedingungen (pl) terms of trade
handelsbezogen mercantile

Handelsbilanz (f)   balance of trade

Handelsdatum (n)   trade date

Handelsgesellschaft (f)   trading company

Handelsgesetz (n)   mercantile law (a specific law)

Handelsgrenze (f)   trading limit

Handelshaus (n)   trade house

Handelskammer (f)   chamber of commerce, merchant guild

Handelskommission (f)   trade commission

Handelskredit (m)   trade credit

Handelsmarke (f)   trademark

Handelsrechnung (f)   commercial invoice

Handelsrecht (n)   mercantile law (in general)

Handelsschranke (f)   trade barrier

Handelssperre (f)   embargo

handelsübliche Qualität (f)   commercial grade

Handelsverband (m)   trade association

Handelsvertrag (m)   trade agreement

Handelsware (f)   commodity

Händler (m)   dealer, merchant, trader

Händlerrabatt (m)   trade discount

Handlung (f)   dealership

Handlungsplan (m)   plan, action

Handlungsreisender (m)   manufacturer's representative

Hardware (f)   hardware (computer)

Hartwährung (f)   hard currency

häufiger Stellenwechsler (m)   job hopper

Hauptausfuhrwaren (f)   key exports

Hauptbuch (n)   ledger

Hauptbucheintragung (f)   ledger entry

Hauptbuchkonto (n)   ledger account

Hauptbüro (n)   head office

Haupteinkäufer (m)   chief buyer

Hauptmarkt (m)   primary market

Hauptrechner (m)   mainframe computer

Hauptsendezeit (f)   prime time

Hauptsitz (m)   headquarters

Haushalt (m)   budget

Haushaltsjahr (n)   financial year

Haushaltsmittelbereitstellung (f)   budget appropriation

Haushaltsvoranschlag (m)   budget forecast

Haussebörse (f)   bull market

Haussemarkt (m)   upmarket

Haussespekulant (m)   bull

Hausverkauf (m)   door-to-door sales

Hebelwirkung (f)   leverage

Heimfall einer Erbschaft an den Staat (m)   escheat

heisses Geld (n)   hot money

hemmender Faktor (m)   disincentive

Herabsetzung (f)   abatement (reduction), writedown

herabziehen   drawdown

herausnehmen   take out (v)

Herkunftsbescheinigung (f)   certificate of origin

Hersteller (m)   manufacturer

Herstellervertreter (m)   manufacturer's agent

Herstellung (f)   production

Herstellungskapazität (f)   manufacturing capacity

herumgehen   go around (v)

hinauswerfen   fire (v)

Hinterlegungsschein (m)   trust receipt

Hochkonjunktur (f)   boom

Höchstgrenze (f)   ceiling

Höchstpreis (m)   top price

Hoheitsgewässer (n)   territorial waters

höhere Gewalt (f)   act of God

Holdinggesellschaft (f)   holding company

Holzhammermethode (f)   hard sell

horten   hoard (v)

Huckepackverkehr (m)   piggyback service

Hundertaktienpaket (n)   round lot

Hybridrechner (m)   hybrid computer

Hypothek (f)   mortgage

Hypothekenbank (f)   mortgage bank

Hypothekenbrief (m)   mortgage bond

hypothekenfrei   free and clear (unmortgaged)

Hypothekenpfandbrief (m)   mortgage debenture

Hypothekenschein (m) mortgage certificate
Hypothekenschulden (f) encumbrance

I

im Börsenhandel eingetragener Verein member firm
im Debet in the red
im Einzug (f) float (outstanding checks)
im Umlauf afloat (in circulation)
im voraus eingegangene Erträge (f) deferred income
immaterielle Werte (f) intangible assets
Import (m) import
importieren import (v)
Importlizenz (f) import license
Impulskauf (m) impulse purchase
in Kommission on consignment
in unabhängiger Datenverarbeitung off line
Index (m) index
Indexierung (f) indexing
Indexoption (f) index option
indirekte Anspruch (m) indirect claim
indirekte Steuer (f) indirect tax
Indossament (n) endorsement
Industrie (f) industry
Industriegenossenschaft (f) trade association
Industriegewerkschaft (f) industrial union
Industrieplanung (f) industrial planning
Industrieprodukte (pl) industrial goods
ineffizient inefficient
Inflation (f) inflation
inflationär inflationary
Informationswege (f) mass media
Infrastruktur (f) infrastructure
Ingenieurwesen (n) engineering
Inhaber (m) bearer, holder, owner, proprietary
Inhaberobligation (f) bearer bond
Inhaberpapier (n) bearer security
Inhaltsverzeichnis (n) table of contents
inländischer Frachtbrief (m) inland bill of lading
inländische Gesellschaft (f) domestic corporation

inländische Steuern und Abgaben (pl) internal revenue tax

Inlandserzeugnis (n) native produce

Inlandwechsel (m) domestic bill

Innenfinanzierung (f) internal funding

inner internal

innerbetriebliche Beziehungen (pl) employee relations

innerbetriebliche Revision (f) internal audit

innerer Wert (m) intrinsic value

insolvent insolvent

Inspektion (f) inspection

Inspektor (m) inspector

instandhalten service (v)

Instandhaltung (f) maintenance

Instandhaltungsvertrag (m) maintenance contract, service contract

institutioneller Investor (m) institutional investor

Interesse (general) (n) interest

Interessenausgleich (m) interest parity

Interessenkonflikt (m) conflict of interest

interimistisch interim

intern internal

internationale Datumsgrenze (f) International Date Line

Internationale Entwicklungsstelle (f) International Development Agency

Internationale Wiederaufbaubank (f) World Bank

interne Rendite (f) internal rate of return

interne Zinsfußrechnung (f) discounted cash flow

Interview (n) interview

Inventar (n) inventory

Inventarstück (n) fixture

investieren invest (v)

Investition (f) investment

Investitionsanalyse (f) investment analysis

Investitionsausgabe (f) capital expenditure

Investitionsbudget (n) capital budget, investment budget

Investitionseinstufung und Bewertung (f) investment grade

Investitionsgüter (pl)   capital goods, industrial goods
Investitionskriterien (f)   investment criteria
Investitionsliste (f)   legal list (fiduciary investments)
Investitionspolitik (f)   investment policy
Investitionsprogramm (n)   investment program
Investitionsstrategie (f)   investment strategy
Investitionstaktik (f)   investment strategy
Investmentfonds (m)   mutual fund
Investmentfonds mit begrenzter Emissionshöhe (m)
  closed-end fund
Investmentgesellschaft (f)   investment company,
  mutual fund
Investmenttreuhandgesellschaft (f)   investment trust
irreführend   misleading
Irrtum (m)   error
Istkosten (pl)   actual costs

J

Jäger auf Nachwuchskräfte (m)   headhunter
Jahr (n)   year
Jahresabrechnung (f)   annual accounts
Jahresabschluß (m)   annual accounts
Jahresabschluß (m)   year-end
Jahresbericht (m)   annual report
Jahresende (n)   year-end
Jahresprüfung (f)   annual audit
Jahresrente (f)   annuity
jahreszeitlich   seasonal
jährlich   annual
Jasonsklausel (f)   Jason clause
Joint-venture (n)   joint venture
Journal (n)   journal
Juniorpartner (m)   junior partner
juristische Person (f)   legal entity

K

Kabel (n)   cable
Kabelfernsehen (n)   television, cable
Kaffeepause (f)   coffee break
Kai (m)   wharf

Kaigebühren (pl) wharfage charges
Kannossementsgarantie (f) letter of indemnity
Kapazität (f) capacity
Kapazitätsausnutzung (f) capacity utilization
Kapazitätsausnutzungsgrad (m) load factor
Kapital (n) capital
Kapital blockieren lock in
Kapitalanlage (f) investment
Kapitalanlage ohne geborgte Mittel (f) gearless
Kapitalaufbringung (f) raising capital
Kapitalaufnahme (f) raising capital
Kapitalaufwand (m) capital expenditure
Kapitalaufwendungen (pl) capital spending
Kapitalausfuhr (f) capital exports
Kapitalerhöhung (f) capital increase
Kapitalertrag (Kapitalverlust) (m) capital gain (loss)
Kapitalflußrechnung (f) cash flow statement
kapitalintensiv capital-intensive
Kapitalisierung (f) capitalization
Kapitalismus (m) capitalism
Kapitalkoeffizient (m) capital-output ratio
Kapitalkonto (n) capital account
Kapitalkosten (pl) cost of capital
Kapitalmarkt (m) capital market
Kapitalrendite (f) return on capital
Kapitalrückflußdauer (f) payout period
Kapitalstruktur (f) capital structure
Kapitalüberschuß (m) capital surplus
Kapitalverzinsung (f) return on investment
Kartell (n) cartel, combination
Kartellgesetze (f) antitrust laws
Kassabuch (n) cash book
Kassamarkt (m) spot market
Kassakonto (n) cash discount
Kasse (f) fund
Kassenbestand (m) cash balance
Kasseneintrag (m) cash entry
Kassenhaltung (f) cash management

Kassenreserven (f)   primary reserves
Kassenscheck (m)   cashier's check, counter check
Kassenvoranschlag (m)   cash budget
Kassette (f)   cassette
Kassierer für Auszahlungen (m)   paymaster
Katalog (m)   catalog
Katalogisierung (f)   listing
Kaufauftrag (m)   purchase order
Kaufbrief (m)   deed of sale
kaufen   purchase (v)
Käufer (m)   buyer
Käuferaufgeld (n)   buyer's premium
Käufermarkt (m)   buyer's market
Käuferoption (f)   buyer's option
Kaufhaus (n)   department store
Kaufinteressent (m)   potential buyer
Kaufkraft (f)   purchasing power
Kaufmann (m)   merchant
kaufmännisch   mercantile
Kaufmannsinnung (f)   merchant guild
Kaufpreis (m)   purchase price
Kaufvertrag (m)   bill of sale
Kaution (f)   deposit
Kautionsversicherungsgesellschaft (f)   guaranty company, surety company
kein Problem   no problem
kennzeichnen   earmark (v)
Keynessche Wirtschaftslehre (f)   Keynesian economics
Klage (f)   lawsuit, legal action
Klartext (m)   hard copy
Kleidung (f)   apparel
Kleinaktie (f)   penny stock
Kleinanzeige (f)   classified advertisement, want-ad
Kleinbetrieb (m)   small business
kleiner Diebstahl (m)   pilferage
knapp bei Kasse   short of cash
Knappheit (f)   short supply
Kodizill (n)   codicil

Kohle (f) coal

Kollege (m) colleague

Kollektivversicherung (f) blanket insurance

Kommanditgesellschaft (f) limited partnership

Kommissionär (m) factor (agent)

kommissionsweise on consignment

Kommunalobligation (f) municipal bond

Kommunalsteuer (f) local tax

Kompensationshandel (m) compensation trade

Konferenzraum (m) conference room

Konflikt (m) dispute

Konjunkturindikatoren (f) economic indicators

Konjunkturspritze (f) pump priming

Konjunkturzyklus (m) business cycle

Konkurrent (m) competitor

Konkurrenz (f) competition

konkurrenzfähiger Preis (m) competitive price

Konkurrenzstudie (f) competitor analysis

Konkurs (m) bankruptcy, failure

Können (n) know-how

konsolidierte Bilanz (f) consolidation

konsolidierter Finanzbericht (m) consolidated financial statement

Konsortium (n) consortium, syndicate

Konsulatsfaktura (f) consular invoice

Konsumentenkredit (m) consumer credit

Konsumgüter (pl) consumer goods

Kontingent (n) quota

Kontingentierungssystem (n) quota system

Konto (n) account

Kontoauszug (m) bank statement, statement of account

Kontokorrentguthaben (n) compensating balance

Kontokorrentkonto (n) open account

Kontokorrentkreditlinie (f) demand line of credit

Kontonummer (f) account number

Kontostand (m) account balance

Kontrahent (m) party

kontrollieren manage (v) (control)

kontrollierter Kassenvorschuß (m)   managed float

kontrollierte Kosten (pl)   managed costs

Kontrolliste (f)   checklist

konvertierbare Vorzugsaktie (f)   convertible preferred stock

konvertierbare Obligationen (pl)   convertible debentures

Konzern (m)   combination

Konzernabschluss (m)   consolidation, group account

Konzerngesellschaft (f)   affiliate, subsidiary

Konzernunternehmen (n)   associate company

Konzessionsbetrieb (m)   franchise

Kooperationsabkommen (n)   cooperation agreement

Kopfjäger (m)   headhunter

Kopplungsgeschäft (n)   package deal

Korn (n)   grain

körperliche Inventur (f)   physical inventory

Körperschaftssteuer (f)   corporate tax

Korrespondenz (f)   correspondence

Korrespondenzbank (f)   correspondent bank

Kosten (pl)   cost

Kosten und Fracht   cost and freight

Kostenanalyse (f)   cost analysis

Kostenaufteilungsverfahren (n)   absorption costing

Kostendeckung (f)   recovery of expenses

Kostendeckungspunkt (m)   break-even point

Kosteneinsparung (f)   cost reduction

Kostenfaktor (m)   cost factor

kostenintensiv   cost effective

Kostennutzenanalyse (f)   cost-benefit analysis

Kostenpreisschere (f)   cost-price squeeze

Kostenrechnung (f)   cost accounting

Kostenüberwachung (f)   cost control

Kostenzuteilung (f)   allocation of costs

Kraftfahrzeugsammelpolice (f)   fleet policy

Krämer (m)   merchant

Krankheitsurlaub (m)   sick leave

Kredit (m)   credit

Kreditanstalt (f)   credit bureau

Kreditbank (f)   credit bank
Kreditbedingungen (pl)   credit terms
Kreditbrief (m)   letter of credit
Krediteinschätzung (f)   credit rating
Kreditkarte (f)   credit card
Kreditkäufer (m)   credit buyer
Kreditkonto (n)   charge account
Kreditkontrolle (f)   credit control
Kreditkündigung mit Geldforderung (f)   margin call
Kreditlinie (f)   credit line
Kreditreferenz (f)   credit reference
Kreditsaldo (n)   credit balance
Kreditsicherungsgrenze (f)   lending margin
Kreditüberschreitung (f)   overdraft
Kreditverein (m)   credit union
Kreditversicherung (f)   credit insurance
Kreditverwaltung (f)   credit management
Kreisdiagramm (n)   pie chart
Krise (f)   depression
Kukuruz (m)   maize
Kulturbesitz (m)   cultural property
kumulativ   cumulative
kumulative Vorzugsaktie (f)   cumulative preferred
  stock
kündbare Obligation (f)   redeemable bond
Kunde (m)   customer
Kundenbetreuer (m)   account executive
Kundendienst (m)   after-sales service, customer
  service
Kundenkredit (m)   consumer credit
kündigen   call (v), terminate (v) (employment)
Kündigungsklausel (f)   call feature
Kündigungspreis (m)   call price
Kündigungsregel (f)   call rule
Kündigungsschutz (m)   call protection
Kündigungstarif (m)   call rate
Kunjunkturabschwung (m)   downswing
künstliche Fasern (pl)   manmade fibers
Kunststoffe (pl)   manmade

Kurier (m) courier

Kurs (m) rate

Kurs-Ertragsverhältnis (n) price/earnings (p/e)

Kursfestsetzer (m) market-maker

Kurssicherung (f) forward cover

Kursstützung (f) pegging

Kursverlust (m) exchange loss

Kurswert (m) market value (stocks)

kurz- und mittelfristige Verbindlichkeiten (pl) accounts payable

kurzfristig above-the-line (short term)

kurzfristige Finanzierung (f) short-term financing

kurzfristiges Kapitalkonto (n) short-term capital account

kurzfristiges Umlaufvermögen (n) current assets, floating assets

kurzfristige Verbindlichkeit (f) current liabilities

kurzfristige Verschuldung (f) short-term debt

kurzlebiges Wirtschaftsgut (n) wasting asset

Kurzversicherung (f) term insurance

L

Laden (m) store

Ladenbesitzer (m) merchant

Ladung (f) cargo

Ladungsfähigkeit (f) tonnage

Ladungsriemen (f) strapping

Lager (n) go down

Lageraufseher (m) warehousekeeper

Lagerhaus (n) warehouse

Lagerkosten (pl) carrying charges

Lagerumschlag (m) inventory turnover, stock turnover

Lagerumschlag des Grossisten (m) jobber's turn

Lagerung (f) storage

Land (n) land

Land-Seewegverkehr (m) fishyback service

Landungsgebühren (f) landing charges

Landwirtschaft (f) agriculture

landwirtschaftliches Akzept (n) agricultural paper

landwirtschaftliche Erzeugnisse (pl)   agricultural products

Landzuteilung (f)   land grant

lange diskutieren   jawbone (v)

langfristig   below the line

langfristiges Kapitalkonto (n)   long-term capital account

langfristige Planung (f)   long-range planning

langfristige Schuld (f)   long-term debt

langfristiger Terminkauf (m)   long hedge

langfristige Verbindlichkeit (f)   fixed liability

langfristige Verzinsung (f)   long interest

langfristige Vermögenswerte (pl)   noncurrent assets

langlebige Gebrauchsgüter (pl)   durable goods

lastenfrei   free and clear (unencumbered)

Lastschrift (f)   debit entry

Lastschriftanzeige (f)   debit note

Lastwagenladung (f)   truckload

laufende Ausgaben (pl)   fixed expenses, on cost

laufende Kosten (pl)   standing charges

laufende Rendite (f)   current yield

laufende Unkosten (f)   running expenses

laufendes Konto (n)   open account

laut Bericht   as per advice

Lauterkeit des Wettbewerbs (f)   fair trade

Lebensdauer (f)   life cycle, product life

Lebenshaltungsindex (m)   consumer price index

Lebenshaltungskosten (pl)   cost of living

Lebenslauf (m)   curriculum vitae

Lebensmittel (pl)   foodstuffs

Lebensstandard (m)   standard of living

Lebensversicherungspolice (f)   life insurance policy

Leckage (f)   leakage

Leerfracht (f)   dead freight

Leerverkauf (m)   short sale

Leerverkaufsposition (f)   short position

Lehrling (m)   apprentice

Lehrmodell (n)   mock-up

Leibrentenempfänger (m)   annuitant

Leistungsfähigkeit (f) efficiency
leiten manage (v)
leitender Angestellter (m) executive
Leiter (m) leader, manager
Leiter der Exportabteilung (m) export manager
Leiter der Finanzabteilung (m) treasurer
Leiter des Rechnungswesens (m) controller
Leitkurs (m) central rate
Leitung (f) management
Leitung durch Röhren (f) pipage
Leitungsschicht (f) management team
Leitzinssatz (m) prime rate
Lernkurve (f) learning curve
letzter Termin (m) deadline
Lieferant (m) supplier
Lieferpreis (m) deliverey price
Lieferschein (m) delivery notice
Liefertermin (m) date of delivery
Lieferung (f) delivery
Lieferungsangebot (n) tender offer
Liegegeld (n) demurrage (fee for)
Liegetage (pl) laydays
Liegezeit (f) lay time
limitierter Börsenauftrag (m) stop-loss order
limitierte Börsenorder (f) limit order
lineare Programmierung (f) linear programming
lineare Schätzung (f) lineal estimation
lineare Bedingungen (pl) linear terms
Liniendirektor (m) line executive
Linienmanagement (n) line management
Liquidität (f) cash flow, liquidity
Liquiditätsbevorzugung (f) liquidity preference
Liquiditätsgrad (m) current ratio, liquidity ratio
Listenpreis (m) list price
Lizenz (f) license
Lizenzaustausch (m) cross-licensing
Lizenzbetrieb (m) franchise
Lizenzgebühr (f) royalty (patent)

Lizenzgebühren (pl)   license fees
LKW-Ladung (f)   truckload
Locher (m)   keypuncher
Lochkarte (f)   punch card
Lochstreifen (m)   paper tape
Lockartikel (m)   leader, loss leader
Lockvogelangebot (n)   loss leader
Logistik (f)   logistics
Lohn (m)   wage
Lohn-Preis-Spirale (f)   wage-price spiral
Löhne (pl)   wages
Lohnempfänger (m)   wage earner
lohnintensiv   labor-intensive
Lohnliste (f)   payroll
Lohnniveau (n)   wage level
Lohnrichtung (f)   wage drift
Lohnrückstand (m)   back pay
Lohnskala (f)   wage scale
Lohnsteuer (f)   payroll tax
Lohnstopp (m)   wage freeze
Lohnstreit (m)   wage dispute
Lohnstruktur (f)   wage structure
Lohnunterschied (m)   wage differential
Lohnzuschlag (m)   double time
Lombardwert (m)   loan value
Los (n)   lot
Löschkosten (pl)   landing costs
Löschschein (m)   landing certificate
Löschungskosten (pl)   wharfage
Löschzeit (f)   laydays
Lotsengeld (n)   pilotage
Lufteilgut (n)   air express
Luftexpress (m)   air express
Luftfracht (f)   air freight
Luftfrachtsendung (f)   air shipment
lustloser Markt (m)   thin market
Luxussteuer (f)   luxury tax
Luxuswaren (pl)   luxury goods

M

Magnetband (n) magnetic tape
Magnetplatte (f) disk
Magnetplattenantrieb (m) disk drive
Magnetspeicher (m) magnetic memory
mahnen drängen dun (v)
Mais (m) maize
Makler (m) broker
Maklerdarlehen (n) day loan
Makroökonomie (f) macroeconomics
Management (n) management
Manager (m) management
Mandat (n) mandate
Mangel (m) shortage
mangelhaft defective
Manteltarifabkommen (n) master agreement
Mantelvertrag (m) collective agreement
Manuskript (n) script
Marge (f) spread
marginale Preisfestsetzung (f) marginal pricing
Marke (f) brand
Markenanerkennung (f) brand recognition
Markenimage (n) brand image
Markentreue (f) brand loyalty
Marketing (n) marketing
Markt (m) market
Marktanteil (m) market share
Marktbericht (m) market report
Marktdurchdringung (f) market penetration
Marktdynamik (f) market dynamics
Markteinschätzung (f) market appraisal
Marktforschung (f) market research
Marktkonzentration (f) market concentration
Marktkräfte (pl) market forces
Marktlage (f) market position
Marktleitung (f) market management
Marktplan (m) market plan
Marktplatz (m) marketplace

Marktpotential (n)   market potential
Marktpreis (m)   market price
Marktprognose (f)   market forecast
Marktsättigung (f)   market saturation
Marktstudie (f)   market survey
Markttendenzen (f)   market trends
Marktübersicht (f)   market survey
Marktwert (m)   market value (general)
Maschinenbau (m)   mechanical engineering
Maschinenpark (m)   machinery
Maschinenschreiber (m)   typist
Maß (n)   ratio
Massenabsatz (m)   mass marketing
Massenkommunikation (f)   mass communications
Massenmedien (f)   mass communications, mass media
Massenproduktion (f)   mass production
Maßstab (m)   yardstick
Materialien (pl)   materials
mathematisches Modell (n)   mathematical model
Matrixbilanz (f)   spreadsheet
Matrizenüberwachung (f)   matrix management
Medien (pl)   media
Mehrfachbesteuerung (f)   multiple taxation
Mehrprogrammverarbeitung (f)   multiprogramming
mehrseitige Abkommen (n)   multilateral agreement
mehrseitige Handel (m)   multilateral trade
Mehrumsatz (m)   add-on sales
Mehrwertssteuer (f)   value-added tax (VAT)
Meinungsbeeinflussung (f) der Abgeordneten   lobbying
Meinungsforschung (f)   public opinion poll
meistbegünstigtes Land (n)   most-favored nation
Meistbietende (m) (f)   highest bidder
Meldung (f)   report
Menge (f)   quantity
Mengenrabatt (m)   quantity discount, volume discount
messen   measure (v)
Metalle (pl)   metals

Methode (f)   method

Metrifikation (f)   metrification

Metallwaren (pl)   hardware

Miete (f)   rent

mieten   lease (v), rent (v) (rent from)

Mieter (m)   lessee

Mieter (m)   tenant

Mietsvertrag mit Bestimmungen für Ankauf (m)   leveraged lease

Mietvertrag (m)   lease

Mikrochip (m)   chip, microchip

Mikrocomputer (m)   microcomputer

Mikrofiche (n)   microfiche

Mikrofilm (m)   microfilm

Mikroprozessor (m)   microprocessor

Minderheitsanteil (m)   minority interest

Minderlieferung (f)   short delivery

Mindersendung (m)   short shipment

minderwertig   second rate

Mindestbetrag (m)   cover charge

Mindesteinschuß (m)   margin requirements

Mindesteinzahlungsbetrag (m)   margin

Mindestlohn (m)   minimum wage

Mindestpacht (f)   dead rent

Mindestreserven (pl)   minimum reserves

Minicomputer (m)   minicomputer

Mischindex (m)   composite index

Mischkonzern (m)   conglomerate

Mischkosten (pl)   mixed costs

Mißerfolg (m)   failure

mißlingen   fail (v)

Mißverständnis (n)   misunderstanding

mit   on line (computer)

mit Bindestrich schreiben   hyphenate (v)

mit Dividende   cum dividend

mit Durchschnittsberechnung   with average

mit Latten versehen   batten fitted

mit Vorrechten ausgestattete Wertpapieremission (f)   senior issue

Mitarbeiter (m) colleague
Miteigentum (n) co-ownership
Miteigentümer (m) joint owner
Mitglied auf Lebenszeit (n) life member
Mitgliedsfirma (f) member firm
mittelfristig medium term
Mittelmanagement (n) management, middle management
Mittelmann (m) middleman
Mittelstand (m) small business
Mittelverwendung (f) resource allocation
mittlere Führungsschicht (f) middle management
Mitversicherung (f) coinsurance
Mobiliarhypothek (f) chattel mortgage
Modell (n) model
Modem (m) modem
modernisieren streamline (v)
modifizieren renegotiate (v)
Möglichkeiten (f) facilities (possibilities)
Molkereiprodukte (f) dairy products
Monopol (n) monopoly
Monopsonie (f) monopsony
Montage (f) assembly
Montagebahn (f) assembly line
Monte Carlo Methode (f) Monte Carlo technique
montieren assemble (v) (things)
Moratorium (n) moratorium
Motivationsstudie (f) motivation study
Müdigkeit nach dem Flug (f) jet lag
Müllerei (f) grain mill
multinationale Gesellschaft (f) multinational corporation
Multiplikator (m) multiplier
Multiwährung (f) multicurrency
mündelsichere Anlage (f) gilt-edged investment
mündlich bestätigter Scheck (m) voiced check
Münzamt (n) mint
Münzstätte (f) mint
Muster (n) design, model, pattern

Musterbrief (m)   form letter
Musterkollektion (f)   sample line
Muttergesellschaft (f)   parent company
Mutterschaftsurlaub (m)   maternity leave

N

nach Sicht Akzept (n)   after-sight
Nachahmung (f)   counterfeit, imitation
nachbestellen   reorder (v)
Nachbestellung (f)   repeat order
nachbörsliche Umsätze (f)   after-hours trading
nachdatieren   afterdate (v)
nachdatiert   postdated
nachfassen   follow up (v)
Nachflugerschöpfung (f)   jet lag
Nachfrage   elasticity (of supply or demand)
nachhängender Konjunkturindikator (m)   lagging indicator
Nachfrage (f)   demand
Nachkaufsmietung (f)   sell and lease back
Nachlaß (m)   estate (testamentary)
nachlässig   negligent
Nachlaßsteuer (f)   estate tax, inheritance tax
Nachnahme (f)   collect on delivery
Nachnahmesendung (f)   cash on delivery
nachrangige Hypothek (f)   second mortgage
Nachricht (f)   report
nachsenden   forward (v)
Nachtdepot (n)   night depository
Nachteil (m)   drawback (disadvantage), handicap
Nahrungsmittel (pl)   foodstuffs
Namenspapier (n)   registered security
Namensscheck (m)   registered check
Nationalbank (f)   government bank
Nationalismus (m)   nationalism
Naturschätze (f)   natural resources
neben   alongside
Nebenausgaben (pl)   incidental expenses
Nebenbetrieb (m)   ancillary operation

Nebeneinkünfte (pl)   perks
Nebenprodukt (n)   by-product
Nebenvergütungen (f)   fringe benefits
Nebenvertrag (m)   subcontract
negativer Zahlungsstrom (m)   negative cash flow
Nennertrag (m)   nominal yield
Nennwert (m)   face value, par value
nennwertlose Aktie (f)   no par value
netto   net
Nettoänderung (f)   net change
Nettobargeldstrom (m)   net cash flow
Nettobarwert (m)   net present value
Nettobetriebskapital (n)   net working capital
Nettoeigenkapital (n)   net equity assets
Nettoeinkommen (n)   net income
Nettofremdkapitalreserven (pl)   net borrowed reserves
Nettogehalt (n)   take-home pay
Nettogewinn (m)   net profit
Nettogewinnspanne (f)   net margin
Nettoinvestition (f)   net investment
Nettostand eines Maklers (m)   net position of a trader
Nettoumsatz (m)   net sales
Nettowert (m)   net worth
Netz (n)   network
neu verhandeln   renegotiate (v)
Neuausgabe (f)   new issue
Neubegebung (f)   new issue
neubestellen   reorder (v)
Neubestellung (f)   repeat order
Neubewertung (f)   revaluation
neues Geld (n)   new money
Neuemission (f)   new issue
Neuerung (f)   innovation
Neufinanzierung (f)   recapitalization
Neugestaltung (f)   reorganization
nicht auf Gewinn ausgerichtet   non-profit
nicht ausgeschüttete Dividende (f)   passed dividend
nicht eingetragen   unlisted

nicht einlösen dishonor

nicht entnommener Gewinn (m) paid-in surplus

nicht frei konvertierbare Währung (f) blocked currency

nicht honorieren dishonor

nicht sonst im Namenregister verzeichnet not otherwise indexed by name

nicht verdienter Wertzuwachs (m) unearned increment

nicht verzeichnet unlisted

Nichterfüllung (f) nonfeasance

nichtig void

nichtkumulative Vorzugsaktie (f) noncumulative preferred stock

Nichtmitglied (n) nonmember

niedrige Einkommenstufe (f) low income

niedrigverzinsliche Obligationen (pl) low-yield bonds

niedrigverzinsliche Darlehen (pl) low-interest loans

noch nicht erledigter Auftrag (m) back order

noch rechtskräftiger Vertrag (m) outstanding contract

Nominalpreis (m) nominal price

Norm (f) norm

Normalzeit (f) standard time

Normung (f) standardization

Notar (m) notary

Notbehelf (m) makeshift

Notenausgabe ohne Deckung (f) fiduciary issue

Notenbank (m) open market operations

notieren take down (v)

Notierung (f) quotation (stock exchange)

Novation (f) novation

null und nichtig null and void

Nutzlast (f) payload

Nutzung noch nicht realisierter Gewinne (f) pyramiding

Nutzungsdauer (f) life cycle, useful life

O

obenerwähnt above mentioned

obengenannt above mentioned

oberste Führungsschicht (f) top management

Obligation (f) bond, debebture

Obligation ohne aufgelaufene Zinsen (f) flat bond

offener Güterwagen (m) flatcar

offene Handelsgesellschaft (f) general partnership

Offenmarkt (m) open market

Offenmarktpolitik (f) open market operations

öffentliche Arbeiten (pl) public works

öffentliche Meinungspflege (f) public relations

öffentliche Mittel (pl) public funds

öffentliche Versteigerung (f) public auction

öffentlicher Bereich (m) public sector

öffentlicher Lagerbetrieb (m) regular warehouse

öffentlicher Verkauf (m) public sale

öffentliches Angebot (n) public offering

öffentliches Verkehrsunternehmen (n) common carrier

Öffentlichkeitsarbeit (f) public relations

Offsetdruck (m) offset printing

offshore Gesellschaft (f) offshore company

ohne Dividende ex dividend

ohne Geschäftsbucheintragung off-the-books

ohne Rechte ex rights

ohne Testament intestate

Ökonometrie (f) econometrics

Oligopol (n) oligopoly

Oligopsonie (f) oligopsony

Opportunitätskosten (f) opportunity cost

Option (f) option

Orderlimit (n) position limit

Organisation (f) organization

Organisationsplan (m) organization chart

Organisationsschema (n) organization chart

Ortsgebräuche (pl) local customs

P

Pacht (f) lease

pachten lease (v)

Pächter (m) lessee

Packkiste (f) packing case
Packzettel (m) packing list
Paketpost (f) parcel post
Palette (f) pallet
palettierte Ladung (f) palletized freight
Panzerkasten (m) safe deposit box
Papier (n) paper
Papierband (n) ticker tape
pari par
Parität (f) parity
Paritätseinkommenverhältnis (n) parity income ratio
Paritätspreis (m) parity price
Pariwert (m) par value
Partieware (f) job lot
Parzellierung (f) acreage allotment
Passierschein (m) entry permit
Patent (n) patent
Patentabgabe (f) patent royalty
Patentanmeldung (f) patent application
patentiertes Verfahren (n) patented process
Patentrecht (n) patent law
Patentverletzung (f) patent infringement
Pattsituation (f) deadlock
Pauschalbetrag (m) flat yield, lump sum
Pauschale (f) flat rate
Pauschalversicherung (f) floater
Pauschalversicherung (f) open cover
Pensionskasse (f) pension fund
Periode (f) period
periodische Bestandsaufnahme (f) periodic inventory
permanente Buchinventur (f) perpetual inventory
Personal (n) personnel
Personalabteilung (f) personnel department
Personalausweis (m) pass (written permit)
Personalbestand (m) manpower
Personalleitung (f) personnel management

Personalwechsel (m)   labor turnover

personenbezogene Aktiengesellschaft (f)   closely held corporation

Personengesellschaft (f)   partnership

persönlicher Abzug (m)   personal deduction

persönliche Einkommensteuer (f)   personal income tax

persönlicher Freibetrag (m)   personal exemption

persönliche Haftpflicht (f)   personal liability

Persönlichkeitsprüfung (f)   personality test

petrochemisch   petrochemical

Petrodollars (pl)   petrodollars

Petroleum (n)   petroleum

Pfand (n)   pledge

Pfandbriefe (pl)   backup bonds

Pfandrecht (n)   lien

Pflicht (f)   duty (obligation)

pflichtwidrige Unterlassung (f)   nonfeasance

Plan (m)   plan

planen   project (v)

Plankosten (pl)   standard costs

Planwirtschaft (f)   managed economy

Platzlieferung (f)   spot delivery

Plenarsitzung (f)   plenary meeting

Police (f)   policy (insurance)

Policeinhaber (m)   policyholder

Politik (f)   policy (action)

Politik der offenen Tür (m)   open door policy

Portefeuille (n)   portfolio

Portefeuilleverwaltung (f)   portfolio management

Portefeuilletheorie (f)   portfolio theory

positiver Zahlungsstrom (m)   positive cash flow

Postanweisung (f)   money order

Posten (m)   item, lot

Postleitzahl (f)   ZIP code

Postversand (m)   mail order

Postversandliste (f)   mailing list

Postversandwerbung (f)   direct mail

potentieller Kunde (m)   potential buyer

potentieller Umsatz (m)   potential sales
Praktik (f)   practice
Praktikant (m)   trainee
praktisch   practical
Prämie, die Gratifikation (f)   bonus (premium)
Prämienzahlung (f)   premium payment
Präsident (m)   president
Preis (m)   price
Preis-Einnahmen Verhältnis (n)   price/earnings (p/e) ratio
Preis-Gewinn Verhältnisse (pl)   multiples
Preisaufschlag (m)   markup
Preisbindung (f)   fair trade, price fixing
Preiselastizität (f)   price elasticity
Preiserhöhung (f)   price increase
Preisgabe (f)   abandonment
Preisgrenze (f)   price limit
Preisherabsetzung (f)   markdown
Preisindex (m)   price index
Preiskrieg (m)   price war
Preislage (f)   price range
Preisliste (f)   price list
Preisnachlaß (m)   price abatement, rebate
Preissenkung (f)   markdown, price cutting, rollback
Preisskala (f)   price range
Preisstop (m)   price freeze
Preisstützung (f)   pegging, price support
Preisunterschied (m)   price differential
Preisverzeichnis (n)   catalog, price list
Preiszettel (m)   price tag
Primärreserven (f)   primary reserve
Priorität (f)   priority
Privateigentum (n)   personal property
Privatflotte (f)   private fleet
Privatmarke (f)   private label (or brand)
Privatplazierung (f)   private placement (finance)
Privatwirtschaft (f)   free enterprise
pro Anteil   per share
pro Kopf   per capita

pro Tag per diem
Probe (f) sample
Probebilanz (f) trial balance
probieren sample (v)
Problem (n) problem
Problemanalyse (f) problem analysis
Problemlösung (f) problem solving
Produkt (n) product
Produktdynamik (f) product dynamics
Produktentwicklung (f) product development
Produktgestaltung (f) product design
Produktgruppe (f) product group
Produktion (f) production
Produktion am laufenden Band (f) production line
Produktionsaufwand (m) production costs
Produktionskapazität (f) manufacturing capacity
Produktionslenkung (f) production control
Produktionsmittel (f) facilities (means of production)
Produktivität (f) productivity
produktivitätsabhängige Leistungsprämie (f) accelerating premium
Produktivkapital (n) instrumental capital
Produktmanagement (n) product management
Produktrentabilität (f) product profitability
Produktsortiment (n) product line
Proformarechnung (f) pro forma invoice
Prognose (f) forecast
Programm (n) program
Programmablauf (m) routine
programmieren program (v)
Projektplanung (f) project planning
Prospekt (m) prospectus
Protektionismus (m) protectionism
Protokolldatum (n) record date
protokollierter Importeur (m) importer of record
Provision (f) commission (fee)
Provision des Verladers (f) address commission
Provisionseinkünfte (pl) percentage earnings

Prozent (n) percent
Prozentpunkt (m) percentage point
Prozeß (m) lawsuit, legal action
prüfen assay (v), audit (v)
Prüfung (f) inspection
Prüfungsbeamte (m) inspector
Prüfungsweg (m) audit trail
Publicitymanager (m) advertising manager
Publizität (f) publicity

Q

Qualifikation (f) qualification
Qualitätskontrolle (f) quality control
Qualitätswaren (pl) quality goods
Quantität (f) quantity
quasi-öffentliche Betrieb (m) quasi-public company
Quellensteuer (f) withholding tax
Quittung (f) receipt (paper)
Quote (f) quota

R

Rabatt (m) allowance, discount
Rabatt je Verladeeinheit (m) unit load discount
Ramschwaren (pl) job lot
Randmarkt (m) fringe market
Randmaschinen (f) peripherals
Rangiergebühren (f) switching charges
Rate (f) rate
rationalisieren streamline (v)
Rationierung (f) rationing
Realeinkommen (n) real income
Realgewinn nach Steuern (m) after-tax real rate of
  return
Realinvestition (f) real investment
Reallöhne (f) real wages
Realzeit (f) real time
Rechenanlage (f) computer
Rechenfehler (m) miscalculation
Rechenschaft ablegen account for (v)
rechenschaftspflichtig accountable

Rechner (m) calculator
Rechnung (f) bill, invoice
Rechnungsabschnitt (m) accounting period
Rechnungsjahr (n) fiscal year
Rechnungsprüfer (m) comptroller
Rechnungsschluß (m) end of period
Rechnungswesen für Betriebsführungsbedürfnisse (n) management accounting
rechtmäßiger Inhaber (m) holder in due course
Rechtsanwalt (m) attorney, lawyer
Rechtsbehelf (m) remedy (law)
Rechtsmängelversicherung (f) title insurance
Rechtsmittel (n) remedy (law)
Rechtsstreit (m) litigation
Rechtstitel (m) title
Rediskontsatz (m) rediscount rate
Refinanzierung (f) refinancing
Reflation (f) reflation
Regelung (f) settlement
Regelungsausloser (m) adjustment trigger
Regierung (f) government
Regierungssektor (m) public sector
Regierungstelle (f) government agency
registrieren index (v)
Regressionsanalyse (f) regression analysis
Regreßrecht (n) right of recourse
Reichtum (m) wealth
Reife (f) maturity (due debts)
rein net
reines Risiko (n) pure risk
Reingewinn (m) net profit
Reinverlust (m) net loss
Reinvermögen (n) net assets
Reinvermögenswert (m) net asset value
Reisebüro (n) travel agency
Reisescheck (m) traveler's check
Reklame (f) advertisement
Reklametext (m) copy (advertising text)
Rendite (f) yield

Rentabilität (f) profitability
Rentabilitätsanalyse (f) profitability analysis
Rentabilitätsrate (f) rate of return
Reportprämie (f) contango
Reproduktion (f) reproduction
Reservefonds (m) contingent fund
Resolution (f) resolution
Rest (m) remainder
restaurieren restore (v)
Restkaufgeldhypothek (f) purchase money mortgage
Restposten (m) job lot
retten salvage (v)
revolvierender Kredit (m) revolving credit
revolvierendes Akkreditiv (n) revolving letter of credit
Rezession (f) recession
richterliche Verfügung (f) injunction
Richtlinie (f) guideline
Richtpreis (m) target price
Risiko (n) risk
Risiko übernehmendes Land (n) country of risk
Risikoanalyse (f) risk analysis
Risikoeinschätzung (f) risk assessment
Risikokapital (n) risk capital, venture capital
Rohgewicht (n) gross weight
Rohgewinn (m) gross profit
Rohrensystem (n) pipage
Rohstoffe (f) raw materials
Rollgeld (n) drayage
Routine (f) routine
Rückerstattung (f) refund, (money) drawback
Rückerstattung im voraus (f) advance refunding
Rückgang (m) recession, slump
Rückgriff (m) recourse
Rückgriffsanspruch (m) rights of recourse
Rückkaufswert (m) cash surrender value
Rücklage (f) reserve
Rückstand (m) backlog
Rückstände (pl) arrears
rückständiges Konto (n) delinquent account

Rücktrittsklausel (f)   escape clause
Rückverkaufen (n)   back selling
Rückversicherer (m)   reinsurer
rückwirkend   retroactive
rückwirkende Steuer (f)   regressive tax
Rückwirkung (f)   feedback
rückzahlbare Staatsubvention (f)   revolving fund
Rückzahlung (f)   refund
Ruhestand (m)   retirement
Ruhetag (m)   holiday
Rundschreiben (n)   memorandum
Rüstkosten (f)   set-up costs
Rüstung (f)   armaments

S

Sachanlagen (pl)   fixed assets
Sachanlagevermögen (n)   tangible assets
Sachleistung (f)   payment in kind
saisonal   seasonal
saisonbedingt   seasonal
Sammelfonds (m)   pool of funds
Satzung (f)   by-laws, charter (written instrument), statute
Säulendiagramm (n)   bar chart
Schachtelaufsichtsrat (m)   interlocking directorate
Schaden (m)   damage
Schaden aus allgemeiner Havarie (m)   general average loss
Schaden in besonderer Havarie (m)   particular average loss
Schadennachweis (m)   proof of loss
Schalterbeamter (m)   teller
Schankkonzession (f)   excise license
schätzen   estimate (v)
Schatzmeister (m)   treasurer
Schätzpreis (m)   estimated price
Schätzung (f)   appraisal, estimate
Schatzwechsel (pl)   treasury bills
Schätzwert (m)   estimated price
Schaubild (n)   flow chart

Schaufensterdekoration (f)   window dressing
Scheck (m)   check
Scheckkonto (n)   checking account
Scheingewinn (m)   paper profit
Schicht (working hours) (f)   shift
Schiedsabkommen (n)   arbitration agreement

Schiedsrichter (m)   arbitrator
Schiedsverfahren (n)   arbitration
Schiffahrtsvertrag (m)   maritime contract

Schiffsfrachtvertrag (m)   affreightment
Schirmherr (m)   sponsor
Schlange stehen   stand in line (v)
schlecht bezahlt   underpaid
Schleuderausfuhr (f)   dumping (goods in foreign market)
Schlichtungsverfahren (n)   grievance procedure
schlüsselfertiger Vertrag (m)   turn-key contract
Schlüsselstellungen   key man insurance
Schlußkurs (m)   closing price
Schmiergeld (n)   kickback
Schmuggelwaren (pl)   prohibited goods
Schneeballverkaufssystem (n)   pyramid selling

Schnellspeicher (m)   direct access storage
Schnittwaren (f)   dry goods
Schriftführer (m)   secretary
schriftliche Vereinbarung (f)   written agreement

schriftlicher Vertrag (m)   written agreement
Schrottwert (m)   salvage value (junk, scrap)
Schubverarbeitung (f)   batch processing

Schuld (f)   debt
Schuldbetrag (m)   amount due
schuldenfrei   afloat (debt-free), free and clear (debt free)
Schuldentilgung (f)   retirement (debt)
Schuldschein (m)   promissory note

Schuldübernahme (f)   novation
Schuldverschreibung (f)   bond, debenture
Schuldverschreibungsvollmacht (f)   bond power

Schutentransport (m)   lighterage

schützen   safeguard (v)

Schutzmarke (f)   trademark

schutzzollbedürftige Industrie (f)   infant industry

Schutzzollsystem (n)   protectionism

schwacher Markt (m)   thin market

schwankende Einfuhrabschöpfung (f)   variable import levy

schwankender Kurs (m)   variable rate

Schwarzmarkt (m)   black market

schwebende Belastung (f)   floating charge

schwebende Schuld (f)   floating debt

Sehwemme (f)   glut

Schwerarbeiter (m)   manual worker

Schwergutaufschlag (m)   heavy lift charge

Schwerindustrie (f)   heavy industry

schwören   swear (v)

Seemeile (f)   knot (nautical)

Seetransportversicherung (f)   marine cargo insurance

Seeversicherer (m)   marine underwriter

Sekretärin (f)   secretary

selbständig   autonomous, self-employed

Selbstbedienung (f)   self-service

selbstfinanzieren   plow back earnings (v)

Selbstkosten (f)   actual costs, prime costs

Selbstschätzung (f)   self-appraisal

Sendung (f)   consignment, shipment

Serienanleihen (pl)   serial bonds

Serienproduktion (f)   batch production

Serienspeicherung (f)   serial storage

sich anmelden   check in (v)

sich einmischen   intervene (v)

sich gegen Verluste sichern   hedge (v)

sich gegenseitig beeinflussen   interact (v)

sich sammeln   rally (v)

Sicherheit (f)   collateral, security

Sicherheitskoeffizient (f)   margin of safety

sichtbare Handelsbilanz (f)   visible balance of trade

Sichteinlage (f)   demand deposit

Sichtwechsel (m)   bill of sight, sight draft

sieben   screen (v)

simulieren   simulate (v)

Sitzung (f)   meeting

Sitzungsraum (m)   boardroom

Sitzungssaal (m)   conference room

so bald wie möglich   as soon as possible

so schnell wie möglich   as soon as possible

Software (f)   software

Soll (n)   debit

Sollsaldo (m)   adverse balance

sonstige Verbindlichkeiten (pl)   other assets (other liabilities)

sonstiges Vermögen (n)   other assets (other liabilities)

Spanne (f)   spread

Sparbuch (n)   passbook

Sparkasse (f)   mutual savings bank, savings bank

Sparkonto (n)   savings account

Spediteur (m)   carrier, forwarding agent, shipping agent

Speicher des Computers (m)   computer memory

speichern   store (computer)

Speicherung (f)   storage (computer)

Spekulant (m)   speculator

Spekulativhändler (m)   scalper

Spesen (pl)   charges

Spesenkonto (n)   expense account

Spezialerzeugnisse (pl)   specialty goods

spezifizierte Rechnung (f)   itemized account

Spitzenbelastung (f)   peak load

Spitzenpreisansetzung (f)   premium pricing

Spitzenqualität (f)   top quality

Spontankauf (m)   impulse purchase

Spontanstreik (m)   wildcat strike

sprunghafte Börsenmarktlage (f)   volatile market

Sprungkosten (f)   semivariable costs

staatlicher Grundbesitz (m)   public domain

Staatsanleihen (pl)   government bonds, treasury bonds

Staatsbank (f) government bank, national bank
Staatseigentum (n) public property
Staatsobligationen (pl) treasury notes
Staatspapiere (pl) government bonds
Staatsschuldverschreibung (f) savings bond
Staatssozialismus (m) nationalism (economic)
Staatsverschuldung (f) national debt
Stab (m) staff
Stab und Linie staff and line
Stabsassistent (m) staff assistant
Stabsorganisation (f) staff organization
Stadtausbreitung (f) urban sprawl
Stadterneuerung (f) urban renewal
Staffelhypothek (f) variable rate mortgage
Staffeltarif (m) adjusted rate, flexible tariff
Stagflation (f) stagflation
Stahlkammer (f) safe deposit box
Stammaktie (f) capital stock, common stock
Stammkapital (n) corpus, ordinary capital
Standardabweichung (f) standard deviation
Standardbrief (m) form letter
Stapelverarbeitung (f) batch processing
starre Nachfrage inelastic demand
starres Angebot inelastic supply
starten take off (v)
Statistik (f) statistics
Statut (n) charter (written instrument), law
Statuten (pl) by-laws
Stauerlohn (m) stowage charges
Staulücken (pl) broken stowage
steigern maximize (v)
Steigerungsklausel (f) escalator clause
Stellage (f) straddle
Stellagegeschäft (n) put and call
Stellenbeschreibung (f) job description
Stellenvermittlung (f) placement (personnel)
Stellenvermittlungsbüro (n) employment agency
stellvertretender Generaldirektor (m) assistant general manager

stellvertretender Geschäftsführer (m) assistant manager, deputy manager

stellvertretender Vorsitzender (m) deputy chairman

Steuer (f) duty, tax

Steuerabzug (m) tax deduction

steuerbegünstigte Anlagemöglichkeit (f) tax shelter

Steuerbremse (f) fiscal drag

Steuereinnehmer (m) tax collector

steuerfrei tax-free

Steuerfreibetrag (m) exemption (tax exemption), tax allowance

steuerfreies Einkommen (n) tax-free income

Steuerhinterziehung (f) tax evasion

Steuerknüppel (m) joystick

Steuerlast (f) tax burden

steuerliche Veranlagung (f) assessed valuation

Steuern erheben levy taxes (v)

Steuernachlaß (m) remission of a tax

Steuernachlaß (m) tax abatement

Steueroase (f) tax haven

steuerpflichtig liable for tax

steuerpflichtige Bruttoeinkommen (n) adjusted gross income

Steuerrückstände (pl) back taxes

Steuerschulden (pl) accrued taxes

Steuervergünstigung (f) tax allowance, tax relief

Steuerzahler (m) taxpayer

Steuerzuschlag (m) surtax

Stichprobe (f) random sample

Stichprobenprüfung (f) acceptance sampling

Stichprobenumfang (m) sample size

Stichtag (m) deadline

Stiftung (f) endowment

stiller Gesellschafter (m) silent partner

stille Reserve (f) hidden asset

Stilliegen (n) down period (factory)

stillschweigendes Einverständnis (n) implied-agreement

stimmaktiviert voice-activated

Stimmrecht (n) voting right

Stimmrechtsermächtigung (f) proxy

Störung (f) bug (computers)

Störungen auffinden und beseitigen troubleshoot (v)

Strafklausel (f) penalty clause

Straftat (f) tort

Strafverfahren wegen Unterschlagung (n) penalty-fraud action

strategische Artikel (pl) strategic articles

Streikbrecher (m) strikebreaker

streiken strike (v)

Streikpostenkette (f) picket line

Streit (m) dispute

streiten dispute (v)

Streßbewältigung (f) stress management

Stromverbrauch (m) power consumption

Stück (n) part

Stückarbeit (f) piecework

Stückgutfracht (f) berth terms

Stückgutsendung (f) less-than-carload

Stückkosten (pl) unit costs

Stückpreis (m) unit price

Stückzoll (m) specific duty

Studie (f) analysis

stufenweise einführen phase in (v)

stufenweise einstellen phase out (v)

Stundenlohn (m) hourly earnings

Stundung (f) moratorium

Stützkurs (m) pegged price

Stützpreis (m) pegged price

Submissionsgarantie (f) performance bond

Subunternehmer (m) subcontractor

Subvention (f) price support, subsidy

Suchanzeige (f) want-ad

Suche nach Führungskräften (f) executive search

Syndikat (n) syndicate

synthetische Stoffe (pl) manmade

Systemanalyse (f) systems analysis

Systemerarbeitung (f) systems engineering

Systemgestaltung (f) systems design

Systemsteuerung (f) systems management

T

Tagesauftrag (m) day order

Tagesbestellung (f) order of the day

Tagesgeld (n) day loan

Tagesordnung (f) agenda

Tagesordnungspunkt (m) point of order

täglich daily

täglich kündbares Geld (n) call money

tägliches Geld (n) demand deposit

Tagung (f) meeting

Tanker (m) tanker

Tarif (m) tariff

Tarifstreitigkeit (f) labor dispute

Tarifverhandlungen (pl) collective bargaining

Tarifvertrag (m) collective agreement, union contract

tatsächlicher Gesamtverlust (m) actual total loss

tatsächliche Haftpflicht (f) actual liability

tauschen barter (v), exchange (v)

Tauschhandel (m) barter

Tauschmittel (n) medium of exchange

Tauschwert (m) exchange value

technisch technical

Technologie (f) technology

Teil (m) part

Teilfracht (f) part cargo

Teilhaber (m) partner, shareholder

Teilhaberschaft (f) partnership

Teilladung (f) part cargo

Teilwert (m) going concern value

Teilzahlung (f) partial payment

Teilzahlungskredit (m) installment credit

Teilzahlungsplan (m) installment plan

Telefon (n) telephone

Telegramm (n) cable, telegram

telegraphische Überweisung (f) cable transfer, wire transfer

Telekommunikation (f) telecommunications

Telex (n) telex
Tendenz (f) trend
Terminabschluss (m) forward contract
Terminal (n) terminal
Termindeckung (f) forward margin
Termingeschäfte (pl) futures
Terminkauf (m) forward purchase
Terminmarkt (m) forward market
Terminoption (f) futures option
Terminsendung (f) forward shipment
Testament (n) will
Testamentsanhang (m) codicil
Testamentseröffnung und Bestätigung (f) probate
Testamentsvollstrecker (m) executor (of an estate)
Textilien (pl) dry goods, soft goods
Textverarbeitungsgerät (n) word processor
thesaurieren hoard (v)
thesaurierte Gewinne (pl) retained earnings
tilgen pay off (v)
Tilgung (f) amortization
Tilgungsfonds (m) redemption fund, sinking fund
tilgungsfreie Zeit (f) grace period
Tochtergesellschaft (f) affiliate, associate company, subsidiary
Tonnage (f) tonnage
Topmanagement (n) management, top management
Totalverlust (m) total loss
tragen bear (v)
Tranche (f) tranche
Transitkonnossement (n) through bill of lading
Transitlager (n) bonded warehouse
transitorische Passiva (pl) unearned revenue
Transport (m) transportation
Transporthaftung (f) carrier's risk
Transportunternehmer (m) carrier
Tratte (f) draft
Trennung (f) separation

treuer Gehilfe (treue Gehilfin) (m)   man (gal)
  Friday
Treuhänder (m)   fiduciary, trustee
treuhänderisches Darlehen (n)   fiduciary loan
Treuhandfonds (m)   trust fund
Treuhandgesellschaft (f)   trust company
Treuhandkonto (n)   escrow account
Treuhandverhältnis (n)   trust
Treuhandverhältnis unter Lebenden (n)   living trust
Treuhandvertrag (m)   deed of trust, escrow
Trockenladung (f)   dry cargo

U

über dem Strich   above-the-line
über der Linie   above-the-line
über Nacht   overnight
über pari   above par
Überalterung (f)   obsolescence
Uberangebot (n)   glut, oversupply
Überbetrag (m)   overage
Überbewerten   overvalue (v)
Überbieten   outbid (v)
Übereinkommen (n)   understanding (agreement)
Übereinstimmung (f)   agreement
überfällig   overdue, past due
Überfluß (m)   overstock
überfordern   overcharge (v)
übergreifen   overlap
übergroße Artikel (f)   outsized articles
überhängen   overhang
überkapitalisiert   overcapitalized
überlangen   overlap
überlappen   overlap
Überliegezeit (f)   demurrage (period of)
Übernahme (f)   buyout, takeover
Übernahmeangebot (n)   takeover bid
Übernehmer (m)   assignee
übernommene Verpflichtung (f)   assumed liability
Überraschungsanruf (m)   cold call

Überschlagsrechnung (f)   rough estimate
Übersetzer (m)   translator
Überstunden (f)   overtime
Übertrag (m)   transfer
übertragbar   negotiable (convertible, transferable)
übertragbare Wertpapiere (pl)   negotiable securities
übertragen   assign (v), carry forward (v), transfer (v)
Übertragungsurkunde (f)   deed of transfer
überweisen   transfer
Überzahlung (f)   overpayment
überzeichnen   oversubscribe (v)
Überziehung (f)   overdraft
üblicher Satz (m)   going rate (going price)
übliches Verfahren (n)   standard practice
Übrige (n)   remainder
Umfang (m)   volume
umgekehrter Markt (m)   inverted market
Umlagekosten (pl)   joint cost
Umlaufsvermögen (n)   working capital, liquid assets
Umorganisierung (f)   reorganization
Umsatz (m)   sales
Umsatzrendite (f)   return on sales
Umsatzschätzung (f)   sales estimate
Umsatzselbstkosten (pl)   cost of goods sold
Umsatzsteuer (f)   sales tax
umschichten   restructure (v)
Umschlag (m)   turnover
Umschreibstelle für Effekten (f)   tranfer
umstrukturieren   restructure (v)
umwandeln in eine Aktiengesellschaft   go public (v)
Umwertung (f)   revaluation
Umzugskosten (pl)   moving expenses
unabhängiger Arbeitsplatz (m)   stand-alone workstation
unbefristete Order (f)   open order
unbegleitete Waren (pl)   unaccompanied goods
unbeschränktes Akzept (n)   general acceptance
Unbeständigkeit (f)   instability
unbezahlte Rechnung (f)   delinquent account

undurchführbar   unfeasible

uneinbringliche Forderung (f)   bad debt

uneinbringliche Forderungen (pl)   uncollectible accounts

uneingeschränkte Urkunde (f)   clean document

unentwickelt   undeveloped

unerwarteter Gewinn (m)   windfall profit

Unfallschaden (m)   accident damage

Unfallversicherung (f)   casualty insurance

unfundierte Schuld (f)   floating debt

ungefähr schätzen   guesstimate

ungelernte Arbeitskräfte (pl)   unskilled labor

ungenutzte Kapazität (f)   idle capacity

ungerade Menge (f)   odd lot

ungesicherte Anleihe (f)   unsecured loan

ungesicherte Haftung (f)   unsecured liability

ungleichartige Stichprobenauswahl (f)   mixed sampling

ungültig   void

ungültig machen   invalidate (v)

ungünstig   unfavorable

unlauterer Wettbewerb (m)   unfair competition

unmittelbar geleistete Arbeitszeit (f)   direct labor

unmittelbare Aufwendungen (pl)   direct expenses

unreines Konnossement (n)   foul bill of lading

unseren Erwartungen entsprechend   up to our expectations

unsichtbar   invisible

unter dem Strich   below the line

unter der Norm   substandard

unter pari   below par

unterbewerten   undervalue (v)

unterbezahlt   underpaid

unterbieten   undercut (v)

unterkapitalisiert   undercapitalized

Unterlassungsversprechen (n)   negative pledge

Unterlieferant (m)   jobber

unternehmen   undertake (v)

Unternehmen (n)   enterprise

Unternehmensberater (m)   management consultant

Unternehmenswachstum (n)   corporate growth
Unternehmer (m)   entrepreneur
Unterpacht (f)   sublease
Unterredung (f)   interview
unterrichten   instruct (v) (teach)
unterschätzen   underestimate (v)
Unterschlagung (f)   embezzlement
Unterschrift (f)   signature
Unterstützungstätigkeiten (pl)   support activities
Untersuchung (f)   analysis, inspection
Untervermietung (f)   sublease
Unterversorgung (f)   short supply
unterwegs   in transit
unterzeichnet   undersigned
unvorhergesehene Ausgaben (pl)   contingencies
unvorteilhaft   unfavorable
unzulänglich   inadequate
unzureichende Aktiva (pl)   insufficient assets
Urheberrecht (n)   copyright
Urkunde (f)   deed, document, instrument (document)
Urlaub (m)   leave of absence
ursprüngliche Fälligkeit (f)   original maturity
Ursprungsland (n)   country of origin
Ursprungszeugnis (n)   certificate of origin
Urteil (n)   adjudication

V

validieren   validate (v)
variabler Erlösüberschuß (m)   variable margin
Verabredung (f)   appointment (engagement)
Veralten (n)   obsolescence
veralteter Scheck (m)   stale check
veränderliche Jahresrente (f)   variable annuity
veränderliche Kosten (pl)   variable costs
veränderliche Parität (f)   moving parity, sliding parity
Veränderung (f)   variance
Veranlagung (f)   assessment
verantwortlich   liable to (responsible)

Verantwortung des Käufers (f)   buyer's responsibility

Verantwortungsverteilung (f)   allocation of responsibilities

verarbeiten   process

verbessern   improve upon (v)

Verbesserung (f)   improvement

Verbindung (f)   liaison

Verbraucher (m)   consumer

Verbraucherannahme (f)   consumer acceptance

Verbraucherforschung (f)   consumer research

Verbraucherpreisindex (m)   consumer price index

Verbraucherzufriedenstellung (f)   consumer satisfaction

Verbrauchsabgabe (f)   excise duty

Verbrauchsgüter (pl)   nondurable goods

Verbrauchssteuer (f)   excise tax

verbriefte Rechte (pl)   vested rights

verbriefte Schuld (f)   funded debt

verbuchen   (bookkeeping) post (v)

Verderb (m)   spoilage

Verdienst (m)   profit

Verdienstspanne (f)   margin, profit margin

verdrängen   supersede (v)

vereidigen   swear

Vereinbarung (f)   agreement, settlement, implied agreement

Vereinbarung auf Treu und Glauben (f)   gentleman's agreement

Vereinheitlichung (f)   standardization

Vereinigung (f)   amalgamation, combination, merger

Verfahren (n)   method

Verfahrensfrage (f)   point of order

Verfall (m)   maturity

Verfalltag (m)   expiry date, maturity date

verfolgen   follow up (v)

verfügbares Bargeld (n)   ready cash

verfügbares Einkommen (n)   disposable income

Vergleichsjahr (n)   base year

vergrössern   enlarge (v)

Vergütung für leitende Angestellte (f) executive compensation

Vergütung (f) compensation, gratuity, remuneration

Verhältnis (n) ratio

verhandeln negotiate (v)

Verhandlung (f) negotiation

verhandlungsfähig negotiable (subject to discussion)

Verhandlungspaket (n) package deal

Verhandlungsstärke (f) bargaining power

Verkauf (m) marketing

Verkauf durch Versandgeschäft (m) mail-order sales

Verkauf durch Vertreter (m) door-to-door sales

Verkauf gegen Barzahlung und Selbstabholung (m) cash-and-carry

verkaufen market, sell (v)

verkaufen und anschließend mieten sell and lease back

Verkäufer (m) vendor

Verkaufsagent (m) distributor

Verkaufsbedingungen (pl) terms of sale

Verkaufsforderung (f) sales promotion

Verkaufsgebühr (f) load (sales charge)

Verkaufsoption (f) put option

Verkaufspersonal (n) sales force

Verkaufsprognose (f) sales forecast

Verkaufspunkt (m) point of sale

Verkaufsquote (f) sales quota

Verkaufsstelle (f) outlet

Verkaufstermin (m) on-sale date

Verkaufsurkunde (f) bill of sale

Verkaufsvolumen (n) sales volume

Verkehrswesen (n) transportation

Verladekosten (pl) shipping expenses

verlangen demand (v)

Verlängerungsabschnitt (m) allonge

Verleumdung (f) libel

Verlust (m) loss

Verlustsaldo (m) adverse balance

Verlustvortrag (m) carryover

Vermächtnis (n) bequest, legacy
vermehren increase (v)
Vermehrung (f) increase
vermieten rent (v) (rent to)
Vermieter (m) lessor
Verminderung (f) cutback
Vermischtes miscellaneous
Vermittler (m) intermediary, middleman
Vermittlung (f) mediation
Vermögen (n) wealth
Vermögensstück (n) asset
Vermögensübertragung gegen Aktien (f) spin off
Vermögensumsatz (m) asset turnover
Vermögensverwalter (m) trustee
Vermögensverwaltung (f) portfolio management
Vermögenswert (m) asset value
vermuten guesstimate (v), project (v)
verpachten farm out (v)
Verpackung (f) packaging
Verpfändung (f) hypothecation
Verpflichtung (f) commitment, obligation
Verringerungskontrolle (f) depletion control
versammeln assemble (v) (people)
Versammlung (f) assembly, meeting
Versand (m) dispatch
Versandanweisungen (pl) shipping instructions
Versandbehälter (m) shipping container
Versandhandel (m) mail order
Versandkosten (pl) shipping charges
Verschiedenes miscellaneous
Verschleiß (m) wear and tear
Verschuldung (f) indebtedness
Versender (m) shipper, shipping agent
Versicherer (m) insurance underwriter
versicherter Bote (m) bonded carrier
Versicherung (f) insurance
Versicherung auf Zeit (f) term insurance
Versicherung für Personen in Schlüsselstellungen (f)
  key man insurance

Versicherungsbeitrag (m)   insurance premium
Versicherungsgesellschaft (f)   insurance company
Versicherungskasse (f)   insurance fund
Versicherungsmakler (m)   insurance broker
Versicherungsmathematiker (m)   actuary
Versicherungspolice (f)   insurance policy
Versicherungsprämie (f)   insurance premium
Versicherungsschutz (m)   coverage (insurance)
Versicherungsstatistiker (m)   actuary
Versicherungswert (m)   actual cash value
versiegeltes Angebot (n)   sealed bid
versorgen   service (v)
Versorgungsbetrieb (m)   public utility, utility
Verstaatlichung (f)   nationalization
Verstauung (f)   stowage
verteilen   allot (v)
Verteiler (m)   distributor
Verteilung (f)   allotment
Verteilungsbogen (m)   spreadsheet
Verteilungsnetz (n)   distribution network
vertikale Verflechtung (f)   vertical integration
Vertrag (m)   agreement (written), contract, covenant (promises), treaty
vertraglicher Frachtführer (m)   contract carrier
vertragsgemäß arbeiten   work by contract
Vertragsmonat (m)   contract month
Vertragspartei (f)   party (contract)
Vertragsurkunde (f)   indenture
Vertrauensorder (f)   discretionary order
vertraulich   confidential
vertreiben   market (v)
vertretbar   fungible
Vertreter (m)   agent, representative
Vertreter des Fiskus (m)   fiscal agent
Vertretung (f)   agency
Vertretungsgebühr (f)   agency fee
Vertrieb (m)   marketing
Vertriebshändler (m)   distributor
Vertriebskosten (pl)   distribution costs

Vertriebsleitung (f) sales management

Vertriebspolitik (f) distribution policy

verwalten manage (v) (administrate)

Verwalter (m) administrator, manager

Verwaltung (f) administration, management

Verwaltungsbehörde (f) government agency

Verwaltungsgebühr (f) management fee

Verwaltungskosten (pl) administrative expenses

verwaltungsmäßig administrative

verweigerte Zahlung (f) payment, refused

Verwicklung (f) implication (involvement)

verzeichnen index (v)

Verzeichnung (f) listing

Verzichtsklausel (f) waiver clause

Verzinsung (return on capital) (f) interest

Verzinsungszeitraum (m) interest period

Verzögerung (f) delay

Veto (n) veto

Vizepräsident (m) vice-president

Volkswirtschaftslehre (f) economics

voll bezahlt paid in full

voll eingezahltes Kapital (n) paid up capital

volle Zahlung (f) payment in full

völlig gedeckte Anleihe (f) back-to-back loan

völliger Stillstand (m) deadlock

Vollmacht (f) power of attorney

Vollmacht haben (f) authority, to have (v)

Vollmachtsformular (n) proxy statement

Vollmachtsüberschreitung (f) ultra vires act

vollständig bezahlen pay up (v)

vollständiger Ausgleich (m) settlement in full

Vollversammlung (f) plenary meeting

Volumen (n) volume

Voluntär (m) trainee

Vorankündigung (f) advance notice

Voranschlag (m) rough estimate

Vorarbeiter (m) foreman

vorausbezahlte Fracht (f) advance freight, freight prepaid

Vorausbezahlung (f)   cash in advance
Vorausbezahlung der (f)   front-end financing
vorausgezahlte Aufwendungen (f)   prepaid expenses (balance sheet)
voraussagen   forecast
voraussichtliche Abfahrt (f)   estimated time of departure
voraussichtliche Ankunft (f)   estimated time of arrival
vorauszahlen   prepay (v)
Vorauszahlung (f)   advance payment
vorbehaltich der Verfügbarkeit   subject to availability
vorbehaltlos   down the line
vorbeugende Instandhaltung (f)   preventive maintenance
Vorbilanz (f)   trial balance
Vorbild (n)   model
Vorentwurf (m)   rough draft
Vorfahrt (f)   right of way
Vorfertigung (f)   modular production
Vorfertigung (f)   prefabrication
vorgeben   simulate (v)
Vorhaben (n)   project
Vorindikator (m)   leading indicator
Vorkaufsrecht (n)   preemptive right
vorläufig   temporary
Vorlaufzeit (f)   lead time
Vorprospekt (m)   preliminary prospectus
Vorrang (m)   priority
Vorrat (m)   inventory, stock
Vorratsaktien (pl)   treasury stock
Vorratskauf (m)   stock purchase
vorsätzliche Ladungsbeschädigung (f)   barratry
Vorschau (f)   forecast
vorschießen   advance (v) (money)
Vorschrift (f)   regulation
Vorschriften (pl)   by-laws
Vorschriften über die Anstellung von Frauen und Minoritäten (pl)   affirmative action
Vorsitzender (m)   president

Vorstand (m) board of directors, executive board

Vorstandsmitglied (n) director

Vorstandssitzung (f) board meeting

Vorstandsvorsitzender (m) chief executive, chairman of the board

vortragen carry forward (v)

vorübergehend temporary

Vorvertrag (m) binder

vorzeitig kündbarer Kredit (m) call loan

Vorzugsaktie (f) preferred stock

Vorzugsaktien erster Ausgabe (pl) first preferred stock

Vorzugsrecht (n) priority

Vorzugszoll (m) preferential tariff

W

Wachstum (n) growth

Wachstumsaktie (f) growth stock

Wachstumsgebiet (n) growth area

Wachstumsindex (m) growth index

Wachstumsindustrie (f) growth industry

Wachstumspotential (n) growth potential

Wachstumsrate (f) rate of growth

Wagenladung (f) carload

Wagenpark (m) rolling stock

Wagniskapital (n) venture capital

Währung (f) currency

Währungseinheit (f) monetary standard

Währungsgruppe (f) currency band

Währungsklausel (f) currency clause

Währungskredite (pl) monetary credits

Währungsrisiko (n) exchange risk

Wandelobligationen (pl) convertible debentures

Waren (pl) goods, merchandise, field warehousing

Waren ohne Gewähr (pl) as is goods

Waren unter Zollverschluß (pl) bonded goods

Warenanalyse (f) product analysis

Warenbestand (m) stock-in-trade

Warenbörse (f) commodity exchange

Warenhaus (n) department store

Warenüberschuß (m) surplus goods

Warenumsatz (m) sales turnover

Warenwechsel (m) trade acceptance

Wartekosten (pl) opportunity cost

Wartezeit (f) attended time

Wartung (f) maintenance

Wartungsvertrag (m) maintenance contract

Wechsel (m) acceptance bill, bank draft, bill of exchange

Wechselbank (f) acceptance house

Wechseldiskont (m) exchange discount

Wechselkredit (m) acceptance credit

Wechselkurs (m) exchange rate

Wechselmakler (m) bill broker

wechselnde Kosten (pl) controllable costs

Wechselprotest (m) protest (banking, law)

Wechselreiterei (f) kiting

Wechselstube (f) money shop

weiche Verkaufstour (f) soft sell

weiche Währung (f) soft currency

Weise (f) mode

Weiterverkauf (m) resale

Weiterverkaufsgewinner (m) scalper

Weltbank (f) World Bank

Weltwährungsfonds (m) International Monetary Fund

Werbeagentur (f) advertising agency

Werbebudget (n) advertising budget

Werbeetat (m) advertising budget

Werbeforschung (f) advertising research

Werbekampagne (f) advertising campaign

Werbekosten (pl) advertising expenses

Werbeleiter (m) advertising manager

Werbesendung (f) commercial (broadcasting)

Werbetext (m) copy (advertising text)

Werbetextprüfung (f) copy testing

Werbeträger (f) advertising media, mass media, media

Werbung (f) advertisement

Werkleiter (m) plant manager

Werkmeister (m)   foreman

Werkstatt (f)   workshop

Werkstoffe (pl)   materials

Werksvertreter (m)   manufacturer's agent

Werkzeuge (pl)   tools

Wert (m)   value

Wertanalyse (f)   value engineering

Wertberichtigung auf das Anlagevermögen (f)   accumulated depreciation

wertlos   worthless

Wertpapier nachgeordneter Sicherheit (n)   junior security

Wertpapierberater (m)   account executive

Wertpapiere   securities

Wertpapieremissionsanzeige (f)   tombstone advertisement

Wertpapierhandel (securities) (m)   secondary market

Wertplanungstechnik (f)   value engineer

Wertsteigerung (f)   appreciation

Wertzoll (m)   ad valorem duty

Wertzuwachs (m)   appreciation

Wettbewerbsstrategie (f)   competitive strategy

Wettbewerbsvorteil (m)   competitive advantage

widerrufliches Treuhandverhältnis (n)   revocable trust

wieder ausführen   reexport (v)

wiederaufnehmen   resume (v)

Wiederbeschaffungskosten (pl)   replacement cost

Wiedererlangung (f)   recovery

Wiederherstellung (f)   reproduction

Wiederholungsauftrag (m)   repeat order

Wiederinbesitznahme (f)   repossession

Wiederverkauf (m)   resale

wilder Streik (m)   wildcat strike

Wille (m)   will

Wink (m)   tip (inside information)

wirken auf   impact on (v)

wirkungslos   inefficient

wirtschaftlich   economic

wirtschaftliche Lebensdauer (f)   economic life

wirtschaftliche Nutzungsdauer (f)   economic life

wirtschaftliche Unabhängigkeit (f)   autarchy

Wirtschaftslehre (f)   economics

Wirtschaftsprüfer (m)   accountant (CPA), certified public accountant, chartered accountant

Wirtschaftsteil (m)   financial pages, newspaper

Wissen (n)   know-how

wohlerworbene Rechte (pl)   vested interests

Wohn- und Industriebaubestimmungen (pl)   zoning laws

Wohnungsamt (n)   housing authority (residential)

Wucher (m)   usury

Z

zahlbar bei Sicht   payable on demand

zahlen   pay (v)

zahlenmäßige Steuerung (f)   numerical control

Zahler (m)   payer

Zahlung (f)   payment

Zahlung bei Lieferung (f)   cash on delivery

Zahlung verweigern (f)   refuse payment (v)

Zahlungen einstellen (pl)   suspend payment (v)

Zahlungsanweisung (f)   money order

Zahlungsaufschub (m)   moratorium

Zahlungsbestätigung (f)   acknowledgement of payment

Zahlungsbilanz (f)   balance of payments

Zahlungsempfänger (m)   payee

Zahlungsfähigkeit (f)   ability-to-pay concept

Zahlungsfähigkeit (f)   solvency

Zahlungshaushalt (m)   cash budget

Zahlungsmeister (m)   paymaster

zahlungsunfähig   insolvent

zahlungsunfähig werden   default (v)

Zeichnungsangebot (n)   prospectus

Zeichnungspreis (m)   subscription price (securities)

Zeit- und Bewegungsstudie (f)   time and motion study

Zeitplan (m)   schedule, timetable

Zeitraum (m)   period (time)

Zeitwechsel (m)   time bill of exchange

zeitweilig   temporary

zeitweilig nicht einlösbare Aktiva (pl)   deferred assets

Zeitzone (f)   time zone

Zentralbank (f)   central bank, government bank, national bank

Zentrale (f)   head office, headquarters

Zentralisierung (f)   centralization

Zentralrecheneinheit (f)   central processing unit

Zentralwert (m)   median

Zeuge (m)   witness

Zeugnis (n)   certificate

Zins (m)   interest

Zinsabschnitt (m)   coupon (bond interest)

Zinsarbitrage (f)   interest arbitrage

Zinsaufwendungen (pl)   interest expenses

zinsbegünstigtes Darlehen (n)   soft loan

Zinsertrag (m)   interest income

Zinseszins (m)   compound interest

Zinsfuß (m)   rate of interest

Zinskoupon (m)   coupon (bond interest)

Zinssatz (m)   interest rate, rate of return

Zivilklage (f)   civil action

Zivilunrecht (n)   tort

Zoll (m)   customs, customs duty, tariff

Zollagent (m)   customs broker

Zollagerhaus (n)   bonded warehouse

Zollangleichung (f)   tariff adjustment

Zolleinnehmer (m)   customs collector

Zolleinstufung (f)   tariff classification

Zollerklärung (f)   customs entry

Zollerlaß (m)   remission of a customs duty

zollfrei   dutyfree

Zollgebühr (f)   customs duty

Zollgebühr (f)   tariff charge

Zollkrieg (m)   tariff war

Zollpapier für vorübergehende zollfreie Einfuhr (n)   carnet

zollpflichtige Waren (pl)   bonded goods

Zollschranken (pl)   tariff barriers

Zollspeicher (m)   bonded warehouse

Zollunterschied (m)   tariff differential

Zollverein (m)   customs union

Zollware (f)   tariff commodity

Zollwert (m)   value for duty

Zone (f)   zone

zu den Akten legen   file (v) (papers)

zu pari   at par

zu stark gekauft   overbought

zu stark verkauft   oversold

Zuerstentnahme der älteren Vorräte (f)   first in-first out (FIFO)

Zuerstentnahme der neuen Vorräte (f)   last in-first out (LIFO)

Zuführungsverhältnis (n)   feed ratio

Zugabenangebot (n)   premium offer

Zugartikel (m)   loss leader

zugeschrieben   imputed

Zulassungsschein (m)   permit

Zulieferant (m)   subcontractor

zum Bestkauf   at or better

zum Marktpreis   at the market price

zum Nennwert   at par

zum Verkauf anbieten   offer for sale

zur Ausfuhr   for export

zur Emissionszeit   when issued

zur Verfügung stellen   make available (v)

Zurichtung (f)   make-ready

zurückbehaltene Gewinne (pl)   retained profits

Zurückbehaltungsrecht des Handwerkers (n)   mechanic's lien

zurückbringen   carry back (v)

zurückdatieren   back date (v)

zurückgestellte Steuerzahlung (f)   deferred tax

zurückkaufen   buy back (v)

Zurücknahme (f)   withdrawal

zurückrufen   call back (v)

Zurückstufung (f)   demotion

zurücktragen   carry back (v)

zurückzahlen   reimburse (v), repay (v)

Zurückzahlungszeitraum (m)   payback period

zusammenlegen   pool (v)

Zusatz (m)   addendum

Zusatzdividende (f)   extra dividend

Zusatzklausel (contracts) (f)   rider

Zusatzleistungen (pl)   fringe benefits

Zusatzsteuer (f)   surtax

Zuschuß (m)   allowance (subsidy)

zustammenstellen   assemble (v) (things)

Zustellung (f)   delivery

Zustimmung (f)   approval, endorsement (approval),
   implied-agreement

Zuteilungsschein (m)   allotment letter

zuverlässige Quelle (f)   reliable source

zuviel fordern   overcharge

Zuwachs (m)   accretion

Zuwachsrate (f)   growth rate, rate of increase

zuweisen   allot (v), assign (v)

Zuweisung (f)   allotment

zuzüglich aufgelaufener Zinsen   plus accrued interest

Zwang (m)   duress

Zwangseinziehung (f)   mandatory redemption

Zweck-Gebrauch Schein (m)   end-use certificate

zweckgebundene Anleihe (f)   tied loan

zweckmäßig   practical

Zweiggeschäft (n)   branch office

Zweigstelle (f)   branch office

Zweigstellenunternehmen (n)   chain store group

zweistufiger Markt (m)   two-tiered market

zweite Hypothek (f)   second mortgage

zweitrangig   second rate

zweitstellig   second position

zwischen Banken   interbank

Zwischenabschluß (m)   interim statement

Zwischenbilanz (f)   interim statement

Zwischenhändler (m)   middleman, purchasing agent

Zwischenhaushalt (m)   interim budget

zwischenstaatlicher Handel (m)   interstate commerce

Zwischenwaren (pl)   intermediary goods

zwischenzeitlich   interim

Chemicals — German to English

Ammoniak (n) ammonia

Analyse (f) analysis

analytische Chemie (f) analytic chemistry

anfallen yield (v)

Äthan (n) ethane

Äther (m) ether

Atom (n) atom

atomar atomic

atomisch atomic

(Auf) Lösung (f) solution

aufgelöste Stoff (m) solute

Azetatsäure (f) acetic acid

Base (f) base

Benzol (n) benzene

Biochemie (f) biochemistry

Biologe (m) biologist

Biologie (f) biology

Chemie (f) chemistry

chemisch chemical

Chlorid (n) chloride

Chloroform (n) chloroform

Dichte (f) density

Dosierung (f) dosage

Dosis (f) dosage

einbringen yield (v)

Elektrolyse (f) electrolysis

Elektron (n) electron

Element (n) element

Enzym (n) enzyme

Erdöl (n) petroleum

Experiment (n) experiment

experimentell experimental

Formel (f) formula

Forschung (f) research

Gemisch (n) compound

Grad (m) degree

Grammolekül (n) mole

Homogenität (f) homogeneity

Hydrolyse (f) hydrolysis

Ingenieur (m) engineer

Isotop (n) isotope

Katalysator (m) catalyst

Kohlenstoff (m) carbon

Kohlenwasserstoff (m) hydrocarbon

Komponente (f) component

Kozentration (f) concentration

Krachverfahren (n) cracking

Kristallisierung (f) crystalization

Labor (n) laboratory

Löslichkeit (f) solubility

Lösungsmittel (n) solvent

Maßanalyse (f) titration

Naturgas (n) natural gas

organische Chemie (f) organic chemistry

Phosphat (n) phosphate

polymeren Körper (f) polymer

Produkt (n) product

Purifikation (f) purification

Raffinerie (f) refinery

raffinieren refine (v)

Raffinierung (f) refinery

Reagenzglas (n) test tube

Reduktion (f) reduction

Reinigung (f) purification

Säure (f) acid

Salpetersäure (f) nitric acid

Salz (n) salt

Salzsäure (f) hydrochloric acid

Schwefelsäure (f) sulfuric acid

Titrierung (f) titration

unorganische Chemie (f) inorganic chemistry

Unreinheit (f) impurity

Verbindung (f) compound

Verbrennungshilfsstoff (m) reactant

Verdampfung (f) evaporation

veredeln refine (v)

Verseifung (f) saponification

Zusammensetzung (f) composition

Chinaware and Tableware — English to German

bone china das feine Porzellan
bowl die Schale
breadbasket der Brotkorb
butter dish die Butterdose
candlestick der Kerzenständer
carving knife das Tranchiermesser
champagne glass das Sektglas, das Champagnerglas
cheese-tray das Käsebrett
china das Porzellan
chinaware die Porzellanwaren, das Porzellan
coffeepot die Kaffekanne
crystal glass manufacturing die Kristallglasherstellung
cup die Tasse
cutlery das Eßbesteck
decanter die Karaffe
dessert plate der Dessertteller
dinner plate der Teller
dish die Schüssel, der Teller
earthenware die Töpferware
espresso cup die Espressotasse
flute die Flöte
fork die Gabel
glass das Glas
gravy boat die Soßenschüssel
hand-painted handbemalt
hand-blown glass das handgeblasene Glas

knife das Messer
lace die Spitze
linen das Leinen
napkin die Serviette
napkin ring der Serviettenring
oilcloth das Wachstuch
pastry server der Tortenheber
pepper mill die Pfeffermühle
pepper shaker der Pfefferstreuer
pitcher der Krug, die Kanne
place setting die Tischordnung
plate der Teller
pottery die Töpferware
salad plate der Salatteller
salt shaker der Salzstreuer
saucer die Untertasse
silverware das Tafelsilber
soup dish der Suppenteller
spoon der Löffel
stoneware das Steingut
sugar bowl die Zuckerdose
tablespoon der Eßlöffel
tablecloth das Tischtuch
teapot die Teekanne
teaspoon der Teelöffel
thread der Faden, das Garn
tureen die Terrine
unbleached linen das ungebleichte Leinen

Major China and Tableware Areas

China
Selb (and environs)
Crystal
Upper Bavaria

Chinaware and Tableware— German to English

Brotkorb (m) breadbasket
Butterdose (f) butter dish
Champagnerglas (n) champagne glass
Dessertteller (m) dessert plate
Espressotasse (f) espresso cup
Eßbesteck (n) cutlery
Eßlöffel (m) tablespoon
Faden (m) thread
Flöte (f) flute
Gabel (f) fork
Garn (n) fork
Glass (n) glass
handbemalt hand-painted
handgeblasene Glas (n) hand-blown glass
Käsebrett (n) cheese-tray
Kanne (f) pitcher
Kaffekanne (f) coffeepot
Karaffe (f) decanter
Kerzenständer (m) candlestick
Kristallglasherstellung (f) crystal glass manufacturing
Krug (m) pitcher
Leinen (n) linen
Löffel (m) spoon
Messer (n) knife
Pfeffermühle (f) pepper mill
Pfefferstreuer (m) pepper shaker
Porzellan (n) china, chinaware

Porzellanwaren (pl) chinaware
Salatteller (m) salad plate
Salzstreuer (m) salt shaker
Schale (f) bowl
Schüssel (f) dish
Sektglass (n) champagne glass
Serviette (f) napkin
Serviettenring (m) napkin ring
Soßenschüssel (f) gravy boat
Spitze (f) lace
Steingut (n) stoneware
Suppenteller (m) soup dish
Tafelsilber (n) silverware
Tasse (f) cup
Teelöffel (m) teaspoon
Teller (m) plate, dinner plate, dish
Terrine (f) tureen
Tischordnung (f) place setting
Tischtuch (n) tablecloth
Teekanne (f) teapot
Töpferware (f) earthenware, pottery
Tortenheber (m) pastry server
Tranchiermesser (n) carving knife
Untertasse (f) saucer
ungebleichte Leinen (n) unbleached linen
Wachstuch (n) oilcloth
Zuckerdose (f) sugar bowl

Electronics — English to German

alternating current der Wechselstrom

amplifier der Verstärker

amplitude modulation (AM) die Amplitudenmodulation

beam die Strahlung, der Strahl

binary code der Binärkode

broadcast (v) senden, ausstrahlen

cable television das Kabelfernsehen

cassette die Kassette

cathode die Kathode

channel der Kanal

circuit die Schaltung, die Fernmeldverbindung

coaxial cable das Koaxialkabel

computer die Rechenanlage

condensor der Kondensator

current der Strom

direct current der Gleichstrom

electricity die Elektrizität

electrode die Elektrode

electron das Elektron

electronic elektronisch

electrostatic elektrostatisch

filter der Filter

frequency die Frequenz

frequency modulation (FM) die Frequenzmodulation

high fidelity die High-Fidelity

induction die Induktion

insulator der Isolator, das Isoliermittel

integrated circuit der integrierte Schaltkreis

kilowatt das Kilowatt

laser der Laser (strahl)

microphone das Mikrofon

microwave die Ultrakurzwelle, die Mikrowelle

optic optisch

oscillator der Oszillator

panel das Schaltfeld, der Schaltkasten

parallel circuit die Parallelschaltung

power die Arbeit (sleistung), die Kraft

printed circuit die gedruckte Schaltung

receiver der Empfänger

record die Schallplatte

record (v) aufnehmen

record player der Schallplattenspieler

resistance der Widerstand

resonance die Resonanz

scanning die (Bild) Abtastung

screen der Bildschirm

semiconductor der Halbleiter

short wave die Kurzwelle

silicon das Silicium

sound der Ton

speaker der Lautsprecher

sterophonic der Stereofon

switch die Umschaltung

tape recorder das Tonbandgerät

telecommunications die Telekommunikation, das Fernmeldewesen

tone der Ton, der Klang

transformer der Umwandler

transmitter der Sender, der Übermittler

tune einstellen (v)

videocassette player das Videokasettengerät

voltage die Stromspannung

wave die Welle, die Schwingung

wire der Draht, das Telegramm

Electronics — German to English

Abtastung (f) (Bild) scanning

Amplituden-modulation (f) amplitude modulation (AM)

Arbeitsleistung (f) power

aufnehmen record (v)

ausstrahlen broadcast (v)

Bildschirm (m) screen

Binärkode (m) binary code

Draht (m) wire

einstellen tune (v)

Elekrizität (f) electricity

Elektrode (f) electrode

Elektron (n) electron

elektronisch electronic

elektrostatisch electrostatic

Empfänger (m) receiver

Fernmeldewesen (n) telecommunications

Filter (m) filter

Frequenzmodulation (f) frequency modulation (FM)

Frequenz (f) frequency

gedruckte Schaltung (f) printed circuit

Gleichstrom (m) direct current

Halbleiter (m) semiconductor

High-Fidelity (f) high fidelity

Induktion (f) induction

integrierte Schaltkreis (m) integrated circuit

Isolator (m) insulator

Isoliermittel (n) insulator

Kabelfernsehen (n) cable television

Kanal (m) channel

Kassette (f) cassette

Kathode (f) cathode

Kilowatt (n) kilowatt

Klang (m) tone

Koaxialkabel (n) coaxial cable

Kondensator (m) condensor

Kraft (f) power

Kurzwelle (f) short wave

Laser (m) laser

Lautsprecher (m) speaker

Mikrofon (n) microphone

Mikrowelle (f) microwave

optisch optic

Oszillator (m) oscillator

Parallelschaltung (f) parallel circuit

Rechenanlage (f) computer

Resonanz (f) resonance

Schallplatte (f) record

Schallplattenspieler (m) record player

Schaltfeld (n) panel

Schaltkasten (m) panel

Schaltung (f) circuit

Schwingung (f) wave

senden broadcast (v)

Sender (m) transmitter

Silicium (n) silicon

Stereofon (m) sterophonic

Strahl (m) beam

Strahlung (f) beam

Strom (m) current

Stromspannung (f) voltage

Telegramm (n) wire

Telekommunikation (f) telecommunications

Ton (m) sound, tone

Tonbandgerät (n) tape recorder

Übermittler (m) transmitter

Ultrakurzwelle (f) microwave

Umschaltung (f) switch

Umwandler (m) transformer

Verstärker (m) amplifier

Videokasettengerät (n) videocassette player

Wechselstrom (m) alternating current

Welle (f) wave

Widerstand (m) resistance

Fashion—English to German

angora   die Angorawolle

belt   der Gürtel

bow tie   die Fliege

button   der Knopf

buttonhole   das Knopfloch

camel's hair   das Kamelhaar

cape   der Umhang

cashmere   die Kaschmirwolle

coat   der Mantel, die Jacke

collar   der Kragen

color   die Farbe

cuff link   der Manschettenknopf

cut (v)   zuschneiden

design (v)   entwerfen

designer   der Modeschöpfer

drape (v)   drapieren

dress   die Kleidung, das Kleid

fabric   der Stoff, das Gewebe

fashion   die Mode

fashionable   modisch, elegant

footage   die Gesamtlänge

handkerchief   das Taschentuch

hem   der Saum

high fashion designer   der Couturier

hood   die Kapuze

jewelry   der Schmuck

length   die Länge

lingerie   die Feinwäsche, die Damenunterwäsche

lining   das Futter, die Ausfütterung

long sleeves   die langen Ärmel

moiré   die Moireseide

necktie   die Krawatte

needle   die Nadel

out of style   außer Mode

pattern   das Muster

pleat   die Falte

pleated   gefaltet

poplin   der Popelin

print   der Druck

raincoat   der Regenmantel

rayon   die Kunstseide

ready-to-wear   von der Stange

scarf   der Schal

sew (v)   nähen

sewing machine   die Nähmaschine

shirt   das Hemd

shoe   der Schuh

short sleeves   die kurzen Ärmel

silk   der Seidenstoff

silk goods   die Seidenwaren

silkworm   die Seidenraupe

silk factory   die Seidenfabrik

silk manufacturers   die Seidenhersteller

size   die Größe

skirt   der Rock

slacks   die lange Hose

socks   die Socken

sportswear   die Sportkleidung

stitch   der Stich, die Masche, die Stichart

stockings   die Strümpfe

style   der Stil

stylist   der Stilist

suede   das Wildleder, das Veloursleder

suit   der Anzug

sweater   der Pullover

synthetic   synthetisch

taffeta   der Taft

tailor   der Schneider

thread   der Faden, das Garn

tuxedo   der Smoking

veil   der Schleier

vest   die Weste

weaver   der Weber

window dresser   der Schaufensterdekorateur

wool   die Wolle

yarn   das Garn

zipper   der Reißverschluß

Fashion—German to English

Angorawolle (f) angora
Anzug (m) suit
außer Mode out of style
Ausfütterung (f) lining
Couturier (m) high fashion designer
Damenunterwäsche (pl) lingerie
drapieren drape (v)
Druck (m) print
entwerfen design (v)
Faden (m) thread
Falte (f) pleat
Farbe (f) color
Feinwäsche (f) lingerie
Fliege (f) bow tie
Futter (n) lining
Garn (n) thread, yarn
gefaltet pleated
Gesamtlänge (f) footage
Gewebe (n) fabric
Größe (f) size
Gürtel (m) belt
Hemd (n) shirt
Jacke (f) coat
Kamelhaar (n) camel's hair
Kapuze (f) hood
Kaschmirwolle (f) cashmere
Kleid (n) dress
Kleidung (f) dress
Knopf (m) button
Knopfloch (n) buttonhole
Kragen (m) collar
Krawatte (f) necktie
Kunstseide (f) rayon
kurze Ärmel (pl) short sleeves
Länge (f) length
langen Ärmel (pl) long sleeves
lange Hose (f) slacks
Manschettenknopf (m) cuff link
Mantel (m) coat
Masche (f) stitch
Mode (f) fashion
modeschöpfer (m) designer
modisch, elegant fashionable

Moireseide (f) moiré
Muster (n) pattern
nähen sew (v)
Nähmaschine (f) sewing machine
Nadel (f) needle
Popelin (m) poplin
Pullover (m) sweater
Regenmantel (m) raincoat
Reißverschluß (m) zipper
Rock (m) skirt
Saum (m) hem
Schal (m) scarf
Schaufensterdekorateur (m) window dresser
Schleier (m) veil
Schmuck (m) jewelry
Schneider (m) tailor
Schuh (m) shoe
Seidenfabrik (f) silk factory
Seidenhersteller (f) silk manufacturers
Seidenraupe (f) silkworm
Seidenstoff (m) silk
Seidenwaren (pl) silk goods
Smoking (m) tuxedo
Socken (pl) socks
Sportkleidung (f) sportswear
Stich (m) stitch
Stichart (f) stitch
Stil (m) style
Stilist (m) stylist
Stoff (m) fabric
Strümpfe (pl) stockings
synthetisch synthetic
Taft (m) taffeta
Taschentuch (n) handkerchief
Umhang (m) cape
Veloursleder (n) suede
von der Stange ready-to-wear
Weber (m) weaver
Weste (f) vest
Wildleder (n) suede
Wolle (f) wool
zuschneiden cut (v)

Iron and Steel—English to German

alloy steel der Legierstahl
aluminum das Aluminium
annealing das Ausglühen, die Härtung
bars die Stangen
billets die Barren
blast furnace der Hochofen
carbon steel der Kohlenstoffstahl, der unlegierte Stahl
cast iron der Eisenguß, das Gußeisen
chromium das Chrom
coil das Gewinde, die Spule
cold rolling das Kaltwalzen
continous mill die kontinuierliche Walzstraße
conveyor das Fördergerät
conveyor belt das Förderband
copper das Kupfer
crucible der Schmelztiegel
cupola die Beobachtungskoppel
electric arc furnace electrodes die Elektroden
electrolytic process der Elektrolyseprozeß
ferroalloys die Eisenlegierung
ferromanganese das Manganeisen
ferronickel das Nickeleisen
finished products die Endprodukte
finishing mill der Schlichfräser
foundry die Gießerei
furnace der Hochofen
galvanizing die Galvanisierung
grinding das Mahlen, das Schleifen
heat der Schmelzgang
hot rolling das Warmwalzen
induction furnace der Induktionsofen

ingot mold die Gußform
ingots die Gußblöcke
iron ore das Eisenerz
limestone der Eisenbitterkalk, der Kalkstein
malleability die Dehnbarkeit, die Formbarkeit
manganese ore das Manganerz
molybdenum das Molybdän
nickel der Nickel
nitrogen der Stickstoff
ore das Erz
pickling das Abbeizen
pig iron das Gußeisen, das Roheisen
plate die Platte
powder das Pulver
pressure der Druck
process der Arbeitsvorgang
refractories die Schamottesteine
rod die Rundstange
rolling mill der Walzwerkbetrieb
scale die Gußhaut
scrap der Abfall
sheet die Platte
slabs die Metallplatten
specialty steels der Spezialstahl
stainless steel der rostfreie Stahl
steel mill das Hüttenwerk, das Stahlwerk
structural shapes das Profileisen
super alloys die Superlegierungen
titanium das Titran
toughness die Zähtestigkeit
tungsten das Wolfram
vacuum melting furnace der Vakuumschmelzofen
vanadium das Vanadium
wire der Stahldraht

Iron and Steel—German to English

Abbeizen (n) pickling

Abfall (m) scrap

Arbeitsvorgang (m) process

Ausglühen (n) annealing

Barren (pl) billets

Beobachtungskoppel (f) cupola

Chrom (n) chromium

Dehnbarkeit (f) malleability

Druck (m) pressure

Eisenbitterkalk (m) limestone

Eisenerz (n) iron ore

Eisenguß (m), Gußeisen (n) cast iron

Eisenlegierung (f) ferroalloys electric arc furnace

Elektroden (pl) electrodes

Elektrolyseprozeß (m) electrolytic process

Endprodukte (pl) finished products

Erz (n) ore

Förderband (n) conveyor belt

Fördergerät (n) conveyor

Formbarkeit (f) malleability

Galvanisierung (f) galvanizing

Gewinde (n) coil

Gießerei (f) foundry

Gußblöcke (pl) ingots

Gußeisen (n) cast iron, pig iron

Gußform (f) ingot mold

Gußhaut (f) scale

Härtung (f) annealing

Hochofen (m) blast furnace

Hüttenwerk (n) steel mill

Induktionsofen (m) induction furnace

Kalkstein (m) limestone

Kaltwalzen (n) cold rolling

Kohlenstoffstahl (m) carbon steel

Kontinuierliche Walzstraße (f) continous mill

Kupfer (n) copper

Legierstahl (m) alloy steel

Mahlen (n) grinding

Manganeisen (n) ferromanganese

Manganerz (n) manganese ore

Metallplatten (pl) slabs

Molybdän (n) molybdenum

Nickel (m) nickel

Nickeleisen (n) ferronickel

Platte (f) plate, sheet

Profileisen (n) structural shapes

Pulver (n) powder

Roheisen (n) pig iron

rostfreie Stahl (m) stainless steel

Rundstange (f) rod

Schamottesteine (pl) refractories

Schleifen (n) grinding

Schlichfräser (m) finishing mill

Schmelzgang (m) heat

Schmelztiegel (m) crucible

Spezialstahl (m) specialty steels

Spule (f) coil

Stahldraht (m) wire

Stahlwerk (n) steel mill

Stangen (pl) bars

Stickstoff (m) nitrogen

Superlegierungen (pl) super alloys

Titran (n) titanium

unlegierte Stahl (m) carbon steel

Vakuumschmelzofen (m) vacuum melting furnace

Vanadium (n) vanadium

Walzwerkbetrieb (m) rolling mill

Warmwalzen (n) hot rolling

Wolfram (n) tungsten

Zähtestigkeit (f) toughness

Leather Goods — English to German

ankle boots die Halbstiefel
astrakan der Astrachan
attaché case die Aktentasche, der Aktenkoffer
beaver der Biber
belt der Gürtel
billfold die Brieftasche
blotter der (Tinten)
Löscher
boot shop der Stiefelladen
bootmaker der Stiefelmacher
boots die Stiefel
briefcase die Aktenmappe
calfskin das Kalbleder
card case das Visitenkartentäschchen
cigarette case das
Zigarettenetui
cowhide das Rindsleder
dye (v) färben
eyeglass case das
Brillenetui
fitch das Iltishaar, die
Iltishaarbürste
fox der Fuchs
gloves die Handschuhe
handbag die Handtasche
holster das Pistolenhalfter
key case das Schlüsseletui
kidskin das Ziegenleder
lamb das Schafleder
leather das Leder
leather goods die Lederwaren
leather jacket die
Lederjacke
lizard (skin) das Eidechsenleder
lynx der Luchs(pelz)
makeup case das
Kosmetiktäschchen
marmot das Murmeltier
mink der Nerz
Morroco leather das
Saffianleder

nutria das Nutriafell
opossum das Opossum
ostrich (skin) der Srauss
otter das Otterfell, der
Otterpelz
passport case das Paßetui
pigskin das Schweinsleder
pocketbook die Hand-
tasche
portfolio die Aktentasche,
die Mappe
purse die Geldbörse, die
Brieftasche
rabbit das Kaninchen, der
Hase
raccoon der Wasch-
bär(pelz)
sable der Zobel(pelz)
saddle der Sattel
saddler der Sattler
scissor case das Scherenetui
sealskin das Seehundsfell,
das Seehundsleder
sewing kit das Nähtäschchen
slippers die Pantoffel
snakeskin das Schlangenleder, die Schlangenhaut
suede das Wildleder, das
Velours(leder)
suede jacket die Wildlederjacke
suitcase der Koffer
tan (v) (Leder) gerben
tanner der Gerber
tannery die Gerberei
tannin (tanin) die
Gerbsäure, das Tannin
tote bag die Einkaufstasche
trunk der Koffer
watch strap das
Uhrenarmband
whip die Peitsche

Leather Goods — German to English

Aktenkoffer (m) attaché case
Aktenmappe (f) briefcase
Aktentasche (f) attaché case, portfolio
Astrachan (m) astrakan
Biber (m) beaver
Brieftasche (f) billfold, purse
Brillenetui (n) eyeglass case
Eidechsenleder (n) lizard (skin)
Einkaufstasche (f) tote bag
färben dye (v)
Fuchs (m) fox
Geldbörse (f) purse
gerben (Leder) tan (v)
Gerber (m) tanner
Gerberei (f) tannery
Gerbsäure (f) tannin (tanin)
Gürtel (m) belt
Halbstiefel (pl) ankle boots
Handschuhe (pl) gloves
Handtasche (f) handbag, pocketbook
Hase (m) rabbit
Iltishaar (n) fitch
Iltishaarbürste (f) fitch
Kalbleder (n) calfskin
Kaninchen (n) rabbit
Koffer (m) suitcase
Koffer (m) trunk
Kosmetiktäschchen (n) makeup case
Leder (n) leather
Lederjacke (f) leather jacket
Lederwaren (pl) leather goods
Löscher (m) (Tinten) blotter
Luchs(pelz) (m) lynx
Mappe (f) portfolio
Murmeltier (n) marmot

Nähtäschchen (n) sewing kit
Nerz (m) mink
Nutriafell (n) nutria
Opossum (n) opossum
Otterfell(n) otter
Otterpelz (m) otter
Pantoffel (pl) slippers
Paßetui (n) passport case
Peitsche (f) whip
Pistolenhalfter (n) holster
Rindsleder (n) cowhide
Saffianleder (n) Morroco leather
Sattel (m) saddle
Sattler (m) saddler
Schafleder (n) lamb
Scherenetui (n) scissor case
Schlangehaut (f) snakeskin
Schlangenleder (n) snakeskin
Schlüsseletui (n) key case
Schweinsleder (n) pigskin
Seehundsfell (n) sealskin
Seehundsleder (n) sealskin
Srauss (m) ostrich (skin)
Stiefel (pl) boots
Stiefelladen (m) boot shop
Stiefelmacher (m) bootmaker
Tannin (n) tannin (tanin)
(Tinten) Löscher (m) blotter
Uhrenarmband (n) watch strap
Velours (leder) (n) suede
Visitenkartentäschchen (n) card case
Waschbär(pelz) (m) raccoon
Wildleder (n) suede
Wildlederjacke (f) suede jacket
Ziegenleder (n) kidskin
Zigarettenetui (n) cigarette case
Zobel(pelz) (m) sable

Motor Vehicles — English to German

air filter   der Luftfilter
alternator   der Wechsel-stromgenerator
assembly line   das Fließband
automatic gearshift   die Schaltautomatik
automobile   das Auto
body   die Karosserie
brake   die Bremse
brake pedal   das Bremspedal
bumper   die Stoßstange
camshaft   die Nockenwelle
car   das Auto, das Kraftfahrzeug
carburetor   der Vergaser
chassis   das Fahrgestell
clutch   die Kupplung
clutch pedal   das Kupplungspedal
connecting rod   die Kurbelstange, die Pleuelstange
convertible   das Kabriolett
crankshaft   die Kurbelwelle, die Anlasserwelle
defroster   der Entfroster, die Enteisungsanlage
designer   der Entwerfer
disc brake   die Scheibenbremse
displacement   der Hubraum
distributor   der Verteiler
driver   der Fahrer
engine   der Motor
exhaust   der Auspuff
fender   der Kotflügel
four-cylinder engine   der Vierzylindermotor
front-wheel drive   der Frontantrieb
gas consumption   der Benzinverbrauch
gasoline   das Benzin
gasoline tank   der Benzintank
gearshift   die Gangschaltung

generator   die Lichtmaschine
grille   das Kühlerschutzgitter
horsepower   die Pferdestärke
ignition   die Zündung
injector   der Einspritzer, die Einspritzelüse
lubrication   die Schmierung, die Ölversorgung
mileage   die Meilenlänge
odometer   der Kilometerzähler
paint   die Farbe
pinion   das Antriebsrad
piston   der Kolben
power steering   die Servolenkung
radial tire   der Gürtelreifen
rear axle   die Hinterachse
seat   der Sitz
shock absorber   der Stoßdämpfer
six-cylinder engine   der Sechszylindermotor
spare tire   der Ersatzreifen
spark plug   die Zündkerze
speedometer   der Geschwindigkeitsmesser
spring   die Feder
starter   der Anlasser
steering   die Steuerung
steering wheel   das Steuerrad
suspension   die Aufhängung
tire   der Reifen
torque   der Drehmoment
V8 engine   der V8-Motor
valve   das Ventil, die Klappe
water pump   die Wasserpumpe
wheel   das Rad
windshield   die Windschutzscheibe

Motor Vehicles — German to English

Anlasser (m) starter
Anlasserwelle (f) crankshaft
Antriebsrad (n) pinion
Aufhängung (f) suspension
Auspuff (m) exhaust
Auto (n) automobile, car
Benzin (n) gasoline
Benzintank (m) gasoline tank
Benzinverbrauch (m) gas consumption
Bremse (f) brake
Bremspedal (n) brake pedal
Drehmoment (m) torque
Einspritzer (m) injector
Einspritzgdüse (n) injector
Enteisungsanlage (f) defroster
Entfroster (m) defroster
Entwerfer (m) designer
Ersatzreifen (m) spare tire
Fahrgestell (n) chassis
Fahrer (m) driver
Farbe (f) paint
Feder (f) spring
Fließband (n) assembly line
Frontantrieb (m) front-wheel drive
Gangschaltung (f) gearshift
Geschwindigkeitsmesser (m) speedometer
Gürtelreifen (m) radial tire
Hinterachse (f) rear axle
Hubraum (m) displacement
Kabriolett (n) convertible
Karosserie (f) body
Kilometerzähler (m) odometer
Klappe (f) valve
Kolben (m) piston
Kotflügel (m) fender
Kraftfahrzeug (n) car
Kühlerschutzgitter (n) grille
Kupplung (f) clutch

Kupplungspedal (n) clutch pedal
Kurbelstange (f) connecting rod
Kurbelwelle (f) crankshaft
Lichtmaschine (f) generator
Luftfilter (m) air filter
Meilenlange (f) mileage
Motor (m) engine
Nockenwelle (f) camshaft
Ölversorgung (f) lubrication
Pferdestärke (f) horsepower
Pleuelstange (f) connecting rod
Rad (n) wheel
Reifen (m) tire
Schaltautomatik (f) automatic gearshift
Scheibenbremse (f) disc brake
Schmierung (f) lubrication
Sechszylindermotor (m) six-cylinder engine
Servolenkung (f) power steering
Sitz (m) seat
Steuerrad (n) steering wheel
Steuerung (f) steering
Stoßdämpfer (m) shock absorber
Stoßstange (f) bumper
V8-Motor (m) V8 engine
Ventil (n) valve
Vergaser (m) carburetor
Verteiler (m) distributor
Vierzylindermotor (m) four-cylinder engine
Wasserpumpe (f) water pump
Wechselstromgenerator (m) alternator
Windschutzscheibe (f) windshield
Zündkerze (f) spark plug
Zündung (f) ignition

Pharmaceuticals—English to German

anaesthetic   das Betäubungsmittel
analgesic   das Analgetikum
antacid   das Antiacidum
anti-inflammatory   entzündungshemmend
antibiotic   das Antibiotikum
anticoagulant   Gegengerinnungsmittel
antidepressant   depressionshemmend
antiseptic   das Antiseptikum
bleed (v)   bluten
blood   das Blut
botanic   botanisch
capsule   die Kapsel
compounds   die Präparate, die Verbindungen
content   der Inhalt
cough (v)   husten
cough drop   die Hustentropfen
cough syrup   der Hustensaft
crude   roh, unbearbeitet
density   die Dichte
disease   die Krankheit
diuretic   das Diuretikum, das harntreibende Mittel
dose   die Dosis
dressing   der Verband
drop   der Tropfen
drug   die Droge, das Medikament
drugstore   die Apotheke
eyedrop   die Augentropfen
hypertension   die Hypertonie
injection   die Spritze
iodine   das Jod
iron   das Eisen
laboratory technician   der Labortechniker
laxative   das Abführmittel
medicine   die Medizin, das Arzneimittel
medication   die Arzneiverordnung, die medizinische Behandlung

morphine   das Morphium
narcotic   das Betäubungsmittel, das Narkotikum
ointment   die Salbe
opium   das Opium
organic   organisch
pellet   die Pille, das Dragée
penicillin   das Penizillin
pharmaceutical   pharmazeutisch
pharmacist   der Apotheker
physician   der Arzt
pill   die Pille
plants   die Pflanzen, die Gewächse
prescription   das Rezept
purgative   das Abführmittel
remedies   die Heilmittel
salts   das Salz
salve   die Salbe
sedative   das Beruhigungsmittel
serum   das Serum
sinus   der Sinus
sleeping pill   die Schlaftablette
sneeze (v)   niesen
starch   die Stärke, die Kohlenhydrate
stimulant   das Anregungsmittel
sulphamide   das Sulfamid
synthesis   die Synthese
syringe   die Spritze
tablet   die Tablette
thermometer   das Thermometer
toxicology   die Toxikologie, die Giftkunde
toxin   das Toxin, der Giftstoff
tranquilizer   das Beruhigungsmittel
vaccine   der Impfstoff, die Vakzine
vitamin   das Vitamin
zinc   das Zink

Pharmaceuticals — German to English

Abführmittel (n) laxative, purgative

Analgetikum (n) analgesic

Anregungsmittel (n) stimulant

Antiacidum (n) antacid

Antibiotikum (n) antibiotic

Antiseptikum (n) antiseptic

Apotheke (f) pharmacy

Apotheker (m) pharmacist

Arzneimittel (n) medicine

Arzneiverordnung (f) medication

Arzt (m) physician

Augentropfen (m) eyedrop

Beruhigungsmittel (n) tranquilizer

Beruhigungsmittel (n) sedative

Betäubungsmittel (n) anaesthetic, narcotic

Blut (n) blood

bluten bleed (v)

botanisch botanic

depressionshemmend antidepressant

Dichte (f) density

Diuretikum (n) diuretic

Dosis (f) dose

Dragée (n) pellet

Droge (f) drug

entzündungshemmend anti-inflammatory

Eisen (n) iron

Gegengerinnungsmittel (n) anticoagulant

Gewächse (pl) plants

Giftkunde (f) toxicology

Giftstoff (m) toxin

harntreibende Mittel (n) diuretic

Heilmittel (pl) remedies

husten cough (v)

Hustensaft (m) cough syrup

Hustentropfen (m) cough drop

Hypertonie (f) hypertension

Impfstoff (m) vaccine

Inhalt (m) content

Jod (n) iodine

Kapsel (f) capsule

Kohlenhydrat (n) starch

Krankheit (f) disease

Labortechniker (m) laboratory technician

Medikament (n) drug

Medizin (f) medicine

medizinische Behandlung (f) medication

Morphium (n) morphine

Narkotikum (n) narcotic

niesen sneeze (v)

Opium (n) opium

organisch organic

Penizillin (n) penicillin

Pflanzen (pl) plants

pharmazeutisch pharmaceutical

Pille (f) pellet, pill

Präparate (pl) compounds

Rezept (n) prescription

roh, unbearbeitet crude

Salbe (f) ointment, salve

Salz (n) salts

Schlaftablette (f) sleeping pill

Serum (n) serum

Sinus (m) sinus

Spritze (f) injection, syringe

Stärke (f) starch

Sulfamid (n) sulphamide

Synthese (f) synthesis

Tablette (f) tablet

Thermometer (n) thermometer

Toxikologie (f) toxicology

Toxin (n) toxin

Tropfen (m) drop

Vakzine (f) vaccine

Verband (m) dressing

Verbindungen (pl) compounds

Vitamin (n) vitamin

Zink (n) zinc

Printing and Publishing — English to German

acknowledgment die Anerkennung

art die Kunst

black and white schwarz-weiß

bleed über den Rand gedruckt

blowup die Vergrößerung

boldface der Fettdruck

book das Buch

capital der Großbuchstabe

chapter das Kapitel

circulation die Auflage

coated paper das gestrichene Papier

color separation der Farbauszug

composition der Schriftsatz

copy die Kopie, das Exemplar

copy (v) Abzüge machen

copyright das Urheberrecht

cover die Titelseite

crop die Masse, die Ausbeute schneiden

distribution der Vertrieb

dummy der Probeband, die Puppe

edit (v) herausgeben, redigieren

edition die Ausgabe

editor der Redakteur

engrave (v) gravieren

font der Schriftsatz

form die Gestalt

format das Format

four-color vierfarbig

galley proof die Fahne, der Fahnenabzug

glossy glänzend, glatt

grain die Faserung

hardcover das Hardcover

headline die Überschrift

inch der Zoll

ink die Tinte

insert die Einlage, die Beilage

introduction die Einführung

italic kursiv

jacket der Mantel

justify (v) justieren

layout das Layout

letter der Buchstabe

line die Linie

line drawing die Federzeichnung

lower case Kleinbuchstaben

matrix die Matrize

negative negativ

newsprint das Zeitungspapier

page makeup die Seitenaufmachung

pagination die Paginierung

pamphlet die Broschüre

paper das Papier

paperback das Paperback

perfect binding die perfekte Bindung

pica die Pica

pigment das Pigment

plate die Platte

positive das Positiv

preface das Vorwort

press book das Pressebuch

print run der Drucklauf, die Auflage

printing der Druck, die Auflage

proofreading das Korrekturlesen

publisher der Verleger

ream das Ries

scanner der Abtaster

sewn geheftet, broschiert

sheet das Blatt

size die Größe

spine der Buchrücken

table of contents das Inhaltsverzeichnis

title der Titel

Printing and Publishing— German to English

Abtaster (m) scanner
Abzüge (pl) machen copy (v)
Anerkennung (f) acknowledgment
Auflage (f) circulation, print run, printing
Ausbeute (f) schneiden crop
Ausgabe (f) edition
Beilage (f) insert
Blatt (n) sheet
broschiert sewn
Broschüre (f) pamphlet
Buch (n) book
Buchrücken (m) spine
Buchstabe (m) letter
Druck (m) printing
Drucklauf (m) print run
Einführung (f) introduction
Einlage (f) insert
Exemplar (n) copy
Fahne (f) galley proof
Fahnenabzug (m) galley proof
Farbauszug (m) color separation
Faserung (f) grain
Federzeichnung (f) line drawing
Fettdruck (m) boldface
Format (n) format
geheftet sewn
Gestalt (n) form
gestrichene Papier (n) coated paper
glänzend glossy
glatt glossy
gravieren engrave (v)
Größe (f) size
Großbuchstabe (m) capital
Hard cover (n) hardcover
herausgeben edit (v)
Inhaltsverzeichnis (n) table of contents
justieren justify (v)
Kapitel (n) chapter
Kleinbuchstaben (pl) lower case
Kopie (f) copy
Korrekturlesen (n) proofreading
Kunst (f) art
kursiv italic
Layout (n) layout
Linie (f) line
Mantel (m) jacket
Matrize (f) matrix
negativ negative
Paginierung (f) pagination
Paperback (n) paperback
Papier (n) paper
perfekte Bindung (f) perfect binding
Pica (f) pica
Pigment (n) pigment
Platte (f) plate
positiv positive
Pressebuch (n) press book
Probeband (m) dummy
Puppe (f) dummy
Redakteur (m) editor
redigieren edit (v)
Ries (n) ream
Schriftsatz (m) composition, font
schwarzweiß black and white
Seitenaufmachung (f) page makeup
Tinte (f) ink
Titel (m) title
über den Rand gedruckt bleed
Überschrift (f) headline
Urheberrecht (n) copyright
Vergrößerung (f) blowup
Verleger (m) publisher
Vertrieb (m) distribution
vierfarbig four-color
Vorwort (n) preface
Zeitungspapier (n) newsprint
Zoll (m) inch

Winemaking — English to German

acid content der Säuregehalt
acre die Aubaufläche
aging das Altern
alcohol der Alkohol
alcoholic content der Alkoholgehalt
blend (v) verschneiden
biological diacidizing die biologische Entsäuerung
body der Gehalt
bottle die Flasche
bouquet das Bukett
case die Kiste
cask (225 litres) das Faß
centiliter der Zentiliter
character der Charakter
classified sparkling wine der Qualitätsschaumwein
climate das Klima
cooper der Küfer, der Faßbinder
cork der Korken
corkscrew der Korkenzieher
country das Gebiet
draw off ausdestillieren
dregs die Hefe
drink (v) trinken
dry wine der trockene Wein
estate (or chateau) das Gut
estate bottled auf dem Gut abgefüllt
ferment das Ferment
fruity fruchtig
grape die (Wein) Rebe, die Weinbeere
grape bunch die (Wein) Traube Weintraube
grape harvest die (Wein) Lese
hectare das Hektar

label das Etikett
liter der Liter
magnum die Zweiquartflasche
neck (of bottle) der Flaschenhals
pasteurized pasteurisiert
production die Produktion, die Herstellung
ripe reif
skin der (Wein) Schlauch
sparkling wine der Schaumwein
sugar content der Zuckergehalt
tannin das Tannin
tasting die (Wein) probe
temperature die Temperatur
type of vine die Weinart
unfermented grape juice der unfermentierte Rebensaft
vat das grosse Faß
vine die (Wein) Rebe, der Weinstock
vineyard der Weinberg
vintage die Weinernte
vintage year der Jahrgang
vintner der Weinhändler
wine Der Wein
wine cellar der Weinkeller
wine cooperative die Weinkooperative
winegrower der Weinbauer
wine steward der Tafelmeister
winemaker der Weinhersteller
winepress die Weinpresse, das Weinkelter
yeast die Hefe
yield der (Wein) Ertrag

Major Wine-Growing Areas

Ahr
Baden
Hessische Bergstraße
Fanken
Mosel-Saar-Ruwer
Mittelrhein

Nahe
Rheingau
Rheinhessen
Rheinpfalz
Württemberg

Winemaking—German to English

Alkohol (m)   alcohol
Altern (n)   aging
Aubaufläche (f)   acre
auf dem Gut abgefüllt   estate bottled
ausdestillieren   draw off
Baden
Bukett (n)   bouquet
Charakter (m)   character
content der Alkoholgehalt   alcoholic
content der Säuregehalt   acid
diacidizing die biologishe Entsäuerung   biological
Etikett (n)   label
Fanken
Fass (n)   cask (225 litres)
Fassbinder (m)   cooper
Ferment (n)   ferment
Flasche (f)   bottle
Flaschenhals (m)   neck (of bottle)
fruchtig   fruity
Gebiet (n)   country
Gehalt (m)   body
gross Faß (n)   vat
Gut (n)   estate (or chateau)
Hefe (f)   dregs, yeast
Hektar (n)   hectare
Herstellung (f)   production
Jahrgang (m)   vintage year
Kiste (f)   case
Klima (n)   climate
Korken (m)   cork
Korkenzieher (m)   corkscrew
Küfer (m)   cooper
Liter (m)   liter
pasteurisiert   pasteurized
Produktion (f)   production
Qualitätsschaumwein (m)   classified sparkling wine

reif   ripe
Schaumwein (m)   sparkling wine
Tafelmeister (m)   wine steward
Tannin (n)   tannin
Temperatur (f)   temperature
trinken   drink (v)
trockene Wein (m)   dry wine
unfermentierte Rebensaft (m)   unfermented grape juice
verschneiden   blend (v)
Wein (m)   wine
(Wein) Ertrag (m)   yield
(Wein) Lese (f)   grape harvest
(Wein) Probe (f)   tasting
(Wein) Rebe (f)   grape, vine
(Wein) Schlauch (m)   skin
(Wein) Traube (f)   grape bunch
Weinart (f)   type of vine
Weinbauer (m)   winegrower
Weinbeere (f)   grape
Weinberg (m)   vineyard
Weinernte (f)   vintage
Weinhändler (m)   vinter
Weinhersteller (m)   winemaker
Weinkeller (m)   wine cellar
Weinkelter (f)   winepress
Weinkooperative (f)   wine cooperative
Weinpresse (f)   winepress
Weinstock (m)   vine
Zentiliter (m)   centiliter
Zuckergehalt (m)   sugar content
Zweiquartflasche (f)   magnum

Agriculture, Industry and Resources

The economic map of Germany will give you a good idea of German industrial geography.

MAJOR MINERAL OCCURRENCES

Ag	Silver	K	Potash
Ba	Barite	Lg	Lignite
C	Coal	Na	Salt
Cu	Copper	O	Petroleum
Fe	Iron Ore	Pb	Lead
G	Natural Gas	U	Uranium
Gr	Graphite	Zn	Zinc
⚡	Water Power	⬚	Major Industrial Areas

GENERAL INFORMATION

ABBREVIATIONS

a.a.   always afloat
a.a.r.   against all risks
a/c   account
A/C   account current
acct.   account
a.c.v.   actual cash value
a.d.   after date
a.f.b.   air freight bill
agcy.   agency
agt.   agent
a.m.t.   air mail transfer
a/o   account of
A.P.   accounts payable
A/P   authority to pay
approx.   approximately
A.R.   accounts receivable
a/r   all risks
A/S, A.S.   account sales
a/s   at sight
at. wt.   atomic weight
av.   average
avdp.   avoirdupois
a/w   actual weight
a.w.b.   air waybill

bal.   balance
bar.   barrel
bbl.   barrel
b/d   brought down
B/E, b/e   bill of exchange
b/f   brought forward
B.H.   bill of health
bk.   bank
bkge.   brokerage
B/L   bill of lading
b/o   brought over
B.P.   bills payable
b.p.   by procuration
B.R.   bills receivable
B/S   balance sheet
b.t.   berth terms
bu.   bushel
B/V   book value

ca.   circa; centaire
C.A.   chartered accountant
c.a.   current account
C.A.D.   cash against documents
C.B.   cash book
C.B.D.   cash before delivery
c.c.   carbon copy
c/d   carried down
c.d.   cum dividend
c/f   carried forward
cf.   compare
c & f   cost and freight
C/H   clearing house
C.H.   custom house
ch. fwd.   charges forward
ch. pd.   charges paid
ch. ppd.   charges prepaid
chq.   check, cheque
c.i.f.   cost, insurance, freight
c.i.f. & c.   cost, insurance, freight, and commission
c.i.f. & e.   cost, insurance, freight, and exchange
c.i.f. & i.   cost, insurance, freight, and interest
c.l.   car load
C/m   call of more
C/N   credit note
c/o   care of
co.   company
C.O.D.   cash on delivery
comm.   commission
corp.   corporation
C.O.S.   cash on shipment
C.P.   carriage paid
C/P   charter party
c.p.d.   charters pay duties
cpn.   corporation
cr.   credit; creditor
C/T   cable transfer

c.t.l.   constructive total loss
c.t.l.o.   constructive total loss only
cum.   cumulative
cum div.   cum dividend
cum. pref.   cumulative preference
c/w   commercial weight
C.W.O.   cash with order
cwt.   hundredweight

D/A   documents against acceptance; deposit account
DAP   documents against payment
db.   debenture
DCF   discounted cash flow
d/d   days after date; delivered
deb.   debenture
def.   deferred
dept.   department
d.f.   dead freight
dft.   draft
dft/a.   draft attached
dft/c.   clean draft
disc.   discount
div.   dividend
DL   dayletter
DLT   daily letter telegram
D/N   debit note
D/O   delivery order
do.   ditto
doz.   dozen
D/P   documents against payment
dr.   debtor
Dr.   doctor
d/s, d.s.   days after sight
d.w.   deadweight
D/W   dock warrant
dwt.   pennyweight
dz.   dozen

ECU   European Currency Unit
E.E.T.   East European Time
e.g.   for example
encl.   enclosure
end.   endorsement

E. & O.E.   errors and omissions excepted
e.o.m.   end of month
e.o.h.p.   except otherwise herein provided
esp.   especially
Esq.   Esquire
est.   established
ex   out
ex cp.   ex coupon
ex div.   ex dividend
ex int.   ex interest
ex h.   ex new (shares)
ex stre.   ex store
ex whf.   ex wharf

f.a.a.   free of all average
f.a.c.   fast as can
f.a.k.   freight all kinds
f.a.q.   fair average quality; free alongside quay
f.a.s.   free alongside ship
f/c   for cash
f.c. & s.   free of capture and seizure
f.c.s.r. & c.c.   free of capture, seizure, riots, and civil commotion
F.D.   free delivery to dock
f.d.   free discharge
ff.   following; folios
f.g.a.   free of general average
f.i.b.   free in bunker
f.i.o.   free in and out
f.i.t.   free in truck
f.o.b.   free on board
f.o.c.   free of charge
f.o.d.   free of damage
fol.   following; folio
f.o.q.   free on quay
f.o.r.   free on rail
f.o.s.   free on steamer
f.o.t.   free on truck(s)
f.o.w.   free on wagons; free on wharf
F.P.   floating policy
f.p.   fully paid
f.p.a.   free of particular average
frt.   freight

frt. pd. freight paid
frt. ppd. freight prepaid
frt. fwd. freight forward
ft. foot
fwd. forward
f.x. foreign exchange

g.a. general average
g.b.o. goods in bad order
g.m.b. good merchantable brand
g.m.q. good merchantable quality
G.M.T. Greenwich Mean Time
GNP gross national product
g.o.b. good ordinary brand
gr. gross
GRT gross register ton
gr. wt. gross weight
GT gross tonnage

h.c. home consumption
hgt. height
hhd. hogshead
H.O. head office
H.P. hire purchase
HP horsepower
ht. height

IDP integrated data processing
i.e. that is
I/F insufficient funds
i.h.p. indicated horse-power
imp. import
Inc. incorporated
incl. inclusive
ins. insurance
int. interest
inv. invoice
I.O.U. I owe you

J/A, j.a. joint account
Jr. junior

KV kilovolt
KW kilowatt
KWh kilowatt hour

L/C, l.c. letter of credit
LCD telegram in the language of the country of destination
LCO telegram in the language of the country of origin
ldg. landing; loading
l.t. long ton
Ltd. limited
l. tn. long ton

m. month
m/a my account
max. maximum
M.D. memorandum of deposit
M/D, m.d. months after date
memo. memorandum
Messrs. plural of Mr.
mfr. manufacturer
min. minimum
MLR minimum lending rate
M.O. money order
m.o. my order
mortg. mortgage
M/P, m.p. months after payment
M/R mate's receipt
M/S, m.s. months' sight
M.T. mail transfer
M/U making-up price

n. name; nominal
n/a no account
N/A no advice
n.c.v. no commercial value
n.d. no date
n.e.s. not elsewhere specified
N/F no funds
NL night letter
N/N no noting
N/O no orders
no. number
n.o.e. not otherwise enumerated
n.o.s. not otherwise stated
nos. numbers

NPV   no par value
nr.   number
n.r.t.   net register ton
N/S   not sufficient funds
NSF   not sufficient funds
n. wt.   net weight

o/a   on account
OCP   overseas common point
O/D, o/d   on demand; overdraft
o.e.   omissions excepted
o/h   overhead
ono.   or nearest offer
O/o   order of
O.P.   open policy
o.p.   out of print; overproof
O/R, o.r.   owner's risk
ord.   order; ordinary
O.S., o/s   out of stock
OT   overtime

p.   page; per; premium
P.A., p.a.   particular average; per annum
P/A   power of attorney; private account
PAL   phase alternation line
pat. pend.   patent pending
PAYE   pay as you earn
p/c   petty cash
p.c.   percent; price current
pcl.   parcel
pd.   paid
pf.   preferred
pfd.   preferred
pkg.   package
P/L   profit and loss
p.l.   partial loss
P/N   promissory note
P.O.   post office; postal order
P.O.B.   post office box
P.O.O.   post office order
p.o.r.   pay on return
pp.   pages
p & p   postage and packing
p. pro   per procuration
ppd.   prepaid
ppt.   prompt

pref.   preference
prox.   proximo
P.S.   postscript
pt.   payment
P.T.O., p.t.o.   please turn over
ptly. pd.   partly paid
p.v.   par value

qlty.   quality
qty.   quantity

r. & c.c.   riot and civil commotions
R/D   refer to drawer
R.D.C.   running down clause
re   in regard to
rec.   received; receipt
recd.   received
red.   redeemable
ref.   reference
reg.   registered
retd.   returned
rev.   revenue
R.O.D.   refused on delivery
R.P.   reply paid
r.p.s.   revolutions per second
RSVP   please reply
R.S.W.C.   right side up with care
Ry   railway

s.a.e.   stamped addressed envelope
S.A.V.   stock at valuation
S/D   sea damaged
S/D, s.d.   sight draft
s.d.   without date
SDR   special drawing rights
sgd.   signed
s. & h. ex   Sundays and holidays excepted
shipt.   shipment
sig.   signature
S/LC, s. & l.c.   sue and labor clause
S/N   shipping note
s.o.   seller's option
s.o.p.   standard operating procedure

spt. spot
Sr. senior
S.S., s.s. steamship
s.t. short ton
ster. sterling
St. Ex. stock exchange
stg. sterling
s.v. sub voce

T.A. telegraphic address
T.B. trial balance
tel. telephone
temp. temporary secretary
T.L., t.l. total loss
T.L.O. total loss only
TM multiple telegram
T.O. turn over
tr. transfer
TR telegram to be called for
TR, T/R trust receipt
TT, T.T. telegraphic transfer (cable)
TX Telex

UGT urgent
u.s.c. under separate cover
U/ws underwriters

v. volt
val. value
v.a.t. value-added tax
v.g. very good

VHF very high frequency
v.h.r. very highly recommended

w. watt
WA with average
W.B. way bill
w.c. without charge
W.E.T. West European Time
wg. weight guaranteed
whse. warehouse
w.o.g. with other goods
W.P. weather permitting; without prejudice
w.p.a. with particular average
W.R. war risk
W/R, wr. warehouse receipt
W.W.D. weather working day
wt. weight

x.c. ex coupon
x.d. ex dividend
x.i. ex interest
x.n. ex new shares

y. year
yd. yard
yr. year
yrly. yearly

WEIGHTS AND MEASURES

U.S. UNIT	METRIC EQUIVALENT
mile	1.609 kilometers
yard	0.914 meters
foot	30.480 centimeters
inch	2.540 centimeters
square mile	2.590 square kilometers
acre	0.405 hectares
square yard	0.836 square meters
square foot	0.093 square meters
square inch	6.451 square centimeters
cubic yard	0.765 cubic meters
cubic foot	0.028 cubic meters
cubic inch	16.387 cubic centimeters

U.S. UNIT	METRIC EQUIVALENT
short ton	0.907 metric tons
long ton	1.016 metric tons
short hundredweight	45.359 kilograms
long hundredweight	50.802 kilograms
pound	0.453 kilograms
ounce	28.349 grams
gallon	3.785 liters
quart	0.946 liters
pint	0.473 liters
fluid ounce	29.573 milliliters
bushel	35.238 liters
peck	8.809 liters
quart	1.101 liters
pint	0.550 liters

TEMPERATURE AND CLIMATE

Temperature Conversion Chart

DEGREES CELSIUS	DEGREES FAHRENHEIT
−5	23
0	32
5	41
10	50
15	59
20	68
25	77
30	86
35	95
40	104

Average Temperatures for Major Cities

	JAN	APR	JULY	OCT
Bonn	38°F (3°C)	50°F (10°C)	68°F (20°C)	54°F (12°C)
Hamburg	32°F (0°C)	50°F (10°C)	68°F (20°C)	50°F (10°C)
Munich	25°F (−3°C)	48°F (9°C)	68°F (20°C)	48°F (9°C)
Vienna	29°F (−2°C)	52°F (11°C)	68°F (20°C)	52°F (11°C)
Zurich	30°F (−1°C)	50°F (10°C)	68°F (20°C)	52°F (11°C)

spring	der Frühling
summer	der Sommer
autumn	der Herbst
winter	der Winter
hot	heiss

sunny	sonnig
warm	warm
cool	kühl
windy	windig
snowing	(es) schneit
raining	(es) regnet

COMMUNICATIONS CODES

Telephones

The German telephone network is almost entirely automated. Coin-operated booths are located on the street with English instructions. International calls can be made from booths marked in green with a sign *Ausland*. Emergency telephone numbers in Germany are 110 (police) and 112 (fire). In Austria they are 133 and 122, and in Switzerland, 117 and 118.

Area Codes within Germany

Bonn	228	Düsseldorf	211
Berlin	30	Frankfurt	611
Hamburg	40	Stuttgart	711
Munich	89	Hannover	511
Cologne	221		

Area Codes within Austria

Linz	723	Vienna	222

Area Codes within Switzerland

Berne	31	Geneva	22
Basel	61	Zurich	1

International Country Codes

Algeria	213	Malta	356
Argentina	54	Mexico	52
Australia	61	Morocco	212
Austria	43	Netherlands	31
Belgium	32	New Zealand	64
Brazil	55	Norway	47
Canada	1	Philippines	63
Chile	56	Poland	48
Colombia	57	Portugal	351
Denmark	45	Saudi Arabia	966
Finland	358	Singapore	65
France	33	South Africa	27
Germany (West)	37	South Korea	82
Germany (East)	49	Spain	34
Gibraltar	350	Sri Lanka	94
Greece	30	Sweden	46
Hong Kong	852	Switzerland	41

Hungary	36	Taiwan	886
Iceland	354	Thailand	255
India	91	Tunisia	216
Ireland	353	Turkey	90
Israel	972	United Kingdom	44
Italy	39	USA	1
Japan	81	USSR	7
Kuwait	965	Venezuela	58
Luxembourg	352	Yugoslavia	38

POSTAL SERVICES

In West Germany

Post offices handle mail, telephone calls, and telegrams. Hours are 8–6, Monday through Friday and 8–noon on Saturday. Some offices have night counters as well. The following are open 24 hours.

Düsseldorf Central Post Office
51 Immermannstrasse

Frankfurt Central Post Office
Hauptbahnhof (main railroad station)

Munich Central Post Office
1 Bahnhofplatz

In Austria

Hours for post offices are 8–6, Monday through Friday, with an hour's lunch break. There is a 24-hour counter in the Vienna central post office.

In Switzerland

The postal service is highly efficient and delivery of regular mail ordinarily takes one day. For more information, contact:

PTT
Generaldirektion
Viktoriastrasse 21
3030 Berne

TIME ZONES

The table on the following page gives the time differences among various countries and major cities of the world, based on Greenwich Mean Time. Remember that from April through September, Daylight Savings Time must be considered.

MAJOR HOLIDAYS
(Observed in all German-speaking areas unless noted)

| January 1 | New Year's Day | Neujahr |
| January 6 | Epiphany (Austria) | Heiligedrei-königstag |

−8 HOURS	−6 HOURS	−5 HOURS	GREEN-WICH MEAN TIME	+1 HOUR	+2 HOURS	+3 HOURS	+ ADDITIONAL HOURS
Los Angeles San Francisco	Chicago Dallas Houston	Boston New York Washington, D.C.	Great Britain Iceland Ireland Portugal	Austria Belgium Denmark France Germany Hungary Italy Luxembourg Malta Monaco Netherlands Norway Poland Spain Sweden Switzerland Yugoslavia	Finland Greece Romania South Africa	Turkey Moscow	Sydney (10 hours) New Zealand (12 hours)

May 1	Labor Day (West Germany/Austria)	Tag der Arbeit
June 15	Corpus Christi Day (Austria)	Fronleichnam
June 17	National Unity Day (West Germany)	Tag der Deutschen Einheit
August 1	National Day (Switzerland)	Nationalfeiertag
August 15	Assumption Day (Austria)	Mariä Himmelfahrt
October 26	Flag Day (Austria)	Nationalfeiertag
November 1	All Saints Day (Austria)	Allerheiligen
December 8	Immaculate Conception (Austria)	Unbefleckte Empfängnis
December 25	Christmas Day	Weihnachtstag
December 26	St. Stephen's Day	Weihnachtstag
March – April	Good Friday	Karfreitag
	Easter	Ostern
	Easter Monday	Ostermontag
40 Days after Easter	Ascension	Christi Himmelfahrt
7 Mondays after Easter	Whitmonday	Pfingstmontag

CURRENCY INFORMATION

Major Currencies of the World

Andorra	French Franc
Austria	Schilling
Belgium	Belgian Franc
Denmark	Danish Krone
Finland	Finnmark
France	Franc
Germany (West)	Mark (DM)
Germany (East)	Mark (M)
Greece	Drachma
Hungary	Forint
Iceland	Krone
Ireland	Punt
Italy	Lira
Liechtenstein	Swiss Franc
Luxembourg	Luxembourg Franc
Malta	Maltese Lira
Monaco	French Franc
Netherlands	Guilder
Norway	Norwegian Krone
Portugal	Escudo
Spain	Peseta

Sweden	Swedish Krone
Switzerland	Swiss Franc
Turkey	Lira
United Kingdom	Pound Sterling
USSR	Ruble
Yugoslavia	Dinar

Major Commercial Banks

In Germany

Deutsche Bank AG
Taunusanlage 12
Postfach 10 06 10
6000 Frankfurt 1

Commerzbank AG
Neue Mainzer Strasse 32-36
Postfach 2534
6000 Frankfurt 1

Dresdner Bank AG
Jurgen-Pronto-Platz 1
Postfach 11 06 61
6000 Frankfurt 1

In Austria

Creditanstalt-Bankverein
Schottengasse 6
Postfach 72
A-1011 Vienna

Girozentrale u. Bank der
  Oesterreichichen
  Sparkassen
Schubertring 5
Postfach 255
A-1011 Vienna

Oesterreichishe
  Kontrollbank
Am Hof 4
A-1010 Vienna

In Switzerland

Union Bank of Switzerland
  (UBS)
Bahnhofstrasse 45
Postfach
CH-8021 Zurich

Swiss Bank Corporation
Postfach
CH-4002 Basel

Credit Suisse
Paradeplatz 8
Postfach
CH-8021 Zurich

MAJOR BUSINESS PERIODICALS

The *International Herald Tribune* is the leading English-language newspaper sold in Europe. It is available at most hotels and newsstands. The *Journal of Commerce* is also widely available.

In Germany

Bild Zeitung
Frankfurter Allegemeine Zeitung
Suddeutsche Zeitung
Die Welt
Capital

In Austria

Weiner Zeitung
Kurier
Die Presse
Kronen Zeitung

In Switzerland

Blick
Tages Anzeiger Zurich
Neue Zercher Zeitung
Schweiz. Handelszeitung
Finanz and Wirtschaft

ANNUAL TRADE FAIRS

In Germany

This listing of exhibitions is a sampling of events. For a complete list, contact the German-American Chamber of Commerce (666 Fifth Avenue, New York, NY 10103).

Berlin

International Tourism Exchange (February–March)
International Audio and Video Fair (August–September)
AAA Automobile Show (October)

Frankfurt

Home and Household Textiles Fair (January)
International Amusement and Vending Trade Fair (January)
Musikmesse (February)
Fur Fair (April)
Clothing Textiles Fair (April)
International Motor Show (September)
Frankfurt Book Fair (October)
Hotel and Restaurant Trade Show (October)
Inter Airport (September)

Hamburg

International Bakery Exhibition (April)
Boat Show (October)

Hanover

International Building Trade Exhibition (February)
Hanover CeBIT Fair (Office Communications) (March)
Industrial Technology Trade Fair (April)
International Aerospace Exhibition (June)
Wood Industries Machinery and Equipment Fair (May–June)

Cologne

International Dental Show (April)
Handicrafts Fair (April)
Ophthalmic Optics Congress (April)
Bicycle and Motor Cycle Exhibition (September)
World Food Market (October)

Munich

International Sports Equipment Fair (February)
International Fashion Fair (March–October)

For additional information, contact: Ausstellungs-und Messe-Ausschuss der Deutschen Wirtschaft e.V. (AUMA), Lindenstrasse 8, D-5000, Cologne 1. telephone: (0221) 21 90 91; telex: 8881507.

In Austria
Vienna

International Furnishing and Interior Design Exhibition
(March)
International Trade Fair (March)
Exhibition for Office Organization and Communications
(May)
International Wine Festival Week (June)
International Trade Fair (September)

Salzburg

Service Station Equipment Exposition (January)
Textiles, Flooring and Carpeting Exhibition (February)
Furniture Exhibition (February)
International Tourist Fair (February)
Souvenirs Exposition (February)
Exhibition of International Young Fashion (Febuary–
March)
Trailers and Recreational Vehicle Trade Fair (March)
International Trade Fair for Footwear, Leather Goods
(March)
Salzburg Antiques Fair (March)
Austrian Handicraft Fair (April)
Packaging and Material Handling Trade Fair (April)

Graz

International Tourist Fair (March)

Innsbruck

Innsbruck Spring Trade Fair (April)

Klagenfurt

Klagenfurter International Fair for Trade and Industry
(October)

For additional information, contact the Austrian Economic
Chamber, Wiedner Hauptstrasse 63, A-1045, Vienna; telephone: 02 22 65 05, department for fairs.

In Switzerland
Basel

International Dog Show (January)
International Coin Fair (January)
Cable and Satellite Television Exhibition (February)
Swiss Industries Fair (March)
International Packaging Exhibition (April)
European Watch, Clock and Jewelry Fair (April)
International Art Fair (June)
Videotext Industry Conference (September)

Hardware and Household Goods Trade Fair (September)
Data Processing Exhibition (September)
Air Cargo Forum (September)
Knee Surgery and Arthroscopy Congress (October)
Swiss Woodworking Fair (October)
Basel Autumn Fair (November)
Wine Fair (November)
Hightech Forum (November)

For more information, contact Schweizer Mustermesse, Messeplatz, CH-4021 Basel. telephone: 061/26 20 20; telex: 62685 fair ch.

Zurich

Industrial Production Engineering Trade Fair (February)
International Art Fair—Forum 86 (February)
International Trade Fair for Semiconductor Technology (March)
Swiss Boat Show (March)
International Fashion Fair (March)
Heating, Air Conditioning and Sanitation Exhibition (April)
Cosmetics, Perfumery and Foot Care Exhibition (May)
International Art and Antiques Fair (May)
Safety and Security Systems Exhibition (May)
Radio, Television and HiFi Exhibition (September)
International Fashion Fair (September)
Precision Engineering and Dimensional Measuring Testing Exhibition (October)
Hairstyling Exhibition and Trade Fair (October)
Medical Equipment Fair (November)
Christmas Collectors' Fair (December)

For additional information, contact: Zuspa, Internationale Fachmessen und Spezial-Ausstellungen Zurich, Thurgauerstrasse 7, Postfach CH-8050 Zurich. telephone: 01311 50 55; telex: 823276 zusp ch.

TRAVEL TIMES

To West Germany

Although there are direct flights to other West German cities, many flights land in Frankfurt. At Frankfurt, you can connect with flights to other German cities, as well as flights to major European, Middle Eastern, and Asian destinations. Trains leave Frankfurt's Rhein/Main Airport every 15 minutes to reach the center of the city 10 km away.

To Austria

At Schwechat Airport, 18 km from Vienna, there are daily flights to other Austrian cities as well as connections with other European cities. There are very few direct flights from the United States to Vienna, however.

To Switzerland

Zurich is the main entryway to Switzerland via air, and there are also a large number of domestic flights to Geneva, Berne, Basel, and Lugano. Kloten Airport is 11 km from the city, with a 10-minute train ride to Hauptbahnhof.

Approximate Flying Times to Key German-Speaking Cities

New York – Frankfurt	7 hours, 30 minutes
Chicago – Frankfurt	8 hours, 45 minutes
Los Angeles – Frankfurt	11 hours
Montreal – Frankfurt	6 hours
Toronto – Düsseldorf	7 hours
London – Berlin	1 hour, 30 minutes
London – Munich	1 hour, 40 minutes
Sydney – Munich	14 hours

Average Flying Times between Major German-Speaking Cities

Düsseldorf – Frankfurt	50 minutes
Munich – Hanover	1 hour, 10 minutes
Stuttgart – Hamburg	1 hour, 10 minutes
Cologne – Munich	1 hour
Munich – Frankfurt	1 hour
Frankfurt – Vienna	1 hour, 20 minutes
Frankfurt – Zurich	55 minutes

Lufthansa serves most cities in West Germany, with flights among Düsseldorf, Frankfurt, Hanover, Munich, Cologne, Nuremburg, and Stuttgart. Lufthansa also offers a Frankfurt–Düsseldorf connection that runs four times a day in both directions. Reservations and information at Lufthansa ticket offices, any IATA travel agency, or Lufthansa Information at the airport of arrival.

Deutsche Bundesbahn is West Germany's other domestic airline. For information on flights, contact Deutsche Bundesbahn, Hauptverwaltung, Friedrich-Ebert-Anl. 43-45, 6000 Frankfurt 11.

There are two major domestic airlines in Austria, listed below. Contact each for information on flights and reservations.

Austrian Airlines	Tyrolean Airways
Oesterreichischer	Luftfahrt Ges.m.b.H. & Co. KG
Luftverkehr AG	Flughafen Innsbruck
Fontanastrasse 1	Fuerstenweg 10
A-1100 Vienna	A-6020 Innsbruck

Swissair is the national airline of Switzerland. For information, contact Swissair, Schweizerische Luftverkehr AG, CH-8058 Zurich. For domestic flights, contact:

Balair AG
Flugplatz Basle-Muehausen
CH-4002 Basel

Crossair
Postfach 630
CH-8058 Zurich

CTA
Case Postale 110
CH-1215 Geneva

MAJOR HOTELS

Berlin

Bristol-Hotel Kempinski
Kurfürstendamm 27 (B 15)
Tel: 88 10 91
Telex: 183553
(Indoor pool)
Major credit cards accepted
Restaurants

Steigenberger Berlin
Los-Angeles-Platz 1 (B 30)
Tel: 2 10 80
Telex: 18144
(Indoor pool)
Major credit cards accepted
Restaurants

Inter-Continental
Budapester Str. 2 (B 30)
Tel: 2 60 20
Telex: 184380
(Indoor pool)
Major credit cards accepted
Restaurant

Düsseldorf

Breidenbacher Hof
Heinrich-Heine-Allee 36
   (D 1)
Tel: 86 01
Telex: 8582360
Major credit cards accepted
Restaurants

Steigenberger Parkhotel
Corneliusplatz 1 (D 1)
Tel: 86 51
Telex: 8582331
Major credit cards accepted
Restaurant

Nikko
Immermannstr. 41 (D 1)
Tel: 88 61
Telex: 8582080
(Indoor pool)
Major credit cards accepted
Restaurant

Inter-Continental
Karl-Arnold-Platz 5
Tel: 4 55 30
Telex: 8584601
(Indoor pool)
Major credit cards accepted
Restaurant

Düsseldorf Hilton
Georg-Glock-Str. 20
Tel: 43 49 63
Telex: 8584376
(Indoor pool)
Major credit cards accepted
Restaurant

Frankfurt

Steigenberger-Hotel
   Frankfurter Hof
Bethmannstr. (33 F 16)
Tel: 2 02 51
Telex: 411806
Major credit cards accepted
Restaurant

Heissischer Hof
Friedrich-Ebert-Anlage 40
   (F 97)
Tel: 7 54 00
Telex: 411776
Major credit cards accepted
Restaurant

Frankfurt Intercontinental
Wilhelm-Leuschner-Str. 43
(F 1)
Tel: 23 05 61
Telex: 413639
(Indoor pool)
Major credit cards accepted
Restaurant

Hamburg

Atlantic-Hotel Kempinski
An der Alster 72 (H 1)
Tel: 24 80 01
Telex: 2163297
(Indoor pool)
Major credit cards accepted
Restaurant

Vier Jahreszeiten
Neuer Jungfernstieg 9 (H 36)
Tel: 3 49 41
Telex: 211629
Major credit cards accepted
Restaurant

Ramada Renaissance Hotel
Grosse Bleichen (H 36)
Tel: 34 91 80
Major credit cards accepted
Restaurant

Hanover

CP Hamburg Plaza
Marseiller Str. 2 (H 36)
Tel: 3 50 20
Telex: 214400
(Indoor pool)
Major credit cards accepted
Restaurant

Maritim
Hildesheimer str. 34
Tel: 1 65 31
Telex: 9230268
(Indoor pool)
Major credit cards accepted
Restaurant

Inter-Continental
Friedrichswall 11
Tel: 1 69 11
Telex: 923656
Restaurant

Munich

Vier Jahreszeiten Kempinski
Maximilianstr. 17 (M 22)
Tel: 23 03 90
Telex: 5235859
(Indoor pool)
Major credit cards accepted
Restaurant

Konigshof
Karlsplatz 25 (M 2)
Tel: 55 84 12
Telex: 523616
Major credit cards accepted
Restaurant

Hilton
Am Tucherpark 7 (M 22)
Tel: 3 84 50
Telex: 5215740
(Indoor pool)
Major credit cards accepted
Restaurants

Bayerischer Hof-Palais
  Montgelas
Promenadeplatz 6 (M 2)
Tel: 2 12 00
Telex: 523409
(Indoor pool)
Major credit cards accepted
Restaurants

Continental
Max-Joseph-Str. 5 (M 2)
Tel: 55 79 71
Telex: 522603
Major credit cards accepted

Stuttgart

Steigenberger-Hotel Graf
  Zeppelin
Arnulf-Klett Platz 7
Tel: 29 98 81
Telex: 722418
(Indoor pool)
Major credit cards accepted
Restaurant

Am Schlossgarten
Schillerstr. 23
Tel: 29 99 11
Telex: 722936
Major credit cards accepted

Vienna

Imperial
Kärntner Ring 16, A-1015
Tel: 65 17 65
Telex: 112630
Major credit cards accepted
Restaurant

Sacher
Philharmonikerstr. 4, A-101
Tel: 52 55 75/5 14 56
Telex: 112520
Major credit cards accepted
Restaurant

Bristol
Kärntner Ring 1, A-1015
Tel: 52 95 52/5 15 16
Telex: 112474
Restaurant

Hotel im Palais
  Schwarzenberg
Schwarzenbergplatz 9,
  A-1030
Tel: 78 45 15
Telex: 136124
Major credit cards accepted
Restaurant

Marriott-Hotel
Parkring 12a, A-1015
Tel: 53 36 11
Telex: 112249
(Indoor pool)
Major credit cards accepted
Restaurant

Hilton International
Landstrasser Haupstr. 2,
  A-1030
Tel: 75 26 52
Telex: 136799
Major credit cards accepted
Restaurant

Intercontinental
Johannesgasse 28, A-1037
Tel: 75 05
Telex: 131235
Major credit cards accepted
Restaurants

Salzburg

Salzburg Sheraton Hotel
Auerspergstr. 4
Tel: 79 32 10
Telex: 632518
Major credit cards accepted
Restaurants

Basel

Trois Rois
Blumenrain 8, 4001
Tel: 25 52 52
Telex: 62937
Major credit cards accepted
Restaurant

Hilton
Aeschengraben 31, 4002
Tel: 22 66 22
Telex: 965555
(Indoor pool)
Major credit cards accepted
Restaurant

Hotel International
Steinentorstrasse 25, 4001
Tel: 22 18 70
Telex: 962370
(Indoor pool)
Major credit cards accepted
Restaurant

Hotel Basel
Münzgasse 12, 4001
Tel: 25 24 33
Telex: 64199
Major credit cards accepted
Restaurant

Euler
Centralbahnplatz 14, 4051
Tel: 23 45 00
Telex: 962215
Major credit cards accepted
Restaurant

Europe
Clarastrasse 43, 4058
Tel: 26 80 80
Telex: 64103
Major credit cards accepted
Restaurant

Schweizerhof
Centralbahnplatz 1, 4002
Tel: 22 28 33
Telex: 962373
Major credit cards accepted

Zurich

Dolder Grand Hotel
Kurhausstr. 65, 8032
Tel: 251 62 31
Telex: 816416
(Outdoor pool)
Major credit cards accepted
Restaurant

Eden au Lac
Utoquai 45, 8023
Tel: 47 94 04
Telex: 816339
Major credit cards accepted
Restaurant

Zurich
Neumühlequai 42, 8001
Tel: 363 63 63
Telex: 56809
(Indoor pool)
Major credit cards accepted
Restaurant

International
Am Marktplatz, 8050
Tel: 311 43 41
Telex: 823251
(Indoor pool)

Baur au Lac
Talstr. 1, 8022
Tel: 221 16 50
Telex: 813567
American Express accepted
Restaurant

Savoy Hotel Baur en Ville
Poststr. 12, 8022
Tel: 211 53 60
Telex: 812845
Major credit cards accepted
Restaurant

Schweizerhof
Bahnhofplatz 7, 8023
Tel: 211 86 40
Telex: 813754
Major credit cards accepted

MAJOR RESTAURANTS

Berlin

Ponte Vecchio—one star
Spielhagenstr. 3 (B 10)
Tel: 3 42 19 99
Diner's Club accepted

Rockendorf's Restaurant—
one star
Düsterhaupstr. 1 (B 28)
Tel: 4 02 30 99
American Express, Diner's
Club accepted

Düsseldorf

Orangerie—one star
Bilker Str. 30 (D 1)
Tel: 13 18 28
Diner's Club accepted

Victorian—one star
Königstr. 3a (D 1)
Tel: 32 02 22
Major credit cards accepted

Im Schiffchen—two stars
Kaiserswerther Markt 9
Tel: 40 10 50
American Express accepted

Frankfurt

Restaurant Francais—one
star
Bethmannstr. 33 (F 16)
Tel: 2 02 51
Major credit cards accepted

Humperdinck—one star
Grüneburgweg 95 (F 1)
Tel: 72 21 22
Major credit cards accepted

Ernos Bistro—one star
Liebigstr. 15 (F 1)
Tel: 72 19 97
Major credit cards accepted

Hamburg

Landhaus Scherrer — one star
Elbchaussee 130 (H 50)
Tel: 8 80 13 25
American Express, Diner's Club accepted

Le Canard — one star
Martinistr. 11 (H 20)
Tel: 4 60 48 30
American Express, Diner's Club accepted

Landhaus Dill — one star
Elbchaussee 404 (H 52)
Tel: 82 84 43
Major credit cards accepted

Hanover

Landhaus Ammann — one star
Hildesheimer Str. 185
Tel: 83 08 18
American Express, Diner's Club accepted

Stern's Restaurant Härke-Stuben — one star
Marienstr. 104
Tel: 81 73 22
American Express, Diner's Club accepted

Munich

Aubergine — three stars
Maximiliansplatz 5 (M 2)
Tel: 59 81 71

Le Gourmet — one star
Ligsalzstr. 46 (M 2)
Tel: 50 35 97
Diner's Club accepted

Sabitzer — one star
Reitmorstr. 21 (M 22)
Tel: 29 85 84
Diner's Club accepted

Boettner — one star
Theatinerstr. 8 (M 2)
Tel: 22 12 10
Major credit cards accepted

Tantris — three stars
Johann-Fichte-Str. 7
Tel: 36 20 61
Major credit cards accepted

Käfer-Schänke — one star
Schumannstr. 1 (M 80)
Tel: 4 16 81
American Express, Diner's Club accepted

Stuttgart

Alte Post — one star
Friedrichstr. 43
Tel: 29 30 79
Diner's Club accepted

Lamm — one star
Mühlstr. 24
Tel: 85 36 15

Hirsch-Weinstuben — one star
Maierstr. 3
Tel: 71 13 75

Vienna

Korso — one star
Mahlerstr. 2, A-1015
Tel: 52 16 42
Major credit cards accepted

Steireck — one star
Rasumofskygasse 2, A-1030
Tel: 73 31 68
American Express accepted

Hauswirth — one star
Otto-Bauer-Gasse 20, A-1060
Tel: 57 12 61
Major credit cards accepted

Mattes — one star
Schönlaterngasse 8, A-1010
Tel: 52 62 75
Major credit cards accepted

Basel

Stucki — two stars
Bruderholzallee 42, 4059
Tel: 35 82 22
Visa accepted

Schloss Binningen
Schlossgasse 5
Tel: 47 20 55
American Express, Visa
  accepted

Zurich

Rebe — one star
Schützengasse 5, 8001
Tel: 221 10 65
Major credit cards accepted

Agnés Amberg
Hottingerstr. 5, 8032
Tel: 251 26 26
Major credit cards accepted

Kronenhalle
Rämistrasse 4, 8001
Tel: 251 02 56
Major credit cards accepted

Petermann's Kunststube —
  two stars
Seestr. 160
Tel: 910 07 15

Sihlhalde — one star
Sihlhaldenstr. 70
Tel: 720 09 27

Ratings extracted from the Red Michelin Guide, *1986.*

USEFUL ADDRESSES

In Germany

Association of German
  Chambers of Industry
  and Commerce
Adenauerallee 148
D-5300 Bonn 1

Federal Association of
  German Industry
Gustav-Heinemann-Ufer
  84-88
Postfach 51 05 48
D-5000 Cologne 51

Central Association of
  German Handicrafts
Johanniterstrasse 1
D-5300 Bonn

Federal Association of
  German Wholesale and
  Foreign Trade
Kaiser-Friedrich-Strasse 13
Postfach 1349
D-5300 Bonn

National Association of
  German Retailers
Sachsenring 89
D-5000 Cologne 1

Federal Association of
  German Banks
Mohrenstrasse 35-41
Postfach 10 02 46
D-5000 Cologne

General Association of
  Insurance Carriers
Ebertplatz 1
D-5000 Cologne 1

Federal Association of
  German Market
  Researchers
Eulenkamp 14
D-2000 Hamburg 70

German Trade Union
  Federation
Hans-Bockler-Strasse 39
D-4000 Düsseldorf 30

In Austria

Ministry of Trade and
  Industry
Export/Import Licensing
  Office
Landstrasse Hauptstrasse
  55-57
1030 Vienna

Federal Economic Chamber
  of Commerce
Wiedner Hauptstrasse 63
A-1040 Vienna

Central Federation of
  Austrian Industry
Bauernmarkt 13
1011 Vienna 1

Austrian National Tourist
Office
Margaretenstrasse 1
A-1040 Vienna

Association of Austrian
Industrialists
Schwarzenbergplatz 4
A-1030 Vienna

In Switzerland

Federal Office for Industry,
Crafts and Labor
Bundesgasse 8
3003 Berne

Federation of Swiss
Employers' Organizations
Florastrasse 44
8034 Zurich

Swiss Federation of
Commerce and Industry
Borenstrasse 26
8022 Zurich

Swiss National Tourist
Office
Bellariastrasse 38
8027 Zurich

In The United States

German-American
Chamber of Commerce
666 Fifth Avenue
New York, New York 10103

German-American
Chamber of Commerce
77 East Monroe Street
Chicago, Illinois 60603

German-American
Chamber of Commerce
One Park Plaza
3250 Wilshire Boulevard,
Suite 2212
Los Angeles, California
90010

German-American
Chamber of Commerce
465 California Street
San Francisco, California
94104

Austrian Trade Commission
845 Third Avenue
New York, New York 10022

Consulate General of
Switzerland
444 Madison Avenue
New York, New York 10022

In Canada and Great Britain

German-Canadian
Chamber of Industry and
Commerce
2015 Peel Street, Suite 1110
Montreal, Quebec H3A 1T8

German Chamber of
Industry and Commerce
12/13 Suffolk Street
St. James'
London SW1 Y4HG

In Australia

German-Australian
Chamber of Commerce
18th Floor, King George
Tower
388 George Street
Sydney, N.S.W. 2000

German-Australian
Chamber of Industry and
Commerce
5th Floor, Hoechst House
606 St. Kilda Road
Melbourne, VIC 3004

MAPS

The following maps of Europe, Germany, Austria and Switzerland will be useful in doing business in German-speaking areas.

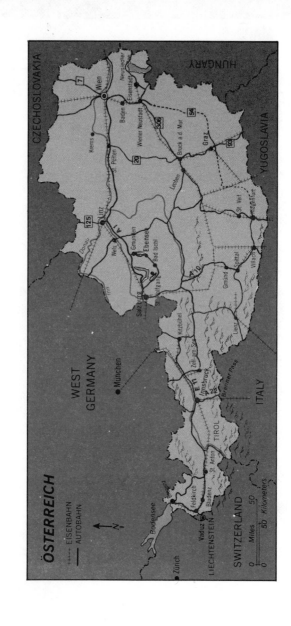

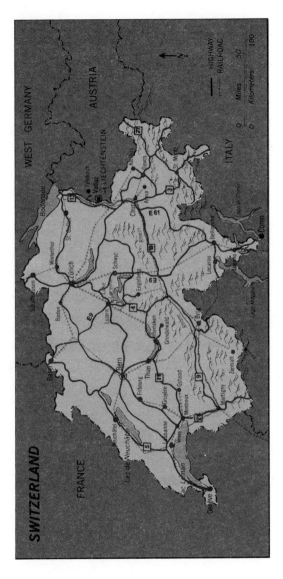

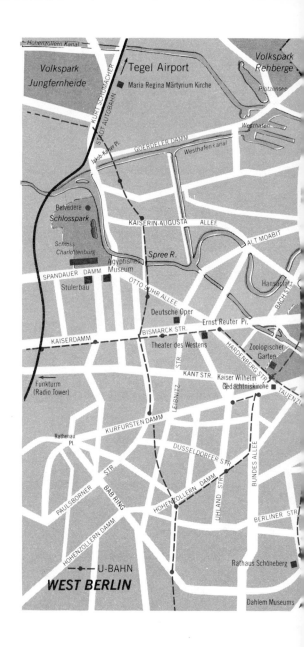

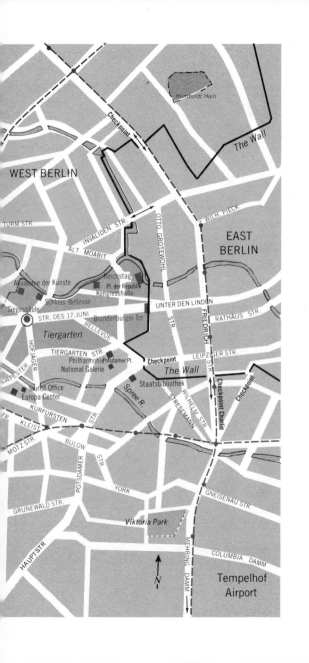

Humboldt Hain

Checkpoint

The Wall

WEST BERLIN

EAST BERLIN

TURM STR.

INVALIDEN STR.

WILH. PIECK

ALT MOABIT

OTTO GROTEWOHL

Akademie der Kunste

Reichstag
Pl. der Republik
Kongresshalle

Schloss Bellevue

Siegessäule

UNTER DEN LINDEN

STR. DES 17. JUNI

Brandenburger Tor

RATHAUS STR.

Tiergarten

BELLEVUE

STR.

FRIEDRICH

HOFJAGER

TIERGARTEN STR.

Philharmonie Potsdamer Pl.
National Galerie

Checkpoint

LEIPZIGER STR.

DAPESTER

The Wall

STR.

Tourist Office
Europa Center

Staatsbibliothek

Spree R.

Checkpoint Charlie

KURFURSTEN

STR.

STRESEMANN STR.

Checkpoint

KLEIST STR.

WILHELM STR.

MOTZ STR.

BULOW

STR.

POTSDAMER

YORK

GNEISENAU STR.

GRUNEWALD STR.

Viktoria Park

HAUPTSTR.

MEHRING DAMM

COLUMBIA DAMM

N

Tempelhof
Airport

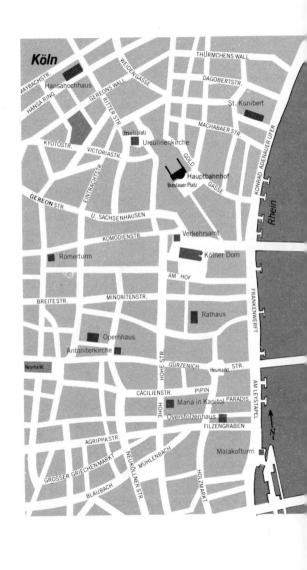

Köln

MAYBACHSTR.

Hansahochhaus

HANSA RING

WEIDEN GASSE

THÜRMCHENS WALL

DAGOBERTSTR.

St. Kunibert

GEREONS WALL

RITTER STR.

MACHABAER STR.

KONRAD ADENAUER UFER

Ursulaplatz

Ursulinenkirche

KYOTOSTR.

VICTORIASTR.

EINTRACHTSTR.

GOLD

Hauptbahnhof

Breslauer Platz

GASSE

GEREONSTR.

Rhein

U. SACHSENHAUSEN

KOMODIENSTR.

Verkehrsamt

Römerturm

Kölner Dom

AM HOF

FRANKENWERFT

BREITESTR.

MINORITENSTR.

Rathaus

Opernhaus

Antoniterkirche

HOHE STR.

GÜRZENICH

Heumarkt STR.

Neumarkt

AM LEYSTAPEL

CÄCILIENSTR.

PIPIN

HOHE

Maria in Kapitol PARADIS.

Overstolzenhaus

FILZENGRABEN

AGRIPPASTR.

MÜHLENBACH

Malakofturm

GROSSER GRIECHENMARKT

NEUKÖLLNER STR.

HOLZMARKT

BLAUBACH

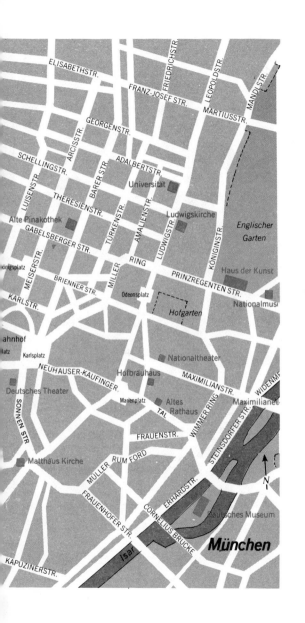

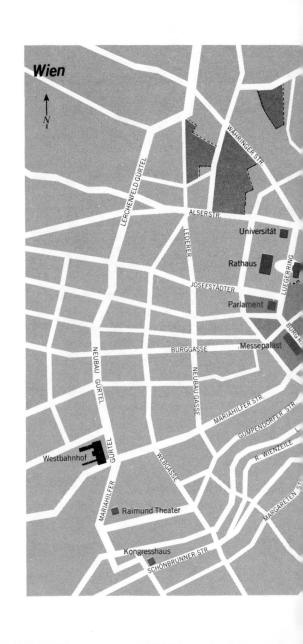